THE
OTHER SIDE
OF THE
COIN

Also by David Orrell

Apollow's Arrow:
The Science of Prediction and the Future of Everything
(*US title*: The Future of Everything)

THE
OTHER SIDE
OF THE
COIN

THE EMERGING VISION OF ECONOMICS AND
OUR PLACE IN THE WORLD

BY DAVID ORRELL

KEY PORTER BOOKS

Library and Archives Canada Cataloguing in Publication

Orrell, David John, 1962-
     The other side of the coin : the emerging vision of economics and our
place in the world / David Orrell.

ISBN 978-1-55263-981-8

     1. Economics. 2. Economics—Sociological aspects. 3. Environmental
economics. I. Title.

HB71.O77 2008   330.1   C2007-905424-2

ONTARIO ARTS COUNCIL
CONSEIL DES ARTS DE L'ONTARIO

The publisher gratefully acknowledges the support of the Canada Council for the Arts and the On-tario Arts Council for its publishing program. We acknowledge the support of the Government of Ontario through the Ontario Media Development Corporation's Ontario Book Initiative.

We acknowledge the financial support of the Government of Canada through the Book Publishing Industry Development Program (BPIDP) for our publishing activities.

Key Porter Books Limited
Six Adelaide Street East, Tenth Floor
Toronto, Ontario
Canada M5C 1H6

www.keyporter.com

Text design and electronic formatting: Alison Carr

Printed and bound in Canada

08 09 10 11 12 5 4 3 2 1

For my mother, Wendy Orrell.

○ ACKNOWLEDGEMENTS

Thanks to my agent Robert Lecker for his enthusiams and support; to Janie Yoon and Jonathan Schmidt for their expert editing; and to the team at Key Porter Books.

Thanks also to Herman Daly and Brian Czech for their valuable comments on portions of the manuscript.

As always, thanks to me wife Beatriz Leon for her careful reading and insightful advice.

Contents

○ INTRODUCTION

The financial market rules everywhere. It doesn't just govern the workings of governments, but also the media, education, even the family. Individuals only have a place in this society if they can produce and buy.
—Subcomandante Marcos, leader of the Zapatista movement in Mexico

And I too welcome wealth. I want, when I leave the bath all perfumed with essences, to feast bravely with my wife and children and to fart in the faces of toilers and Poverty.
—Aristophanes, *Plutus*

It is we alone who have devised cause, sequence, reciprocity, relativity, constraint, number, law, freedom, motive, and purpose; and when we interpret and intermix this symbol-world, as "being-in-itself," with things, we act once more as we have always acted— mythologically.
—Nietzsche, *Beyond Good and Evil*

The beginning is the end.
—Heraclitus, *fragment 70*

THE CROOKED PATH

Something is askew in the global economic system.

This rather unremarkable thought occurred to me as I sat with my wife and infant daughter in the back of an aged Ford Explorer, staring out at the residents of a Latin American barrio from behind sunglasses and tinted windows. Small children hawked goods by the side of the road; an old woman stood in the dark interior of a shed patched together from sheets of corrugated iron and plywood. Above them, ramshackle homes piled one on top of the other, climbing their way up the steep hillside. It didn't look as though anyone had two coins to rub together.

We were on our way to visit my wife's family in Venezuela. We'd just come from a couple of nights at a secluded—and well secured—seaside club near the airport. We were taking this road not by choice, but because the highway from the airport to the capital was closed, after large cracks appeared in the supports of a viaduct that bridged two mountains. The alternate route took several hours longer, and meant passing through the barrios. The area was familiar to my wife from her days as a sociology student conducting surveys, but it was new to me.

Our luggage in the back was covered with a plastic sheet, to shield it from prying eyes. Our driver, a family friend, had also asked me to wear dark glasses to disguise the fact that I was a gringo. He seemed a little paranoid, but the dangers were real enough. Three of my wife's relatives had been subjected to so-called express kidnappings, where captives are held for a few hours until money is handed over, or are marched to the nearest cash machine. They were especially popular around the airport. It was the local idea of a tourist industry.

On the way, as we drove carefully along the narrow, twisting road that led down the mountain towards the capital, our friend told us why the viaduct had failed: untreated sewage from the surrounding barrios had eroded the supports. It seemed ironic that the country could use its oil wealth to build a modern international airport, but it took longer and was far riskier to drive the thirty kilometres to the capital than to fly to New York, all because of a sewage problem. Advanced technology is great at tasks such as keeping an airliner flying several thousand feet in the air, but is easily crippled by social complications.

I felt relieved when we descended from the barrios into the more familiar concrete jungles of the capital, where the roads were straight, the buildings square, and we could roll down the windows and let in the air. I was also appreciative that Canada, my home, is generally dominated by a large middle class rather than the extreme inequalities of wealth that exist in Latin America. But we can't be too smug. From a larger perspective, Canada and other rich countries are like an elite club—literally, a country club. We too are surrounded by barrios, in the form of developing countries; we extract the greatest gains from the international economic system, while the poor struggle to survive.

In the 1960s, there was a hope that the world's problems could be solved through technology, science, and economics. Third world countries would be modernized after the first world example. Free trade and market forces, coupled with advances in energy, transportation, and communication, would propel us into a new era of prosperity. In 1966, *TIME* magazine chose the boomer generation as its "Person of the Year" and predicted, "He is the man who will land on the moon, cure cancer and the common cold, lay out blight-proof, smog-free cities, enrich the underdeveloped world and, no doubt, write finis to poverty and war."[1]

But the dream has not been realized. The global economy powers ahead, but we have little idea of where it is going, or how to correct its excesses. Economic theories of the left or the right have done little to help. The world seems more divided than ever before. Some areas are orderly and secure, like a carefully maintained club, but many are cut off and clamoring to get in, and their numbers are increasing. The slums that surround cities such as Caracas or Delhi or Jakarta or Nairobi now make up about a third of the world's urban areas, and they are growing all the time.[2] We put a man on the moon, but we can't solve more basic problems back here on earth.

Even in rich countries, despite robust growth in economic statistics, such as gross domestic product, and great improvements in technology, many people feel as though they are working longer and harder just to stay at the same level. Most middle-class families rely on two incomes, where one once sufficed. In the United States, productivity growth since the 1960s has benefited primarily the top 10 percent of earners, while the salaries of everyone else have lagged well behind.[3] Wealth disparities have increased, and reported levels of happiness have shown a gradual decline during the past fifty years. There is the sense that, while our economic system has resulted in a material standard of living undreamed of 100 years ago, our actual overall well-being peaked some time ago.

On a global level, our economy is bumping up against the capacity of the planet to support it in the style to which it has become accustomed, and we haven't found a way to reconcile economic growth with environmental protection. The business pages of a newspaper herald the discovery of a new oil field, while the opinion section worries about the effect of burning hydrocarbons on global warming. A 2006 study for the British government claimed, "Climate change is the greatest market failure the world has ever seen."[4] There is a growing suspicion that the problems and contradictions are not just local or political, but are inherent in the world economic system, which sometimes seems as much a source of evil as of good.

The textbook definition of economics is to study and improve the allocation of scarce resources. Governments and institutions such as the World Bank and the International Monetary Fund employ a forbidding array of mathematical and statistical tools to achieve this goal. But something has gone wrong in the equations. Orthodox economic theory imagines a stable world where rational individuals compete on level terms, and the invisible hand of capitalism magically guides the economy to an optimal state of equilibrium. In a world of stark inequities and gyrating asset prices, this picture seems completely out of touch. It doesn't describe Wall Street, let alone the streets of the barrios.

Such economic and social difficulties have been blamed on everything from multinational corporations, to incompetent institutions, to globalization, to the nature of human beings, to government interference with free markets. But I believe a large part of the problem is our dominant economic paradigm—the way we think about money. Not just in an abstract way, but also in the concrete sense of what money is, what it does, what it's for, and how it behaves.

Neoclassical economics, the type most taught and practiced today, was invented in the 1870s. The theory saw the economy as a collection of rational individuals, each one acting solely to further his or her own ends. By aggregating these hypothetical individuals (i.e. taking the whole to be the linear sum of the parts), and assuming the economy was at balanced equilibrium, the neoclassical economists claimed scientifically to prove a number of things about the economy—such as that correctly designed free markets would by themselves lead to an ideal distribution of the world's scarce resources.

The neoclassical theory was intended to be a kind of physics of money that modeled human behavior with a set of equations. The guiding metaphor was of the economy as an efficient machine, where human beings were its cogs and nature was no more than a source of material and energy. Based on the "rational mechanics" of Isaac Newton, and embedded in a tradition of scientific thought that dates back to the ancient Greeks, the aim was to optimize goodness through the use of mathematics, and control the economy as if it were a spaceship. The theory has had enormous ideological impact, teaching us that selfishness is good, and most social policies are inefficient. But can the world really be reduced to numbers, and is the theory really on firm ground? People are increasingly asking whether the traditional physics approach works for human economies. Consider, for example, the following statements from the alternative economics literature:

"We live in an uncertain and ever-changing world that is continually evolving in new and novel ways. Standard theories are of little help in this context. Attempting to understand economic, political and social change requires a fundamental recasting of the way we think."[5] (Douglass North, winner of the Bank of Sweden Prize for Economics.)

"There is a theory that everybody pursuing his self-interest actually serves a common interest, because markets tend towards equilibrium, and equilibrium assures the best allocation of resources. That theory happens to be false."[6] (Former hedge fund manager George Soros.)

"We wish to escape from imaginary worlds!...Call to teachers! Wake up before it is too late!" (A student petition signed by fifteen students at the Sorbonne in Paris, 2000.)

"Money can't buy happiness." (Traditional.)

If the economic world is askew, maybe there is something wrong with the foundations—or perhaps, like those of the viaduct, they just can't stand up to the corrosive effects of social realities. *The Other Side of the Coin* is about a new, emerging vision of economics, society, and our place in the world. It is about an economics that makes room for ethics, social justice, other species, and the rights of future generations—all of which are excluded by the neoclassical approach. And an economics that is in tune with modern science, rather than that of the nineteenth century.

The world is being reshaped, though not in the way that *TIME* envisaged in 1966. A series of new and interconnected ideas from scientific and social movements are profoundly changing the way we think about the economy and our place in the world. The first heroes of this revolution included the astronauts of the moon missions, but also student protesters, environmentalists, rock musicians, stink-bomb-throwing feminists, maverick mathematicians, and dissident scientists. Just as neoclassical economists prepared the ground for twentieth-century capitalism, so the efforts of this disparate band helped forge a new science of money for the dawn of the millennium.

The new type, or types, of economics currently being created go by different names—ecological, post-autistic, complexity, green, feminist. But if there is one thing they have in common, it is that they are all reversing a 2,500-year-old tradition of reductionist, mechanistic thought that goes back to ancient Greece, and a secretive cult led by a demi-god. They are all post-Pythagorean.

THE DNA OF ECONOMICS

Western civilization owes a great deal to Pythagoras. Born around 570 B.C., he was named after the Pythian oracle at Delphi, who had surprised his parents by announcing his imminent birth before his mother knew she was pregnant (his name literally means "the oracle speaks"). His followers later claimed that he was not completely human, but had been sired by the god Apollo, for whom the oracle was the spokesperson.

Pythagoras founded a quasi-mystical cult in southern Italy based on the power of number. He is credited with coining the words "cosmos" and "philosopher." He was involved in government and commerce, and is said to have introduced the first coinage to his region.[7] His efforts kick-started the development of mathematics, music theory, and numerical prediction. Perhaps betraying a family connection, these interests reflected those of Apollo, who was the god, among other things, of reason, music, and prophecy.

Another of Pythagoras' many contributions to civilization, and book publishers, was the idea of the top ten list. The Pythagoreans believed the number ten, which they called the decad, was the most complete number. They composed a list of ten opposing principles that divided phenomena into two classes, one good and the other evil. By aligning themselves with those qualities in the left-hand column, the Pythagoreans believed they could move closer to the gods.

Limited	Unlimited
Odd	Even
One	Plurality
Right	Left
Male	Female
At Rest	In Motion
Straight	Crooked
Light	Darkness
Square	Oblong
Good	Evil

Table 1.1. The Pythagorean list of opposites.

Like two complementary strands of DNA, this list of pairs formed the foundation of Pythagorean philosophy, and its traces are easy to detect throughout Western science. Scientists still seek simple, unvarying principles that reduce a plurality of phenomena to one; they shine the light of linear logic on the darkness of ignorance; they are entranced and inspired by what physicist Leon Lederman called the "symmetry, simplicity and beauty that can be described by abstract mathematics."[8] As the journalist and philosopher Arthur Koestler wrote of Pythagoras, "his influence on the ideas, and thereby on the destiny, of the human race was probably greater than that of any single man before or after him."[9] (The influence has not been universally perceived as positive; for example, the biologist Robert Rosen associates Pythagoras with "a disastrous turn" whose impact "has spread far beyond mathematics."[10])

As I will argue in this book, the orthodox economic theory, in its linearity, rationality, and obsession with concepts such as scarcity and equilibrium, is also Pythagorean to the core—and has been ever since the subject was modeled after physics in the nineteenth century.[11] The new economics, however, is turning the table. It sees the economy not as an efficient and independent machine, but as something more like a living ecosystem. The invisible hand is an emergent property of this system, which never reaches an optimal equilibrium, but instead is fundamentally dynamic and unstable, with complex effects on society. The financial network is both highly creative and prone to seizure-like crashes. The market is not square and balanced, but rather is strongly asymmetrical, with some players—at the top of the food chain—enjoying far more power than others. And in a finite world, uncontrolled growth is no longer the solution to all ills, but rather part of the problem.

This book is not an economics or sociology textbook (I promise!). It does not make one-size-fits-all policy recommendations, or instruct the reader on how to get rich. The aim is to examine the main insights of the new sciences and movements and show how they both reveal the flaws in the neoclassical model and also provide a new way of thinking about money and society. We will see how ecology sheds new light on economic growth, how fuzzy logic affects the national accounts, and how network theory is revealing the value of relationships. We view the economy as a complex, chaotic system where the dice aren't square but crooked. This book will show how the different aspects of this scientific revolution, along with social movements such as feminism and environmentalism, each form a separate strand in a larger pattern, which is slowly inverting our ideas about money, value, and the purpose of society.

I am a mathematician, and in large part this book is also a meditation on number. The notes all have numbers on them, and economics is the place where the world of number collides with human reality. As we'll see, our ideas about money and the economy are strongly influenced by our ideas about the property and behavior of those numbers.

As is appropriate for a book about a complex system such as the economy, the style is linear, periodic, and chaotic at the same time. Each chapter loops back in time—to the birth of Western science in ancient Greece, to the Victorian era, to the 1960s—in order to set the arguments within a historical context. There are also diversions from the road, the better to take in the view, and spot often-unexpected connections. We will explore:

- How the space race changed our ideas about limits and scarcity;
- How Jimi Hendrix subverted both classical logic and the meaning of gross domestic product with his guitar;
- The relationship between networks and net worth;
- Why the invisible hand has a bad case of the shakes;

- Why the price of gold went chaotic;
- What the distribution of craters on the moon tells us about financial risk;
- The connection between book sales and the *Forbes* list of wealthy Americans;
- How Victorian explorers helped pave the way for the efficient market hypothesis;
- How feminists and environmentalists are putting the "eco" back into economics;
- How a new, post-Pythagorean vision of society and the economy is being forged, and what it will mean for governments, businesses, and you.

The ideas and movements discussed here first germinated more than forty years ago, but are only now reshaping finance and economics. It often takes that amount of time for scientific or other insights to filter through to the rest of society, and something happened in the 1960s that produced a cluster of ideas that helped unravel the Pythagorean meme. As seen in the next chapter, their near-simultaneous emergence was linked to a communal, out-of-this-world experience, marred only by another problem with sewage—but it wasn't Woodstock. If anything, it was the opposite of Woodstock.

1 ○ LIMITED VERSUS UNLIMITED
THE SPACEMAN ECONOMY

Picture of an "earthrise" taken by *Apollo 8* astronaut William Anders.
The photographer Gallen Rowell called it "the most influential environmental
photograph ever taken."

*As all things change to fire, and fire exhausted falls back into things,
the crops are sold for money spent on food.*
—Heraclitus, *fragment 22*

You want to live *"according to nature"? O you noble Stoics, what
fraudulent words! Think of a being such as nature is, prodigal beyond
measure, indifferent beyond measure, without aims or intentions,
without mercy or justice, at once fruitful and barren and uncertain;
think of indifference itself as a power—how could* you *live according
to such indifference? To live—is that not precisely wanting to be other*

than this nature? Is living not valuating, preferring, being unjust, being limited, wanting to be different?
—Nietzsche, *Beyond Good and Evil*

Once a photograph of the Earth, taken from the outside, is available—once the sheer isolation of the Earth becomes plain—a new idea as powerful as any in history will let loose.
—Fred Hoyle, astronomer

Money makes the world go round.
—Traditional

THE DAY THE WORLD TURNED

It is impossible to put an exact date on the start of a revolution, especially one that had to wait two and a half millennia. But December 24, 1968, seems as good a place as any to begin.

That Christmas Eve, families everywhere gathered around their television sets to see a historic event. Three men—Frank Borman, James Lovell, and William Anders—sat hunched inside a frail-looking, cone-shaped metal container. It had about as much interior room as a minivan, and was named after a Greek god. The men were performing a television broadcast. And they were doing it from outer space.

"This is *Apollo 8* coming to you live from the moon," began Borman. "We showed you first a view of the earth as we've been watching it for the past sixteen hours. Now we're switching so that we can show you the moon ..."[1]

The crew had just completed a lunar orbit, becoming the first humans to escape the earth's gravity and see the dark side of our constant companion. While on the other side they had been outside radio contact. They described what they had seen, then, in a move unplanned by their NASA controllers, took turns reciting from the Book of Genesis. William Anders read the first lines:

> In the beginning God created the heaven and the earth. And the earth was without form, and void; and darkness was upon the face of the deep. And the Spirit of God moved upon the face of the waters.
> And God said, Let there be light: and there was light.
> And God saw the light, that it was good: and God divided the light from the darkness.

An estimated one billion viewers watched the broadcast—more than a quarter of the world's population. In countries all over the world, people stopped what they were doing to witness the amazing spectacle of these men who had broken free from the planet's bounds.

The *Apollo 8* mission—its badge a figure 8 on its side, the infinity symbol—captured the spirit of the time, and the excitement accompanying the seemingly unlimited promise of technology. This was the Space Age, when many hoped science and automation would put the world to rights. Stanley Kubrick had just released his film *2001: A Space Odyssey* (although it was outgrossed by *The Graduate*, where Dustin Hoffman gets one word of career advice: "Plastics"). *TIME* chose the *Apollo* crew this time as their Men of the Year, and contrasted their can-do, right-stuff attitude with that of the peaceniks and Vietnam War protesters: "For this is what Westernized man can do. He will not turn into a passive, contemplative being; he will not drop out and turn off; he will not seek stability and inner peace in the quest for nirvana … if he knows anything at all, he knows how to challenge nature … He knows how to reach for the moon."[2] Rather than escaping from the earth, the astronauts were defining its future.

The *Apollo* mission was the most dramatic demonstration possible of America's scientific, technological, and economic power. If America could put a man on the moon—as it shortly did with *Apollo 11*—then it could certainly solve the more mundane problems back on earth, such as poverty, pollution, or social unrest. Utopia lay in science, not in society.

Of course, the *Apollo* program also had a strong political and military dimension. In many ways its main motivation was to win a round in the Cold War. Just a few months earlier the Soviets had managed to send a spaceship around the moon with two turtles (or cosmo-turtles) on board. The success of *Apollo* was proof to Americans of the superiority of their capitalist, free market system over that of the communist Russians—and reassurance that they still had the edge on rocket design.

The broadcast on Christmas Eve, therefore, announced a triumph, not just for the space program and the men on board, but for a particular set of values: the light of knowledge over the darkness of ignorance, action over contemplation, right over left, linear science over unruly nature. Above all, as NASA administrator Thomas O. Paine pointed out, it was "the triumph of the squares. The guys with computers and slide-rules who read the Bible on Christmas Eve."[3]

Ironically, though, the fuzzy images of the moon taken from *Apollo 8* were rather disappointing. As crew member Jim Lovell noted, "The moon is essentially gray, no color; looks like plaster of Paris or sort of a greyish beach sand."[4] Bill Anders had a similar impression, saying it "really isn't anywhere near as interesting as I thought it was going to be. It's all beat up."

The star of the show was the earth. It was the first time anyone, let alone the general public, had seen the entire planet from the outside. The astronauts, alone in their capsule, surrounded by infinite space, seemed especially moved by their privileged view of its royal blue oceans and swirling white clouds. Photographer Galen Rowell described the picture taken by Anders that showed the earth partially lit from one side, rising over the moon—thus inverting their usual relationship—as "the most influential environmental photograph ever taken."[5] Lovell told the viewers back home, "The vast loneliness is awe-inspiring and it makes you realize just what you have back there on earth." We had to go to the moon to figure out where we were from.

Even as the astronauts were completing their precisely orchestrated revolutions of the moon, a different sort of revolution was taking place in science. It was not applauded, or even noticed by the editors of *TIME*; it did not capture the spirit of the Space Age. Nor was it limited to one branch of science, but rather broke out in many different, apparently unrelated areas at once.

Science had long been based on the reductionist approach, championed by Descartes and Newton, of breaking complex systems down into their constituent parts, and analyzing their function as one would a machine. Like the Pythagoreans before them, scientists assumed the world was based on number and mathematical laws. To understand and predict a system—be it the movements of a spaceship, the workings of a body, or the fluctuations of the economy—it was only necessary to write out the necessary equations, and solve.

There was little room in this picture for uncertainty or ambiguity. Even the bizarre behavior of quantum systems obeyed strict probabilistic laws. But then came the 1960s. Perhaps inspired by the antics of the student rebels, who were launching sometimes violent antiestablishment protests across the United States and Europe, scientists too began to loosen the shackles of scientific thought and question their own establishment. Fuzzy logic, for example, dared to ask whether the traditional system of logic that underpinned science was compatible with a reality that was never black and white, but only shades of gray. Network theory analyzed systems such as the economy by focusing less on the components themselves than on the relationships between them. Complexity studied emergent properties that could only be understood in a holistic sense; nonlinear dynamics explored new kinds of chaotic motion; fractals were crooked and broken. And for almost the first time, women were making significant inroads into science and questioning many of its tacit assumptions about the nature of reality.

In their different ways, each of these new approaches were challenging the reductionist, mechanistic paradigm—the one that had put a man on the moon. Nowhere was this more true than in the area of economics, where a robust—and still today unsettled—debate was underway.

The argument came down to a basic dichotomy, which in many ways defines the subject of economics—that of limited versus unlimited.

LIMITED VERSUS UNLIMITED

The term "economics" dates from around 1870. It was derived from the Greek words *oikos* (household) and *nomos* (law), and means something like household rule. One textbook describes it as the study of "how society chooses to allocate its scarce resources to the production of goods and services in order to satisfy unlimited wants."[6] In orthodox, neoclassical economics, it is tacitly or explicitly assumed that human wants are infinite. There never comes a point when a household member says enough is enough. Downsizing is not a seriously considered option. So the aim of economics is to reconcile limited supplies with unlimited demands.

For the Pythagoreans, the two qualities, limited (*peras*) and unlimited (*apeiron*), held a somewhat different significance: they were the basic principles that created and defined the universe. According to their version of Genesis, in the beginning there was unity. Unity divided into the limited and the unlimited. The former represented order, and was good; the latter represented chaos, darkness, and plurality. The two opposites then came together to form numbers, which are the stuff of the universe.

The Pythagoreans thought about numbers by arranging pebbles in different configurations. The numbers four and nine, for example, were believed to have special properties of solidity and symmetry because they were square.

The decad was represented by the tetractys, which consisted of four rows of dots (or pebbles on the cave floor), and was used as a sacred symbol. A Pythagorean aphorism read, "What is the Oracle at Delphi? The Tetractys, the very thing which is the Harmonia of the Sirens."

To the Pythagoreans, number was the reality that had crystallized, like the planets themselves, out of a formless void. The pebbles in the tetractys were limited, and the space between them was unlimited. Number was therefore a way of ordering and controlling the universe.

Aristotle wrote in *Nicomachean Ethics*: "Evil belongs to the unlimited, as the Pythagoreans surmised, and good to the limited."[7] The divine patron of the Pythagoreans was Apollo, whose temples were adorned with phrases such as "Nothing too much" and "Observe limit." The perfect example of limited order was the stars, which the Greeks believed moved in a perfectly circular motion. For this reason, the Pythagoreans saw astronomy as the noblest kind of science. *Apollo 8*'s goal of conquering unlimited space through the use of astronomy and technology would have met with approval by the Pythagoreans, as a continuation of their own Apollo mission.

While numbers had a mystical significance to the Pythagoreans, they also had more prosaic uses. As the scholar W. K. C. Guthrie observed, it is likely that "Pythagoras derived his enthusiasm for the study of number from its practical applications in commerce."[8] The Greeks were a nation of merchants, and they needed a monetary system and accounting techniques to manage their businesses. Pythagoras, whose father was a gem engraver, was probably also involved in the design of coinage for his region of southern Italy.

Mathematics was not just about keeping track of where the moon was going, but also where all the money was going. Pythagoras may have been one of the first to extend the use of number beyond commerce, but at heart, he was an economist.

Like number, money is a way of ordering and controlling an ever-shifting reality, of making sense out of the universe. Its value is associated with its scarcity—the more there is around, the less it is worth. It is a way of defining limits.

THE DISMAL SCIENCE

If economics is the study of how society allocates limited resources among different people, then perhaps its most basic questions are: How many resources do we actually have? And how many people?

The English Reverend Thomas Malthus might not have called himself an economist—the term was not used until after his death—but he was certainly concerned with the concept of limits. In particular, he was troubled by some data supplied by Benjamin Franklin, which implied that the pilgrim folk in the newly settled frontier of America were reproducing at the healthy rate of four surviving children per generation. If this kept up, the population would double in size every twenty-five years or so. In two centuries, it would expand by a factor of about 250. In his 1798 *Essay on the Principle of Population*, Malthus argued that the human population would eventually outstrip the availability of food.

Even if the food supply miraculously kept pace, the over-crowding alone would lead to war and disease. As he later wrote, "It is not easy to conceive a more disastrous present, one more likely to plunge the human race in irrecoverable misery, than an unlimited facility for producing food in a limited space."[9]

Until Malthus, population growth had generally been seen in Europe as a positive thing. The power of the state had always been linked with the number of people it could band together to fight wars. And as trade became the main determinant of a nation's wealth and ability to fund conflicts, the need for a large internal market, and a supply of cheap labor, grew even larger. According to the economic theories of the time, wages went down with the number of laborers available, and this increased the profits from trade. The human race could therefore cheer-fully obey the injunction in Genesis to "be fruitful, and multi-ply."[10] As Daniel Defoe put it in 1709, "People are indeed the essential of commerce, and the more people the more trade; the more trade, the more money; the more money, the more strength; and the more strength, the greater the nation."[11]

Malthus's gloomy prognostications were therefore not well received by his Victorian contemporaries. Nor did they gain credence with the passage of time, for he had failed to anticipate changes in the rates of both population growth and food production.

Between 1800 and 1890, the United States population did increase by a factor of about twelve, which was almost exactly in line with a doubling time of twenty-five years. Of course, this increase was due to immigration as well as reproduction. However, after 1890, the rate of growth slowed significantly, to a doubling time of about fifty years. The reason for the change was not because Americans went off sex, but rather because the economy switched its diet. From 1870 to 1900, the Industrial Revolution, which had started in Britain, caught up with the United States. This transformed it from a primarily agrarian society into an industrial powerhouse. Instead of being fueled by agriculture (i.e. the energy stored in plants), the economy was rocket-fueled by carbon, the coal deposits in the ground. Railroads and electricity networks spread their tentacles across the country, and the first industrial giants, such as U.S. Steel and General Electric, were formed.

The effect of all this industrialization was to enrich the population, but also to slow its growth. Demographers have found that economic development tends to be accompanied by reduced birth rates. Some hypothesized reasons are increased opportunities for women in work and education; greater availability of birth control; reduced infant mortality; and the fact that, in an agrarian society, children are seen as an economic asset—more hands to work the fields—while in an industrialized society they are more of an expense. Since the 1960s, the demographic slowdown has been even greater, especially in countries such as Japan or Russia, where the birth rate is now lower than the replacement rate, and populations are falling.

The other flaw in Malthus's argument was that he assumed food production would eventually fall behind population growth. However, in industrialized countries, the price of food has actually dropped as a percentage of wages, because of technologies such as fertilizers, pesticides, and new farming methods. The limit Malthus had foreseen, when mankind would run out of food and space and scores would die from famine, seemed to get further and further away.

SPACE RACE

The Space Age of the 1960s reignited the Malthusian debate— or at least supplied it with a new metaphor.

To the orthodox, neoclassical economists, there was nothing like the moon mission to gird one's faith in human ingenuity and technology. The astronauts were like the first pilgrims to visit America: brave, strong, and guided by a pure spiritual vision. Man could overcome any limit—including the earth's gravity— and so could the economy.

Before the Industrial Revolution, economists had recognized two factors of production: land and labor. The fruit of the soil, and the sweat of the worker. With the development of factories, capital was added to the list. But in the 1960s, with the advent of nuclear power—which its advocates claimed would one day be "too cheap to meter"—it seemed human ingenuity could conjure energy and matter out of thin air. As economist Robert Solow affirmed, "The world can, in effect, get along without natural resources." So land was dropped from the list, and the equations.[12] The human economy was a self-contained system, fully independent from the rest of the planet. Like the astronauts, all we needed were brains, hard work, and a generous amount of financial backing.

But not everyone saw the *Apollo* missions as heralding the triumph of mankind over nature. On the other side of the debate was a new breed of economist, inspired by natural systems. To these economists, nothing brought home the concept of limits more vividly than those television images of the astronauts, suspended in their tiny, fragile craft a quarter million miles from home, and surrounded by infinite space. If there were any kind of malfunction—say, one of the booster rockets failed to work as planned—they could find themselves endlessly circling the moon, or propelled farther and farther into outer space, as their oxygen supply slowly dwindled. In Kenneth Boulding's paper "The Economics of the Coming Spaceship Earth," he imagined a world "in which the earth has become a single spaceship, without unlimited reserves of anything, either for extraction or pollution."[13] Like astronauts, we would have to live in a finite space with limited supplies—and carefully dispose of waste.

One of the less glamorous aspects of *Apollo 8* involved what was known as the craft's waste management system, which was a device for vacuuming human waste into outer space. It worked fine, until Frank Borman suffered the first occurrence of what is now known as space adaptation syndrome. Caused when the balancing system of the inner ear adapts to weightlessness, it affects about a third of people who go into space. Less than a day into the flight, Borman had an attack of vomiting and diarrhea. Soon the astronauts were chasing globs of feces and vomit that floated weightlessly around the cabin. They cleared it up in time for the broadcast.[14]

The situation wasn't quite that bad on earth—at least for first world countries with adequate sewage systems—but pollution was becoming a global issue. Rachel Carson's *Silent Spring*, published in 1962, had exposed the hazards of chemicals such as the pesticide DDT. And while nuclear power held huge potential, people were afraid of the possibility of nuclear conflict, and were beginning to wonder where we would put all that radioactive waste.

Boulding characterized the two sides of the debate as the cowboy economy and the spaceman economy. The cowboys had a frontier mentality, like the pioneers who first settled the open plains of America, and saw the universe as a landscape ready to be plundered. There was no need to worry about availability of resources because they were effectively infinite, and perhaps not even necessary. The spaceman economy, in contrast, was seen as an explicitly open system. In physics terms, the difference between an open and closed system is that the latter is self-contained, while the former experiences flows of matter and energy to and from the outside world. Living things are open systems, because they require an input of food energy at one end, and output waste at the other. For these functions, the human economy relied on the planet—and in the 1960s it was already showing signs of stress. Warning bells were beginning to ring. As the *Apollo 13* astronauts later put it: Houston, we have a problem.

SUPERMAN

After all, as Boulding realized, the fact that Malthus had based his analysis on the agrarian society of his time and had been a little off on his prognostications did not mean his theory was completely wrong, only that it needed to be adjusted.

For one thing, the industrialized countries may have transformed their economies, but even today much of the world is still agrarian—and we still need to eat. Malthusian pressures are therefore more evident in the developing countries, where famine is widespread.

In rich countries, the main issue is not so much population as economic growth. One of the main differences between humans and other animals is that we own and accumulate a lot of physical artefacts. A human being in an industrialized country wears clothes made from advanced fabrics, lives in a house, often owns a car, and has tons of other stuff stashed away in closets or the basement or under the stairs or in a storage locker in the outskirts of town (in the United States alone there is an estimated two billion square feet of rental storage space).[15] In the end, this entire superstructure is fabricated from materials that come out of the ground. So our impact on the environment is a function not just of population, but of how much we acquire and consume. This, in turn, is a function of wealth.

Imagine the economy as a kind of hungry animal. If it grows larger it will consume more energy, and will need more food and other resources. (The first man in space, Yuri Gagarin, was five feet two inches tall, which helped save room on his tiny craft.) If, alternatively, the economy simply becomes more active, then it will still burn off more energy and require more nourishment. The total activity in the economy is typically estimated by the gross domestic product (GDP), which measures the goods and services produced. Figure 1.1 shows GDP in the United States for the postwar period. During that time, it doubled in size approximately every twenty years, growing much more quickly than the population. For a forty-year-old person, the economy has expanded by a factor of four just since he or she was born.

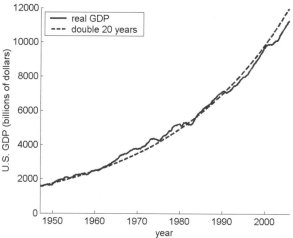

Figure 1.1. Plot of real GDP in the United States for the postwar period, in year 2000 dollars. Dashed line has a doubling time of twenty years.

Our tendency to acquire superstructure—to be super-men—has two implications. At the input end, it means we take in far more matter and energy from the environment than would be required just to feed ourselves. Even if the land's productivity kept up with our stomachs, it may not keep up with our demand for cars, video game consoles, and spacious homes. At the output end, our waste management system has to deal with far more than sewage. All those things eventually need to be disposed of somehow, after they have broken down or we have grown bored with them. People in wealthy countries, therefore, have far more impact on the environment than those in poor countries.[16] The world can support more Haitians than Americans.

The net effect is hard to measure because it depends on a large number of interacting factors. Rich countries may generate more waste, but they also tend to have higher environmental standards, and more efficient technologies. The richer we get, the better we become at taking care of our environment. And local effects matter. The world as a whole may be able to support many more Haitians, but it isn't clear that Haiti can.

The problem with the Malthusian limit was not just that it was moving further away, but that it was vague and ill defined. We could overshoot it, and not learn of the consequences until afterwards.

The reason for this was that the earth wasn't like another spacecraft, with a fixed amount of food and oxygen. It was a living ecosystem.

THE LOGOS

The term "ecology" is from the Greek words *oikos* (household) and *logos* (study or reason), and means something like household study. Like economics, it relates to how we live in our home—the planet. The science of economics was developed first, and ecologists named their field in direct reference to it, as an economics for nature.

If Pythagoras was at heart an economist, then his contemporary Heraclitus was an ecologist. No complete manuscript of Heraclitus survives; his teachings are known to us only as a set of more than 100 separate sentences, similar to the koans of Buddhism. He is best known for his statements "all things change" and "good and evil are one." The two sides of the Pythagorean divide are not separate, but are different aspects of a unified, dynamic whole—they are two sides of the same coin. As Guthrie explains it, Heraclitus saw the world as "a living organism," in which "everything is always moving up and down the path of change, driven thereto by the attacks of its opposites or its own attacks upon them, but all within strict limits." To Heraclitus, *logos*—the root of ecology—represented the divine law of measure and proportion. "Listening not to me but to the *logos*," he wrote, "it is wise to agree that all things are one."

Two and a half millennia ago, Western society chose to follow Pythagoras rather than Heraclitus (it probably didn't help that, according to his biographer Diogenes Laertius, Heraclitus became in his senior years "a complete misanthrope ... spending his time in walking about the mountains; feeding on grasses and plants"[17]). The result was a system of thought that has served us well, and has indeed given us dominion over the rest of the planet. But it also resulted in a kind of mental schism, which reflects the Pythagorean division of phenomena into two opposing classes, and which has divided us against both nature and ourselves. Nowhere is this more obvious than in the split between economics and ecology.

While these two fields initially shared much in common, by the 1960s they had diverged to the point where they were in direct opposition to each other. To orthodox economists, the natural world had no intrinsic value, apart from how it benefited our own species. The market determined an object's price, so if there wasn't a market for a particular type of fish or tree, it followed that it had no value. Pollution was therefore not in itself considered economically harmful, even if it damaged the habitat of local species. As Oxford University economist Wilfred Beckerman put it: "... effluence entering into some remote stream might harm the fish in it, but if the fish were never to be the object of human satisfaction, this would be of no practical consequence."[18] Similarly, if something was non-scarce and freely available—such as sunlight—then it had no economic value.

Economics and ecology were separate disciplines belonging to separate university departments. The division reflected the biblical divide between man and beast. As written in Genesis, man was given "dominion over the fish of the sea, and over the fowl of the air, and over every living thing that moveth upon the earth."[19] Economics was about mankind and all those physical artefacts we owned, and ecology was about every other living thing.

In 1969—the year of the first lunar landing, and, at the other end of the cultural and physical activity spectrum, John Lennon and Yoko Ono's bed-in for peace—the ecologist Eugene Odum published a paper entitled "The Strategy of Ecosystem Development." Odum's father was the sociologist Howard W. Odum, whom he credited for giving him a holistic, interdisciplinary vision of science, and his paper bridged the *nomos/logos* divide by viewing humankind as part of the larger ecosystem. He noted that ecosystems tend to follow a certain developmental path as they become established that involves an interaction between the species and their environment.

All ecosystems ultimately obtain their energy from the sun. Plants absorb the energy directly through photosynthesis and use it to produce organic material. Plants are then eaten by animals, which in turn are eaten by carnivores. Classically, the great chain of eating has been represented by a pyramid, with mankind at the apex, as in Figure 1.2. As Odum pointed out, a more accurate depiction would show the ecosystem as a complex web of relationships.

The energy absorbed from sunshine flows upwards from the base of the pyramid, and circulates through the ecosystem. Mankind has also learned to directly exploit the stored solar energy in oil and coal deposits, which are formed from prehistoric plant matter—but it can all be traced back to the sun. Money may not grow on trees, but, like leaves, each note contains a ray of sunshine (literally, in the case of the U.S. dollar, as shown in the illustration at the start of Chapter 8).[20]

Odum argued that ecosystems—for example the species in a forest—develop so as to achieve "as large and diverse an organic

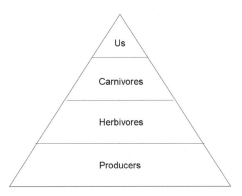

Figure 1.2. The great chain of eating. Solar energy is absorbed by the producers at the bottom, which are typically plants. These are eaten by herbivores, which in turn are eaten by carnivores. We just buy what we want at the store.

structure as is possible within the limits set by the available energy input and the prevailing physical conditions of existence (soil, water, climate, and so on)." In immature ecosystems, at an early stage of their development, the available energy is rapidly exploited to maximize growth and production. They gorge on the plant food, resulting in a transient bloom. A few species tend to dominate this race, so diversity is initially low. As the ecosystem matures, however, it shifts from exploiting resources for growth to maintaining the existing store of biomass. The number of species increases as new ecological niches appear. The food chain switches from a linear one based on grazing to a more web-like structure in which multiple species interact in increasingly complex ways. The waste of one organism is recycled as food for another, and resources, such as nutrients and minerals, are conserved. Such ecosystems tend to become more stable and robust, resulting in "increased control of, or homeostasis with, the physical environment in the sense of achieving maximum protection from its perturbations."

An example of a mature ecosystem is a tropical rainforest.

Most of the nutrients in a patch of rainforest are not in the ground, but rather in the trees and the species that live in the trees. Perhaps, surprisingly, given the abundance of life, the land itself has little agricultural productivity. Farmers who cut down rainforests to grow soy or provide pasture for cattle often have to abandon the land within a few years. Of course, even a mature ecosystem can receive a burst of youth and return to a bloom state if there is a sudden influx of nutrients, as with the blooms of algae caused by fertilizer run-off in lakes.

As Odum notes, the development of ecosystems has a striking parallel with the development of economies. In a society of pioneers, "high birth rates, rapid growth, high economic profits, and exploitation of accessible and unused resources are advantageous." However, as the economy matures, "these drives must be shifted to considerations of symbiosis (that is, civil rights, law and order, education, and culture), birth control, and the recycling of resources."

Odum's paper puts the cowboy/spaceman debate into a new perspective. The cowboy economy is like an ecosystem that has just been inundated with a large but temporary influx of nutrients—namely, the hydrocarbons stored in oil and coal deposits. A spaceman economy is a more mature version of the same thing. Strategies that work in one are less effective in the other. Intensive agricultural techniques that rely on heavily fertilized monocultures, for example, maximize productivity in the short term, but rapidly deplete nutrients from the soil, and are vulnerable to pests or changes in climate.

The other lesson is that the human economy cannot be treated as if it is somehow divorced from the rest of the world. As Odum put it, "Until recently mankind has more or less taken for granted the gas-exchange, water-purification, nutrient-cycling, and other protective functions of self-maintaining ecosystems, chiefly because neither his number nor his environmental manipulations have been great enough to affect regional and global balances. Now, of course, it is painfully evident that such balances are being affected, often detrimentally." The solution was "some form of ecosystem analysis that considers man as a part of, not apart from, the environment."

In other words, the earth isn't an inert spaceship or a lump of rock—it is also a living ecosystem, of which our own economy is just one part. This idea was best captured by the chemist and inventor James Lovelock, who in 1969, after a discussion with novelist William Golding, chose the name Gaia to describe his notion of a living planet.[21] If Apollo is the divine patron of economists, then Gaia, the Greek earth goddess, could be considered the patron of ecologists. Lovelock's Gaia theory proposed that the planetary ecosystem incorporated numerous feedback loops that actively regulate the environment to keep conditions suitable for life. Examples are the planet's temperature, and the salinity of the oceans, both of which are kept within fairly narrow bounds, just as they are in our own bodies. The earth is the ultimate mature ecosystem—but it is saddled with an immature species.

HOLD IT STEADY

So how will the cowboy/spaceman debate play out? Will humanity suddenly run out of resources, or will the cowboy economy shoot down limits as quickly as they appear?

Neoclassical economists argue that as a resource such as oil nears exhaustion, its price will go up. We will therefore learn to conserve, or switch to an alternative. However, as I will discuss later, it isn't clear that the price mechanism really gives much warning. Estimates of supplies are highly error prone, and scarcity only has a secondary effect on the cost of extraction—the fact that a glass is nearly empty doesn't make it harder to drink from. Sellers may continue to sell at the going rate, right up until the resource suddenly runs out.

This argument also assumes that we can continue to find suitable alternative energy sources, necessity being the mother of invention. It is true that in the past we successfully made the transition from wood to coal, or from whale oil to petroleum. But these all represent natural stores of solar energy: they are the low-hanging fruit of the energy world, and there isn't much left. The timing has been wrongly predicted many times before, but one day we really will run out of cheap oil. Indeed, the global rate of oil discovery peaked back in the late 1960s.[22] Nuclear energy is an alternative, but presents huge waste disposal and security problems, which is why it isn't very popular (although this is beginning to change in some countries).

A separate concern is the harmful effect of pollution on the rest of the ecosystem. We rely on the earth not just for natural resources, but also for what economists refer to as "services," such as an amenable climate, productive soil, and healthy oceans. Because mainstream economics radically partitions the world into the human economy and everything else, and relies on scarcity to determine a sense of value, such services are treated as free and therefore expendable. But there's no advantage in discovering a new source of oil if it only means we dump more carbon into the atmosphere and trigger a global warming calamity.

Human activities—in terms of agriculture, engineering, carbon emissions, and so on—have reached a scale where they are comparable to natural processes. It is therefore impossible to study ecology without taking into account our effect on ecosystems. Conversely, it makes no sense to manage the economy as if we were not part of a larger system. Man or beast, we're all in the same boat. Gertrude Stein once said, "The thing that differentiates man from animals is money." But money is just a social convention—and one that is turning out to have hidden costs, both physical and psychological.

The English economist Lionel Robbins said in 1935 that economics is "the science of scarcity."[23] His definition reflects the view of the human economy as a closed system, in which value can flow from one form to another, or from one person to another, but can never be created or destroyed. The only way to get rich is to out-compete your neighbors. This emphasis on scarcity has resulted not just in an age of plenty, but an age of worry. As Barbara Brandt puts it, "It should not be surprising that in affluent modern societies, where there is no such thing as enough, and more is always better, people are constantly plagued by fear of scarcity rather than being able to enjoy the abundance their work and technology have created."[24] If we only value that which is hard to obtain, then we can never be satisfied with what we have. And in an economic system with huge disparities between the rich and the poor, money and resources tend to get sucked up by the small number of people at the top—thus exacerbating scarcity (see the box "Money from nothing").

The alternative to a growth-and-scarcity-driven economy is either one that crashes (not good) or one that maintains a kind of homeostatic balance with the environment. In such a so-called steady state economy, the aim is for internal (creative, spiritual, or intellectual) development rather than material growth. The idea goes back to classical economists such as John Stuart Mill, who wrote in 1848, "A stationary condition of capital and population implies no stationary state of human improvement. There would be as much scope for ever for all kinds of mental culture, and moral and social progress; as much room for improving the Art of Living and much more likelihood of its being improved, when minds cease to be engrossed by the art of getting on."[25] In 1968, the U.S. economist Herman E. Daly revived the concept—and helped create the new field of ecological economics—with his paper "On Economics as a Life Science."[26]

To bring about an economy based on ecological principles, Daly had three controversial proposals: caps on minimum and maximum salaries; transferable birth licenses; and a cap-and-trade auction system for natural resources. (Salary caps are discussed in Chapter 9.) Transferable birth licenses were first suggested by Kenneth Boulding. Each couple could get, say, two licenses to have a child. They could either use them or sell them to another couple. If a couple had an unlicensed child, it would not be taken to a remote mountainside to die from exposure (as weaklings were in ancient Sparta), but rather the parents might get fined or lose economic benefits (as in China and Singapore).

The purpose of the auction system was to set a price for scarce, nonrenewable resources such as oil. The government would cap resource extraction and sell the extraction rights to the highest bidder. It could thus control the rate at which resources are consumed. The money could be used to lower taxes, or set aside to compensate future generations for the depleted resources. Prices of nonrenewable resources would tend to go up until they compared with their nearest renewable alternatives.

These proposals are obviously a hard sell, and they are anathema to neoclassical economists, who carry enormous ideological influence. But it does seem bizarre that governments can set exorbitant prices for frequency bandwidth for radio broadcasters or mobile phone companies, but can't do the same for precious resources such as oil. It's as though we value the ether more than the ground. One area where cap-and-trade systems are being adopted is to limit pollution. For example, in the

United States, regulators now cap the amount of sulfur dioxide that can be emitted by power plants, and the power companies are allowed to trade the permits. Similarly, under the Kyoto protocol, the market in carbon permits motivates countries to reduce their carbon emission levels by allowing them to sell permits to heavy polluters.

Another tool for moderating both resource use and pollution is tax policy. Personal income taxes, sales taxes, or corporate taxes do not explicitly account for costs such as environmental damage or resource depletion (in fact, resource companies often seem as good at extracting massive tax concessions as they are at extracting things from the ground).[27] This is reasonable if resources are viewed as essentially infinite, and pollution a minor side effect; but it now makes more sense to increase tax on resource use and pollution, and compensate with lower taxes on income.

ECO-MONEY

Ecological economics is not a minor adjustment to business-as-usual, but is what Brian Czech of the Center for the Advancement of the Steady-State Economy calls "a post-normal, revolutionary economics" that necessitates a fundamental shift in the way we think about value and prosperity.[28] We tend to associate economic growth with good things, such as health and progress, and a lack of growth with stagnant decline. Politicians and business leaders stake their careers on promises of continuous expansion. But in an ecosystem, excessive growth is also a feature of disease, imbalance, and infestations (my day job currently involves working with mathematical models of cancer cells, which gives one a different perspective on uncontrolled growth). Stability, on the other hand, is like a flowing river in which the inputs and the outputs are in balance.

Instead of conquering limits, the ecosystem approach is about finding ways to live within them, while at the same time celebrating and respecting the amazing abundance of the planet. Worth is determined by something other than market price, so just because something is non-scarce and freely available doesn't mean it is without value. After all, the biggest impact of the moon missions came from the way it showed the earth so strongly and vibrantly alive in the emptiness of space. Just as a person is worth more than the amount in their bank account, so the real wealth of the planet bears little relation to the sum of our gross domestic products.

In 1997, a group of ecological economists led by Robert Costanza tried to make this more explicit, by estimating the total value of the earth's services to humanity. The number they came up with was $33 trillion (so about twice the global GDP at the time). The figure was attacked both by mainstream economists, who questioned the methodology, and by environmentalists, who thought the number was too low or irrelevant. As discussed further in the next chapter, it's impossible to put an exact price on the planet; however, the study did help clarify two basic points: that the planet provides us with very valuable things— such as bountiful food, fresh air, and clean water—and that its capacity to do so is being degraded.

One of the main concepts of ecological economics, developed by Bill Rees of the University of British Columbia, is that of our ecological footprint: how much impact we have on our environmental stomping ground.[29] His analysis shows that if everyone consumed at the same rate as Americans, we would need five earths to support our lifestyle. His former student Mathis Wackernagel recently launched the Global Footprint Network, which works with urban planners and governments to help reduce their footprint.[30] This doesn't necessarily involve a great deal of pain. For example, an Italian person's footprint is about 2.5 times smaller than an American's, but they seem to be doing okay. According to Wackernagel, much of the difference comes down to the way cities are laid out. "Particularly, if you have more compact cities where you can walk around, that are pedestrian-friendly, and where you can live downtown."[31] The trends in urban design and architecture are now towards designing low-footprint communities that exploit new technologies and clever design to minimize the use of nonrenewable energy.[32]

LIMITED *AND* UNLIMITED

During our visit to Venezuela, we spent a couple of weekends at my sister-in-law's cabin, about forty-five minutes east of the capital. When they purchased the cabin about a year earlier, it came with an acre of land on the slope of a small mountain; two Rottweiler guard dogs (one pregnant, so they ended up with five); and a couple with two young children, who lived in a small shack in the garden and looked after the property. The house offered beautiful views over a tree-covered valley. Most amazing were the birds: hummingbirds, falcons, something called a guacharaca, which I never saw but it woke us every morning with an incredibly loud call like an old-fashioned klaxon.

My brother-in-law was trying to get his neighbors interested in a plan to protect the local environment, which the Audubon Society had recognized as an area rich in biodiversity. The area was supposed to be protected by law, but in the frontier-style society of Venezuela, you don't need land to be legal to build on it. Shantytowns were spreading along the valley from the town below. With good access to the highway, it seemed only a matter of time before human habitations took over the area. Trees could also fetch a high price on the market, which encouraged deforestation.

Birth rates are falling in Latin America, but are still high, especially among the less well off. The couple that lived on site, José and Maria, had two kids and a third on the way, and José also had three children in another village from an earlier marriage. He was in his twenties. My brother-in-law was helping them build a proper house adjacent to his own. He was a little worried they would keep having kids, in which case it was going to get crowded.

My wife and I had brought along a telescope as a present for our nephew. The cabin was far from the city lights, so the stars and full moon were strikingly bright in the dark night sky. Our nephew set up the telescope in the garden and aimed it at the moon. We took turns examining its scarred and cratered face, like that of an ancient, pockmarked coin. I thought about the *Apollo 8* astronauts—how strange it must have been to fly silently over its surface, to see up close what had for so long been a thing of mystery and mythology. As psychologist Jules Cashford writes, "the extraordinary and far-reaching powers attributed to the Moon—powers over birth, fecundity, growth, destiny, death and rebirth—amount almost to a world view at the beginning of human history. From a broad perspective, the Moon was just one among many expressions of the culture of the Great Earth Goddess, in which Earth and Moon were understood as one manifestation in dual aspect. But a closer look suggests that the peculiar character of the Moon offered an imaginative scope of its own, both crystallizing the essence of the Goddess myth, and, through the provocative metaphor of the Moon's cycle and phase, exploring ways of thinking about permanence, time and mortality."[33] We gained a lot when we went to the moon, but we lost something too.

I don't think the problems down here on the ground will be solved by amazing technological feats, or by smashing through limits. Ecology tells us that to preserve things we value about the planet, such as biodiversity and productivity, we need to find a way to live within its bounds. Perhaps ironically, the only way to accomplish this is by losing our obsession with conquering scarcity. Rather than exploiting scarce resources until the last drop, we must shift to sustainable energy use, through urban design and the development of alternative energy sources. Like a glass of water that is constantly refilled, or a river that constantly flows, renewable resources are both limited and unlimited. They are limited in the sense that we can only access them at a certain rate—solar energy direct from the source is handed out more parsimoniously than solar energy stored in oil. But they are unlimited because they never run out.

It seems a contradiction to say that something is both limited and unlimited at the same time. To understand the logic, it helps to consider an event in 1969 that offered another communal, out-of-this-world experience ... Woodstock.

MONEY FROM NOTHING

Why do we always seem to feel short of money? Part of the reason is that our financial system was designed to create just that effect.

Suppose you want a new car and apply at a bank for a one-year loan of $10,000. The bank does a credit check and then decides to lend you the money at a set interest rate, say 6 percent. It only needs to back its loan with a small fraction of the total, known as the reserve amount, which is set by the central bank. (One may ask where its money comes from. As with the Pythagorean conception of the birth of number, the ultimate source of all money is the void—it is created from nothing by fiat of the central bank.) You buy the car, and after a year your payments exceed the original loan amount by 6 percent. That extra money wasn't magically produced in the same way—it comes from the pool of money that is out there, which the central bank deliberately keeps scarce to protect its value. So you have to compete with other people to grab your share and pay the interest back. If the economy as a whole is growing, that makes the job easier, but as the author and former banker Bernard Lietaer notes, scarcity is "artificially and systematically introduced and maintained."[34]

Traditionally, religions such as Christianity, Judaism, and Islam prohibited usury and viewed it as a serious sin (Islam still does). In the 1800s the Catholic Church began to relax this dogma, and by the late nineteenth century—when the modern banking system was designed—any concern in the banking community over the ethics of charging interest were apparently forgotten. Because rich people usually lend to (and earn interest from) the poor rather than the other way round, the gulf between the two tends to grow. Many of the features of modern capitalist society, such as the constant pressure of competition, economic inequality, and striving for economic growth, can therefore be traced back to the banking system's dual reliance on scarcity and interest. One of the biggest impediments to a steady state economy is that governments would have to get out of debt before they could afford it.

So does money always have to come with such a heavy price? One idea is a return to 100 percent reserve banking, so that profits from the creation of new money go directly to the government, rather than banks.[35] Another option is to expand the suppliers of new money to include anyone at all. Around the world, some thousands of regions have developed complementary currencies that circulate in parallel with the official currency. An example is Local Exchange Trading Systems (LETS) that act as a kind of exchange network for labor. Under this system, a hairdresser may swap a trim for a credit he can use to pay someone to fix his computer. The credits don't become scarce because they can be created at any time by doing work, and interest is not charged. The money also circulates locally, instead of being siphoned off to some remote corporate headquarters.

Such schemes are not intended to replace a national currency, but they tend to foster a sense of community, and perhaps because they are backed by personal labor rather than the command of a central bank, they are perceived as being somehow warmer and friendlier than cold hard cash. They can also play a valuable backup role during times of financial crisis, when the official currency suddenly becomes hard to find.

HOW TO BE ECOLOGICAL

In the past few years, we have become increasingly aware of our own personal ecological footprint, and also of ways to measure and reduce it.

If you drive a car, buying a hybrid will get you a few more miles per gallon. You can also switch to public transportation, bicycle, walk whenever possible, cut down on airplane trips, or move from a house in the suburbs to an apartment near where you work.

Eating less meat, or being vegetarian, will lighten your footprint (and your weight). You can avoid conspicuous consumption, recycle your bottles, charm friends and family with homemade Christmas gifts, switch off electrical appliances such as stereos instead of leaving them on standby, turn down the heating or air conditioning, insulate your home, and only boil as much water for hot drinks as you actually need.

If you live somewhere sunny, you can hook up some solar panels. If you're having a new home designed, you can insist that it follow the specifications drawn up by organizations such as LEED (in North America) for a green building.

You can lobby the government to impose carbon taxes (and reduce other taxes accordingly), and protest activities that damage the environment.

These are all good things. They will also help create a market for products that benefit the environment, and drive down the prices.

But if you fail at all of them, there is still one surefire strategy that will have a guaranteed effect (if it's not too late), and that is simply to have fewer children. A family that has only one child instead of three can reduce its future emissions by a similar factor, assuming the child doesn't go crazy at the mall spending his or her inheritance. This is the voluntary version of a birth license scheme.

Of course, it involves the thorny issue of birth control. Crafting a new economy is often less about science than politics and personal beliefs.

2 ○ ODD VERSUS EVEN
FUZZY MONEY

Phases of the moon

It is impossible for anyone to suppose that the same thing is and is not, as some people think Heraclitus said.
—Aristotle, *Metaphysics*

Just as the river where I step
is not the same, and is,
so I am as I am not.
—Heraclitus, *fragment 81*

But what is the folk-song in contrast to the wholly Apollonian epos?
What else but the perpetuum vestigium *of a union of the Apollonian and the Dionysian? Its enormous diffusion among all peoples, further re-enforced by ever-new births, is testimony to the power of this artistic dual impulse of Nature: which leaves its vestiges in the folk-song just as the orgiastic movements of a people perpetuate themselves in its music.*
—Friedrich Nietzsche, *The Birth of Tragedy*[1]

Money can't buy happiness.
—Traditional

FUZZ TONE

At nine in the morning on Sunday, August 17, 1969, Jimi Hendrix stood in front of about 30,000 tired, cold, wet, and muddy music fans at a dairy farm in Bethel, New York. Wearing a red head-band and a loose-fitting shirt the same color as the cream Fender Stratocaster in his hands, he launched into a set of six-teen songs, including "Foxy Lady," "Hey Joe," and "Purple Haze." The one that made rock history was his version of "The Star-Spangled Banner." Twisting and distorting the notes as if trying to batter an aural sculpture out of sheet metal, his guitar turned the American national anthem into a searing lament for the Vietnam War, complete with simulated screams and explosions.

The Woodstock Music and Art Fair was intended to be a rel-atively small-scale affair. Up to 50,000 people were expected to show up for the weekend of music. Around half a million came. Hendrix was the headliner, but the playbill contained many of the rock luminaries of the 1960s—Janis Joplin, The Who, Santana. The concert was immortalized in Joni Mitchell's song "Wood-stock," despite the fact that she got stuck in a traffic jam and missed her performance.

The event went off mostly peacefully. There were three acci-dental deaths, two births, and an unrecorded number of concep-tions, accidental or not. The weather was rainy, there wasn't much food, and there was definitely a waste management problem, but the concert was memorable. Or it would have been, if most of the audience hadn't been higher than the astronauts who less than a month before had set foot on the moon. By the time Hendrix reached the stage, nine hours after his scheduled midnight appear-ance, nearly everyone had either gone home or passed out.

Like the *Apollo* astronauts, Hendrix had a military back-ground. In his case, he joined the 101st Airborne as a trainee para-trooper in 1961, in a deal to avoid a two-year sentence for theft. His record was undistinguished. Military archives show he couldn't shoot straight—he was the worst marksman in his unit—and his supervisor thought he was unintelligent and probably crazy, writing: "He has been undergoing group therapy at Mental Hygiene with negative results ... Pvt Hendrix plays a musical instrument during his off hours, or so he says. This is one of his faults, because his mind apparently cannot function while performing duties and thinking about his guitar."[3] He was discharged after a year, and never had to go to Vietnam, though his songs would become favorites of the U.S. soldiers there. A test pilot for his generation, he flew high and died young, at twenty-seven.

Hendrix was a musician who turned the rules of music upside down—literally. He was left-handed, but played a right-handed guitar, so he reversed the string order. This changed the relative position of the pickups, resulting in a unique sound. He could play his guitar behind his back, or with his teeth, and would sometimes end performances by covering his guitar in lighter fluid and setting it alight, smashing it to pieces, or both. And while Hendrix wasn't the first to exploit effects such as feedback and distortion, he took them further than anyone else.

A big fan of Hendrix's music is Seattle software billionaire (and former number two at Microsoft) Paul Allen. He commissioned architect Frank Gehry to build the Experience Music Project, a museum of rock music dedicated to Hendrix and named after his album *Are You Experienced?* Gehry got his inspiration for the design by playing around with the smashed bodies of Fender guitars. The result is a swooping, discordant, multicolored blob, clad in around 21,000 pieces of stainless steel and aluminium—the architectural equivalent of a Hendrix song (appropriately, one of the colors is "purple haze"). The building is penetrated by the once-futuristic Seattle monorail, an inheritance of the 1962 World's Fair, in what Nietzsche might have called "a union of the Apollonian and the Dionysian," a merging of scientific reason with drunken ecstasy.

Gehry's building was made possible by technological developments, such as computer design and fabrication techniques from the airline industry. Hendrix's music was similarly reliant on technology. The electric guitar was first introduced in the 1930s, but large-scale production started with the solid-bodied Fender Stratocaster in 1954. It is similar to its acoustic ancestor, except that the vibration of the strings is sensed by magnetic pickup coils. The signal is then sent to a separate amplifier, but on the way is often subjected to a wide range of distorting effects.

Hendrix pioneered the use of devices including the wah-wah pedal (which makes the guitar sound like a human voice), the octave doubler, and fuzz tone. These were not mere ornamentations, but were the basis of his sound. Most of the songs had a simple musical structure: "Purple Haze," for example, has the chords E, G, and A. As musicologist Sheila Whiteley notes, though, "the underlying logic of the chord progressions is transformed by Hendrix to produce a feeling of intuitive incoherence and lack of rationality through the use of fuzz tones which distorts the hammered and pulled-off notes."[4]

Fuzz effect units were the first to be based on transistors, rather than vacuum tubes. They alter the signal coming from the guitar by clipping and boosting the signal, and add a range of harmonics and cross harmonics that create a dissonant effect. A single note becomes a complex cacophony of sound. Instead of accuracy and precision, the aim is the opposite; an engineer once described the electronics to me as "a circuit designed to screw itself up." The sound is characteristic of many hits from the 1960s, such as "Satisfaction," by the Rolling Stones.

While engineers were attaching Space Age transistor technology to electric guitars to fuzz up their sound, a different kind of engineer was fuzzing up something more basic—the very principles of logic that date back to ancient Greece. Their work would have implications for everything from philosophy to the design of washing machines to how we think about money and make business decisions.

ODD VERSUS EVEN

Question: if you play a note slightly off-key, is it still musical?

If you change the notes of "The Star-Spangled Banner," is it still a national anthem?

If a chapter talks mostly about music, can it still be about money?

Yes or no? Right or wrong?

Western logic has traditionally been based on the idea that just as a coin toss is either heads or tails, so a statement is either true or false, but it can't be a bit of each at the same time. As Aristotle said, "It is impossible for anyone to suppose that the same thing is and is not" (though Heraclitus begged to differ). The dislike of duality can be traced to the Pythagoreans. To them, the number two, or dyad, represented the initial division of the universe, and was the symbol of discord and dissent. The even numbers contained the number two, and were associated with the feminine, the unlimited, and the left hand. The odd numbers were firm and decisive, while the evens were waffling, uncertain, and prone to fall apart. According to Iamblichus, Pythagoras asserted "the right hand is the principle of what is called the odd number, and is divine; but that the left hand is a symbol of the even number, and of that which is dissolved."

The Pythagorean philosophy was forged—literally—in their study of the relationship between number and music, and the discovery that musical harmony obeys mathematical laws. The story goes that Pythagoras was passing a blacksmith's forge, and noticed that the tone produced by hammers depended on the weight of the hammer. Some hammers, when struck together, produced a pleasing harmony, while other combinations sounded discordant. Investigating further, he discovered those that sound good together have weights in a simple ratio, such as 1:2 (which gives an octave). He then applied the same idea to the strings of musical instruments, arguing that two strings, one with twice the tension of the other, will again differ by an octave.

In the sixteenth century, the musician Vincenzo Galilei (father of Galileo) tried to verify the experiment, and found that the tone actually varied with the inverse square of tension. To give an octave, strings had to differ in tension not by a factor two, but by a factor two squared, or four. Isaac Newton noted the correspondence between this and his law of gravity, which stated that gravitational force decreased with the square of distance. A great Pythagorean, Newton argued that Pythagoras was aware of the true relationship, and even of the law of gravity, but opted to keep them secret.

The Pythagoreans correctly stated that a string's tone varies directly with its length, so if a string is fretted at a point halfway along its length (a ratio 1:2), it will produce a tone an octave higher; and they were the first to discover that notes that harmonize together are related by simple mathematical ratios. The position of the frets on a Stratocaster is determined by Pythagorean mathematics. As shown in Figure 2.1, the fret halfway down a string gives a note differing from the open string by one octave. The fret two-thirds of the way down gives a musical fifth, and three-quarters down gives a fourth. Play the three notes together (on different strings) and you have a major chord.

The key musical ratios are therefore 1:1 (the open string), 1:2 (an octave), 2:3 (a fifth), and 3:4 (a fourth). These were represented by the ratios between the four rows of the tetractys. The correspondence between music and mathematics was essential to the Pythagorean worldview. The fact that music—considered the most expressive of art forms—could be reduced to simple ratios reinforced their belief that number was the basis for all reality.

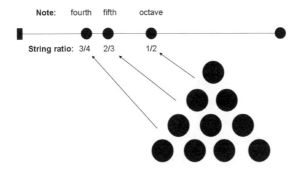

Figure 2.1. Relation between musical harmony and the tetractys. The fourth, fifth, and octave correspond to the ratios between the rows of the tetractys.

Iamblichus wrote that Pythagoras used music as a kind of therapeutic calming device against "every aberration of the soul."[5] On one occasion, walking home from a late-night astronomy session, he came across an irate young man. The fellow had been listening to inflammatory music, and had decided to set fire to the house of his girlfriend, who was with another lover. Pythagoras ordered a piper to play some soothing music, and the lad immediately calmed down: his fury "being immediately repressed, he returned home in an orderly manner."[6] In this fashion, "Pythagoras through music produced the most beneficial correction of human manners and lives." (One doubts the technique would have worked on Hendrix, who had already experienced the army's attempts at mental hygiene.)

So when Hendrix plugged in his specially designed Axis fuzz

unit, he was doing much more than fuzzifying the chords of a song—he was fuzzifying the tetractys. He was playing the spaces between the dots, the sounds between the notes. He was playing the unlimited.

FUZZY THINKING

The word "fuzzy" was first used in a mathematical context in the 1965 paper "Fuzzy Sets" by Lotfi Zadeh at the University of California, Berkeley. In classical logic, sets are defined as a collection of entities. Once a set is defined, it cleanly divides the world into two classes of things—those that are in the set, and those that are outside it. With fuzzy sets, membership is a matter of degree. It is possible to be partly in and partly out. You can talk about finance and listen to music at the same time.

Suppose we consider the collection of musical notes in an octave to make up a set. In traditional instruments in the West, the octave is divided into twelve notes (this number is culture-dependent—Indian music, for example, has twenty-two notes per octave). A composer can write a piece of music using only these notes, and a musician can duplicate it whether their instrument is an electric guitar or an oboe. The exact sound will depend on the instrument, the precise tuning, the skill of the musician, and so on; but in principle, if someone were to listen to the performance and transcribe it note for note, the transcribed version should match the original perfectly.

Hendrix taught himself guitar by playing old blues songs. The basic blues scale is a minor pentatonic scale with an additional note, known as the blue note, which gives blues its distinctive flavor. It is located somewhere between a fourth and a flattened fifth, and can be played on the guitar by bending the string to change the pitch. However, each musician will play it slightly differently. So the set of notes in a blues scale is some-what vaguely defined. It is extremely difficult to transcribe an improvised piece in a way that captures the exact warmth and feel of the music. Two different transcribers may come up with different versions of the song. If electronic effects such as dis-tortion are added, transcription becomes almost impossible. This is because the notes are not exact—they are part of a fuzzy set. Membership is a matter of degree. The blue note almost cor-responds to the fourth in a traditional scale, but not quite. It is slightly off-tetractys.

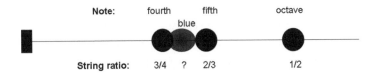

Figure 2.2. The blue note sits somewhere between a fourth and a flattened fifth, and so doesn't quite belong to the set of notes in a traditional scale, and varies slightly with the player. The set of notes in a blues scale is therefore vaguely defined.

As another example, suppose we consider the set consisting of versions of "The Star-Spangled Banner." The song was written by Francis Scott Key during the War of 1812, based on the music of an English drinking tune, and has long been a symbol for American patriotism. At sports events such as baseball games, the anthem is usually performed pretty much note for note, with some small variations, so those renditions definitely belong in the set. However, at the start of game five of the 1968 World Series between St. Louis and the home team, Detroit, the blind Puerto Rican musician José Feliciano broke with tradition by strum-ming a bluesy version, and ended with a laconic "Hey-hey." To some baseball fans, it wasn't the anthem at all. One wrote: "What screwball gave permission to have the national anthem desecrated by singing it in the jazzy, hippy manner that it was sung? It was disgraceful and I sincerely hope such a travesty will never be permitted again."[7] The person who selected Feliciano to perform was called a Communist and nearly lost his job.

Hendrix's version a year later was even more problematic. Are those diving whammy bar bomb effects really part of the tune? And then there was the 1990, deliberately out-of-tune version by comedian Roseanne Barr, which President George Bush called a "disgrace," or the 2006 Spanish-language version, which his son George W. Bush saw as a threat to the "national soul."[8] These might have been based on "The Star-Spangled Banner," but they each departed from the script. Are they the national anthem, or not? Some would say yes, others would say no, and many wouldn't be sure. They are partly in and partly out. They have a partial membership in the fuzzy set of American national anthems.

Another example of fuzzy logic from a different context is the following statement about police horses by a member of the Vancouver Police Mounted Squad: "We're an effective, hard presence but in a soft way. The horses break down barriers. We're sort of a big stick, but a warm, fuzzy big stick."[9] Police horses are intimidating, but at the same time they are kind of cuddly, and they help make a connection with people. They are both hard and soft, imposing but accessible.

Here's another example: Are you happy? Are you a fully paid-up member of the class of happy people? If so, congratulations! But for most people, the answer will again be a matter of degree. They are quite happy, or a bit down, or just kind of so-so. The statement "I am happy" isn't 100 percent true or false. Some people have a permanently sunny disposition, but for most of us, our mood varies more like the phases of the moon (shown at the start of this chapter), which is usually neither completely bright nor completely dark, but rather somewhere in between.

Even apparently simple statements can lead to contradiction if we insist on true/false logic. Consider the statement by Epimenides the Cretan, "All Cretans are liars." Is this statement true or false? If it is true, Epimenides is himself a liar, so the statement must be false (we're taking the word "liar" literally here). On the other hand, if the statement is false, it follows that Cretans are not liars. So it must be true. This is why the statement is called the liar's paradox.

Lotfi Zadeh's fuzzy sets were a way of addressing these shortcomings in traditional logic. Zadeh was born in Soviet Azerbaijan. At age ten he moved to Iran, where he attended a Presbyterian missionary school in Tehran. After getting his degree in electrical engineering, he did his master's at the Massachusetts Institute of Technology (MIT). He was therefore exposed to a mix of Soviet atheism, Protestantism, Muslim fundamentalism, and American technology—which perhaps helped motivate his interest in reconciling opposing ideas.[10]

Fuzzy logic uses the idea of fuzzy sets to assign approximate degrees of truth. For example, the statement "I am happy" may be 70 percent true, and 30 percent false. Everyone, even the suicidally depressed, has a partial membership in the class of the cheerful. Feliciano's "The Star-Spangled Banner" is, let's say, 85 percent national anthem, while Hendrix's is only 70 percent. Viewed in this way, the liar's paradox ceases to be a paradox— as Zadeh reasoned, it is exactly half true, and half false.

The concept of fuzzy logic was not warmly received at the time. One University of California professor wrote: "Fuzzy theory is wrong, wrong, and pernicious. What we need is more logical thinking, not less. The danger of fuzzy logic is that it will encourage the sort of imprecise thinking that has brought us so much trouble."[11] It was the philosophical equivalent of passing "The Star-Spangled Banner" through a fuzz pedal.

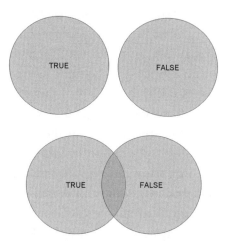

Figure 2.3. In classical logic, the sets of true and false statements are distinct (top). In fuzzy logic, statements can be both partially true and partially false (bottom), just as most phases of the moon are partially light and partially dark.

Of course, Zadeh wasn't the first person to point out that reality was shades of gray, rather than black and white, or that most phenomena cannot be neatly divided into opposing classes. Heraclitus wrote that a flowing river "is not the same, and is." In the 1866 work *Beyond Good and Evil*, Nietzsche mocked the use of antitheses, such as good versus evil, where in fact "there are only degrees and many subtleties of gradation."[12] The Buddhist philosopher D. T. Suzuki describes the fundamental aim of Buddhism as being "to pass beyond the world of opposites." People from political leaders to parents have long applied their own versions of fuzzy thinking.

Even Western science, which was built on the square foundations of classical logic, had to grapple with duality with the 1930s development of quantum physics, in which entities such as electrons appeared to behave like both particles and waves, and can only be described in a probabilistic fashion. However, fuzzy logic isn't concerned with the probability that the blue note belongs to a Pythagorean scale, or that Hendrix's "The Star-Spangled Banner" belongs to the class of American national anthems. The chance of these being completely true is, in either case, zero. We know they don't quite fit. The question is, how close do they come? To what extent are they in, and to what extent are they out? The reason fuzzy logic caused so much controversy was because it went beyond the calculation of probabilities to question the very structure of logical thought.

Fuzzy logic has since found many useful, down-to-earth applications, especially in the area of engineering. Many electronic devices now use it to determine how much detergent to add to a wash cycle, or how to control a thermostat, or focus a digital camera. Instead of invoking rigid mathematical rules, such devices simplify complex problems by following a series of fuzzy steps (see "Fuzzy rules" below).

So what does all this have to with money? It turns out there is a fuzzy connection—this chapter is at least partly about money—and it goes to the very core of neoclassical economics. It is the question of happiness.

THE HAPPY SCIENCE

Economics is often called the dismal science—in part because of people like Malthus—but in fact it is all about happiness.[13] Neoclassical economics is based on the theory of utility, which was first proposed in the late eighteenth century by Jeremy Bentham, the English philosopher and social reformer. Utility was defined as that which appears to "augment or diminish the happiness of the party whose interest is in question."[14] Society's purpose, Bentham argued, was to satisfy the "greatest happiness principle"—in other words, provide the greatest happiness to the most people. The goodness of an action could be assessed by summing over its positive and negative effects on the people involved. Bentham's aim was to put social policy on a rational, enlightened basis.

Before Bentham, classical economists had usually associated an object's value with its cost of production. Neoclassical economists, such as Bentham's follower, William Stanley Jevons, proposed instead that an object's value was determined by its utility, or more specifically its marginal utility—how much additional happiness it could bring to its purchaser. This tends to decrease with the number of units. For a single person, one car is useful, two is nice, but the marginal utility of a third is much lower, especially if you are all out of parking.

Utility theory answered the question of how individuals, businesses, and governments went about dividing scarce resources. The aim of the game for each player was to maximize his or her own utility. The economy could therefore be modeled using what Jevons called "a mechanics of utility and self-interest," similar to Newtonian mechanics.[15]

In mathematical models of physical systems, such as the motion of planets, every quantity has a unit of measurement. In the standard metric system, distances are measured in meters, time in seconds, and speed in meters per second. Utility, in contrast, has no basis in physical reality—there is no yardstick or measuring device for happiness (economists often prefer instead to work with preferences, which simply rank things or desires in order). But as Jevons argues, if utility is equated with value, then it can be inferred from prices: "I hesitate to say that men will ever have the means of measuring directly the feelings of the human heart. A unit of pleasure or of pain is difficult even to conceive; but it is the amount of these feelings which is continually prompting us to buying and selling, borrowing and lending, laboring and resting, producing and consuming; and it is from the quantitative effects of the feelings that we must estimate their comparative amounts. We can no more know nor measure gravity in its own nature than we can measure a feeling; but, just as we measure gravity by its effects in the motion of a pendulum, so we may estimate the equality or inequality of feelings by the decisions of the human mind. The will is our pendulum, and its oscillations are minutely registered in the price lists of the markets."[16] Utility, therefore, could be measured in terms of cash.

As a mathematical model of human behavior, neoclassical economics sits on top of a vast edifice of theory, which in turn relies on a number of assumptions about the behavior of people. Chief among these are that each person: (1) aims to maximize utility (as measured in monetary terms); (2) has fixed preferences; and (3) acts rationally. As seen later, these assumptions have been relaxed somewhat in recent decades, but they are still implicitly assumed to hold, at least to a good degree of approximation, in standard economics. They allow theorists to predict the behavior of consumers and producers, and go on to make claims about the behavior of markets; for example, that free markets effectively optimize the total utility, in the sense that no one can be made better off without making someone else worse off (known as Pareto optimality).

We will go on to discuss assumptions two and three in later chapters. But for now, how happy are we with the first assumption? Is it really true that we act to maximize our own happiness? What does that even mean? Can happiness be measured in units of currency? And how can a supposedly "hard" science be built on something as fuzzy as an emotion?

PAYING FOR PLEASURE

There is something intrinsically upside down and counter-intuitive in the relationship between money and happiness. Most of the audience got into Woodstock free, and the concert lost money on ticket sales (although it eventually made a profit from record and film rights). The music fans didn't purchase their happiness, unless you count the substances consumed.

Many people consider contact with nature essential for happiness. The strongest message to come from the *Apollo 8* mission was how special the earth was in comparison to its sibling planets. The swirling atmosphere, the blue oceans, the green and brown continents—everything that made the planet a hospitable place to live—all of it is free.

In recent years, an international movement has grown up around the idea of slowing the pace of life in order to make it more pleasurable.[17] Slow food, for example, emphasizes organic ingredients, home cooking, leisurely lunch hours, and slowing down the entire process of the production and consumption of food. In economic terms, this is usually equivalent to putting your foot on the brakes, and earning or spending less money.

Much consumption in industrialized countries is driven by mass advertising, which aims to convince us that we won't be happy unless we buy the offered car/holiday/shampoo. Advertising makes a lot of money for publicity companies and their clients, but it doesn't make the rest of us happy, and often we end up buying stuff we don't really want or need (which is the entire point).

A healthy social network of family, friends, and informal acquaintances is an important contributor to happiness. People in poorer countries often maintain strong social support networks, exactly because they need each other's help. The rich elite often ends up cutting itself off from the rest of society in gated communities—for security reasons if nothing else—but risks becoming isolated and unhappy.[18]

Economists usually treat work as a "disutility"—something we do to earn money to spend on things we enjoy. But jobs provide a lot more than money: they also give our lives structure and a sense of meaning. Many people, economists included, are happy when they lose themselves in their work. As economist E. F. Schumacher wrote, a job gives a person "a chance to utilise and develop his faculties," and allows him "to overcome his egocenterdness by joining with other people in a common task."[19] Some even choose to postpone retirement; others retire early only to find they miss their jobs.

My baby daughter appears to be very happy much of the time, and she makes us happy when she laughs, which she often does for no particular reason at all. This has nothing to do with economic transactions.

Most religions see the emphasis given to money in our culture and educational system as a source of problems rather than a route to eternal joy. The Dalai Lama, who seems happy, said at a conference in 2006: "So we get people who just see profit as important. Money, money and more money. That doesn't go together with inner spiritual development ... Sometimes I think compassion is greater among poor people and the uneducated."[20] According to him, "for a successful and happy life much of it depends on our mental outlook. The money, power or even health, I think is secondary. If mental state is calm, at peace, then you really enjoy your life."[21]

Americans care a lot about happiness—the right to "life, liberty, and the pursuit of happiness" is even written into the U.S. Constitution. Since 1972, the General Social Survey has asked the folksy question: "Taken all together, how would you say things are these days, would you say that you are very happy, pretty happy, or not too happy?" The answer has been quite stable over that time—about a third say they are very happy, a little over half are pretty happy, and around 12 percent are not too happy—but the trend is slightly downward.[22] In fact, earlier results from the Gallup organization showed the number of people describing themselves as very happy peaked back in the mid-1950s, at around 45 percent, and then declined in the 1960s. Similar results have been found for Japan and Europe. Cases of clinical depression and suicide, meanwhile, have increased, led by the boomer generation.[23] Antidepressant drugs such as Prozac have become a multi-billion-dollar business.

During the same time period, however, the average annual income in the United States has soared, even after adjustment for inflation, as has the gross domestic product (GDP). So there appears to be no relation between happiness and the overall wealth of the society. If the economy is really a machine for generating happiness, it seems to be failing.

This is also borne out by comparisons between different countries. The inhabitants of New York or London seem little happier than people in poorer countries. For a few years I lived in East London, not far from the financial district. I would often walk to Liverpool Street station to take the underground train. At rush hour, the station and surrounding streets would be packed with bankers and traders and others who worked in the gleaming office towers. Everyone seemed locked into his or her own little world, avoiding eye contact, making the dash home.[25] If there did exist such a thing as a happiness meter, I don't think it would have gone off the scale, despite the huge concentration of wealth. In the barrios of Venezuela, on the other hand, I was struck by the poverty, but the impression wasn't of widespread misery—if anything, people looked pretty content. Maybe it's the weather.

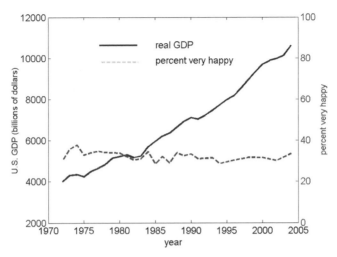

Figure 2.4. Real GDP in the United States (solid line) has more than doubled since 1972, but the percentage of people who consider themselves very happy (dashed line) has a slow downward trend over the same time period.[24]

Indeed, a report from the World Values Survey ranked eighty-two countries in order of their "subjective well-being."[26] The fifteen happiest countries, in order of descending states of bliss, were Puerto Rico, Mexico, Denmark, Ireland, Iceland, Switzerland, Northern Ireland, Colombia, Netherlands, Canada, Austria, El Salvador, Venezuela, Luxembourg, and the United States (Britain, the home of utilitarianism, came in at twenty-five). Venezuelans are on average poorer than Britons, by a factor of around three, but that doesn't make them sadder. In general, income has a strong effect on a country's overall happiness only if it is below a minimum level of around $15,000 per year (starving people aren't happy); and there isn't much gained from having an income above that level.

Of course, one can argue polls are often unreliable, and the answers are highly subjective. However, a large body of research now exists that shows a consistent response among many different countries. Controlled laboratory experiments have also been performed that monitor people's reported happiness while they are subjected to positive or negative stimuli, such as pleasant or disturbing images, and the results are compared with brain scans. The left prefrontal cortex is more active when thinking happy thoughts, while the corresponding area in the right hemisphere is more active when processing negative thoughts (the blue note is presumably a right-brain invention). In any case, while science usually tries to avoid dealing in subjective judgments, with happiness, subjectivity is the entire point: what matters is how you feel, not how you ought to feel.

In general, it seems people are quite capable of judging and reporting how happy they are, and are highly willing to respond to the question. Answers are influenced to a degree by mood and recent events, but these effects should cancel out over a large survey.

So does it then follow that money can never buy happiness? Not quite. Where money seems to have a great effect—especially in materialistic consumer societies—is in boosting one's self-esteem by outdoing the neighbors (as opposed to people in other countries). As John Stuart Mill put it, "Men do not desire to be rich, but to be richer than other men."[27] In the United States, for example, there is a distinct correlation between income and happiness: almost half (49 percent) of those with annual family income greater than $100,000 describe themselves as very happy, compared to only 24 percent with family incomes lower than $30,000. The only factor that has a stronger correlation is health. (It isn't clear whether the ultrarich are happier still— they probably don't answer the phone for surveys.) Unfortunately, there are far fewer rich people than poor (discussed more in Chapter 9), so the net effect is that most people aren't satisfied with their earnings.

It seems, then, that we are sensitive to our level of relative wealth compared to those around us, but not our actual level of wealth.[28] This was illustrated by a U.S. Gallup poll, which asked, "What is the smallest amount of money a family of four needs to get along in this community?" The answer simply tracked the average income.[29] As other people get richer, we feel we must get richer as well just to maintain the same relative position. And by purchasing goods to increase our own utility, the happiness of other people actually declines. If you buy a Mercedes convertible for $95,000, you haven't just increased your own utility by that amount, you've sent a fuzzy but powerful (and damned good-looking) social signal to your colleagues, friends, and people you overtake on the highway, while subtly devaluing their own achievements. A society in which each person is hell-bent on maximizing his or her own utility, may therefore have declining overall utility.

Furthermore, sudden increases in wealth only have a transient effect. As soon as we get used to improvements in living standards, they lose their ability to please or excite. What was once luxury—such as an extra bathroom in the house—is now seen as standard equipment. It seems we care more about changes in conditions than the conditions themselves. Happiness is moving rather than fixed.

If the aim of economics is really to provide the greatest happiness to the most people, then it is rather shocking to discover that economic growth has no net effect on happiness. So what has gone wrong with the neoclassical project?

MEASURING HAPPINESS

While neoclassical economics initially set out to maximize happiness, it did so by equating utility with the numerical price of objects or services. Price is a kind of technique for defuzzifying value; and as economist Herman E. Daly wrote in 1968, economics is based on the "Pythagorean analogy" between "fuzzy" reality and "well-defined, analytic number."[30] In a market economy, anything from food to car maintenance to entertainment has a certain price that is supposed to reflect its underlying utility. In practice, though, emotions such as happiness fall off this numerical grid. We can't really buy happiness—all we can buy are objects or services, in the hope that they will bring us pleasure. Unlike short-term pleasure, happiness is a mental state that relies on a number of factors, such as character (some people are naturally more optimistic), network of friends, family support, health, culture, political system, state of the environment, and so on. It therefore has a fuzzy and often counterintuitive relationship with the material world. Nowhere is this truer than in measurements of the net progress of a nation's economy.

Neoclassical economics was modeled after the hard physical sciences, and favors objective, numerical measurements over subjective judgments. The health of the economy is usually measured in terms of the GDP, which estimates the monetary value of the goods and services produced by a nation in a year. It is therefore a measure of the economy's total activity, rather than the accumulated wealth of individuals. The GDP was initially developed as a planning tool during the buildup to World War II, but has now become a kind of proxy for a society's well-being. A growing GDP is good, while a decrease is bad. The former is associated with growth and robustness, the latter with stagnation and decay.

While GDP gives the impression of being objective, impartial, and exact—i.e. non-fuzzy—its use as a measure for happiness or well-being is equivalent to saying all that counts is what can be counted. It is like attaching motion detectors to a

Buddhist monk in meditation and a child with attention deficit disorder and concluding that the child is happier because he runs around a lot. (The measure is also fuzzier than it looks: in 2006, Greece revised its GDP up by 25 percent after deciding to include activities such as prostitution, cigarette smuggling, and money laundering.[31])

By optimizing such numerical quantities, instead of addressing more fundamental questions of well-being, neoclassical economics has lost track of what it was supposed to be about. As a result, it has produced a greater distortion than anything achieved by Jimi Hendrix with his effects pedals. As Robert F. Kennedy told the University of Kansas in March 1968, the GDP "counts air pollution and cigarette advertising, and ambulances to clear our highways of carnage. It counts special locks for our doors and the jails for those who break them. It counts the destruction of our redwoods and the loss of our natural wonder in chaotic sprawl. It counts napalm and the cost of a nuclear warhead, and armored cars for police who fight riots in our streets ... Yet [it] does not allow for the health of our children, the quality of their education, or the joy of their play. It does not include the beauty of our poetry or the strength of our marriages; the intelligence of our public debate or the integrity of our public officials. It measures neither our wit nor our courage; neither our wisdom nor our learning; neither our compassion nor our devotion to our country; it measures everything, in short, except that which makes life worthwhile."[32] The numbers look good, and we're working hard, but really we're on a treadmill, going nowhere fast. The reason is that economic growth is both good and bad at the same time.

The biggest distortions due to GDP occur in the third world, where much economic activity simply goes unmeasured. A subsistence farmer in a rural area may contribute nothing to the money economy, while if he moves to a squalid slum on the out-skirts of a city, he may make a few dollars a day. In the case of a mass migration from rural areas to slums—as is happening in many areas of the world—the GDP receives a significant boost, but it is far from clear that living standards have actually improved.

If the aim is to improve gross happiness, rather than the GDP, then, it follows, we should moderate growth, reduce social inequalities, and cultivate a nonmaterialistic culture. We should take into account political freedoms, education, literacy, health, and the state of the environment. And if we factor in the hap-piness of future generations, then, like rich people planning a trust fund for their descendants, we need to consider long-term sustainability.

Like happiness, sustainability rests on a number of separate planks, such as land use, pollution, and species protection, whose value cannot be determined by market mechanisms alone. The market is a human invention, and is good at determining appro-priate prices for exchange between people, but it fails completely when the exchange takes place between people and the environ-ment, or between the current generation and future generations. The environment can't walk away from a bad deal, and future generations haven't been born yet. What is the value of a piece of Amazon rainforest? To a soy farmer, very little, but to an ecolo-gist—not to mention the species that call it home—the value is huge. What is the loss of value caused by the deposit of waste chemicals in the deep ocean? If the last of a species of bird dies, is that of no practical concern, or is it worth a great deal? How much does a country lose when its biodiversity falls? And if we empty the world of valuable resources such as oil, how do we set-tle that account with our unborn descendants?

These questions are intrinsically fuzzy and ill defined, so orthodox economics naturally avoids them. The problem is compounded by our highly limited ability to look into the future. We know the supply of oil is finite, but we can't predict exactly when it will run out; we know that destroying rainforest will affect the climate, but we don't know exactly how. Environmental damage is therefore treated as an "externality," and the rights of future generations are written off or "discounted" as if they were bargains in a sale.

Fuzzy logic offers a way to bring these issues back into the picture. In recent years, fuzzy logic programs have been used by social scientists and economists to measure human well-being, to determine the key factors behind ecological sustainability, and so on. Such programs consist of traditional statements of the type used in regular computer programs, with the difference that the rules are expressed in fuzzy terms. The aim is not to come up with a definitive formula for happiness or sustainability, or make precise predictions, but to determine some fuzzy rules that can help move society towards a more congenial setting (see "Warm and fuzzy," below).

Fuzzy logic is also used in the agent-based models discussed later, where agents representing individual people, firms, or nations use fuzzy rules to make their decisions. Of course, any program that uses fuzzy logic doesn't escape the world of numbers altogether. The program can only be run by assigning specific degrees of membership to fuzzy sets. To say that the land quality of a country belongs 30 percent to the set of "very bad" admits a degree of vagueness, but why 30 percent instead of 25 percent or 31.9 percent? In the end, fuzzy logic programs run on computers, which reduce everything to a string of 0's and 1's. They also suffer from the same problems as other mathematical models, in that they fail to capture the true complexity of the underlying system.

Another example of fuzzy thinking, which doesn't specifically rely on fuzzy logic programming, is alternatives to GDP such as the Index of Sustainable Economic Welfare (ISEW).[33] This accounts for factors such as income inequality and environmental degradation. Because it is impossible to accurately quantify the damage caused by carbon dioxide emissions or the elimination of animal species, the ISEW is a fuzzier measure than GDP—but it may be more meaningful. Between 1950 and about 1970 the GDP and ISEW rose together, but since then the ISEW has remained flat or has even declined slightly. Economist Mark Anielski's "genuine wealth" combines human wealth (people), social wealth (relationships), and natural wealth (the environment) with more traditional measures of economic well-being.[34] The country of Bhutan has replaced the GDP with Gross National Happiness, which reflects fuzzy qualities such as sustainability, social equitability, cultural values, and good governance.

Perhaps the greatest contribution of fuzzy logic is to force us to avoid simplistic yes/no reasoning, and accept uncertainty and duality. There is something in duality that seems to repel the Western mind—we tend to search for clarity and directness, and reject statements that are vague or only partly true. This tendency seems particularly strong in traditional economics, whose founders wanted to place it on a firm logical footing. As Jevons wrote in a text on logic, nothing can both "be and not be ... that is to say, what is both A and not A does not exist, and cannot be conceived."[35] But in a complex world, even vague and contradictory statements can have a degree of validity, and fuzzy logic offers a way to work with them. The alternative is an abstract system that has nothing to do with real life. It is better to be fuzzy but relevant than precise but irrelevant. As Herman Daly wrote, "Some would like to abandon the concept of sustainable development altogether, arguing that it adds nothing to standard economics and is too vague to even be useful. But most important concepts are not subject to analytically precise definition—think of democracy, justice, welfare, for example. Important concepts are more dialectical than analytic, in the sense that they have evolving penumbras which partially overlap with their 'other'."[36] In other words, they are fuzzy rather than firm. Neoclassical economics takes the all-or-nothing position that nothing counts unless it can be measured in dollars and cents. It started off being about happiness, but its obsession with objectivity has meant that subjective feelings are now actually sacrificed for the bottom line.

We will never be able to build an accurate model of happiness or well-being, at the individual or societal level. Nor is it obvious that constant happiness should be our main goal in life—it doesn't correlate very well with things like creativity, critical awareness, or good blues music. Just as the moon waxes and wanes, so the human spirit needs to occasionally spend some time in the dark. (Nietzsche, who didn't seem happy, wrote of the followers of Bentham: "Not one of all these ponderous herd animals with their uneasy conscience [who undertake to advocate the cause of egoism as the cause of the general welfare—] wants to know or scent that the 'general welfare' is not an ideal, or a goal, or a concept that can be grasped at all, but only an emetic ...")[37]

All we can do is cultivate the necessary conditions for a reasonably fair, prosperous, diverse, and content society. Like a good song, this depends on having the right elements in place—the basic chords—but also on the warmth, the feel, the color, the minute variations of the performance, the right degree of sustain in the mix. And, as discussed in the next chapter, those warm fuzzy feelings often come not from maximizing our own utility, as a brilliant soloist, but from our collaborations with others.

WARM AND FUZZY

As an example of an engineering application for fuzzy logic, a heater could be programmed with the fuzzy rules depicted in the figure below. The temperature scale is divided into three sets: cold, perfect, and hot. Any temperature can be viewed as being simultaneously cold, perfect, and hot, but to different extents. The temperature 15°C is 100 percent cold, 0 percent perfect, and 0 percent hot, while 17°C is 50 percent cold, 50 percent perfect, and 0 percent hot. Each fuzzy set is associated with a rule: IF cold, THEN run heater at high power; IF perfect, THEN run at medium power; IF hot, THEN turn off. The degree to which the rules are applied depends on the extent to which a given temperature belongs to the fuzzy temperature sets, so at 17°C the heater will be halfway between medium and full power. The advantage of such fuzzy control systems is that they work like a human operator, by breaking complex tasks into simple but fuzzy steps.

Similar methods can be used to estimate more complex phenomena—such as human and ecosystem sustainability. One program published in the journal *Ecological Economics* contains the following instructions:[38]

IF land quality is very bad
OR air quality is very bad
OR water quality is very bad
OR biodiversity is very bad
THEN ecosystem sustainability is very bad

As with the heater, the degree to which the rule is applied depends on the extent to which land quality belongs to the very bad set, and so on. The complete program consists of hundreds of such statements, which together give a kind of fuzzy picture of a society's sustainability.

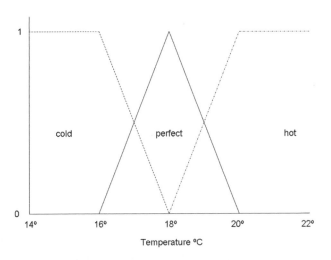

cold   perfect   hot

Temperature °C

HOW TO BE FUZZY

We live in a society that seems increasingly obsessed with numerical targets. Young children are continuously tested at school, with their performances ranked numerically. To go to university in the United States, students must usually excel in their SAT scores. Success in the workplace is measured by salary. Businesses press their employees to meet sales targets or productivity goals, and governments monitor statistics such as GDP to measure the success of their policies. At no time in history has the Pythagorean notion that "number is all" been so rigorously applied.

Numerical measures have advantages. Just as musical notation allows musicians to communicate, numerical scores allow easy comparison and communication of results. But things like wisdom, happiness, or sustainability are not easily measured numerically. Education is about producing rounded human beings, not just expert test-passers. (Indeed, it is a little scary that the United States is run by a group of people who have all done well at a single test—that can't be good for diversity.) Lasting happiness can be elusive, and is rarely induced by something as simple as a salary raise. Businesses that are resilient and successful over the long term often have a strong internal culture with goals and aspirations that go beyond the making of short-term profits.[39]

Some businesses and government organizations are replacing the conventional, bottom-line calculation of profit or loss with the "triple bottom line," which accounts for financial, environmental, and social impacts; or "blended value," which combines the three in a single fuzzy estimate.[40] (Of course, these factors are not incompatible, or independent—being kind to the environment or workers can do much for a company's image, and hence its profitability.) The latest project of Robert Costanza—the economist who came up with the $33 trillion estimate for the planet's services—is the nonprofit company Earth Inc., which is preparing a shareholders report for the planet based on the four factors of natural, human, social, and built capital.[41]

In a fuzzy world, the aim is usually to balance a number of different factors and priorities, some of which may be conflicting. Optimizing for any single target can be a mistake, because it just introduces a distortion. Things like wealth and happiness often go to those who don't directly pursue them.

Well, that's what I think anyway. I'm 80 percent sure.

3 ○ ONE VERSUS PLURALITY
THE VALUE OF NETWORKS

Love of one *is a piece of barbarism: for it is practised at the expense of all others.*
—Nietzsche, *Beyond Good and Evil*

The notion that all these fragments are separately existent is evidently an illusion, and this illusion cannot do other than lead to endless conflict and confusion. Indeed, the attempt to live according to the notion that the fragments are really separate is, in essence, what has led to the growing series of extremely urgent crises that is confronting us today.
—David Bohm, *Wholeness and the Implicate Order*

From out of all the many particulars comes oneness, and out of oneness come all the many particulars.
—Heraclitus, *fragment 54*

It's a small world.
—Traditional

ONE VERSUS PLURALITY

My first full-time job, at the age of sixteen, was at a small camera store in Kensington High Street tube station, London, near where my parents were living for a year. Angie, the manager, hired me to replace a salesperson who had recently quit. It was just she, I, and another guy called Peter. Or that was the way it was supposed to be. On my first day, a young man in his early twenties, dressed smartly in a pin-stripe suit, showed up and announced that the owners were bankrupt and the store was going into receivership. We had to lock the doors immediately and do an inventory.

For the next few days, my task was to help go through the stock of cameras, lenses, films, tripods, filters, cases, and all the other miscellany associated with photography. The accountant, Simon, tallied it all up and compared it with the various invoices and accounts.

It was a strange introduction to working life. At first, there was a good deal of antagonism between Simon and us. He seemed paranoid that we would steal something, and never let us out of his eye for a moment. Angie and Peter resented his presence and were worried about finding another job.

After the inventory was complete, Simon consented to unlock the doors and allow customers in, with the hope that we could sell off some of the stock. He stood stiffly behind the counter in his suit, and even tried gamely to sell cameras. After a while he relaxed enough to leave us alone in the shop, and the mood improved.

I loved photography, and it was great to work—if only for a short time—in a shop full of camera equipment and chat with photographers. I got a good deal through the store on a tele-photo lens, which I tried out in the nearby Kensington Gardens and Hyde Park.

One afternoon—after sharing a carafe or two of wine over lunch with Peter and Angie—I was trying to sell a camera to a customer. I enthusiastically described the various features of the device, a thirty-five-millimetre Pentax SLR. At one point I accidentally banged it on the glass counter, which elicited a chuckle from my tipsy coworkers. The man listened to my spiel with apparent interest, but left without buying the camera, promising to return later. (He didn't.)

Angie gave me some advice: "Don't explain it to them. Let them hold it." For most people, purchasing a camera isn't about the exact specifications or features—even if they think it is. They are far more likely to buy if they feel a camera's weight in their hands, experience the texture, even the smell. This is why real estate agents are in favor of the baking of bread before open houses, and why car salesmen care about that new-car odor. When we consider buying something, we absorb a plurality of information, and integrate it into an emotional response. We use our nose as much as our eyes, our heart as much as our head.

After a few weeks of less than stunning sales performance, the doors were locked for the last time, and the remaining stock taken away. Simon was on better terms with us by then, and seemed almost sorry to see the store close. In his briefcase, he held the final accounts, which he would report to his superiors. All the camera gear, the labor, the customer contacts, the unclaimed developed films, everything that made up the business had been reduced to a single profit/loss number (with an emphasis on loss). The plurality had become one.

Money is the great reducer. It's a way of shrinking reality down to a single point, just as a photograph shrinks time down to a single instant—except instead of having a unique record of an event, you have a number. As Aristotle said, "All things are measured by money."[1]

But as someone later told me at the end of another project, "It's the people that matter—that's what you remember about a job." So how much are relationships worth? Hard to answer, outside the kidnapping business. In this chapter, we look at the structure of networks—the ties that bind together a team of workers, or schoolchildren in a park, or a money-trading economy. For even money itself has no value if there is no network of people to recognize it.

CONFIDENCE TRICK

The first coins were made from precious metals such as silver and gold. They appeared around 630 B.C. in what is now Turkey, and rapidly spread around the civilized world. Pythagoras may have introduced the first coinage to his region, and money no doubt influenced his thoughts on the power of number. As classicist W. K. C. Guthrie noted, "The impact of monetary economy, as a comparatively recent phenomenon ... might well have been to implant the idea that one constant factor by which things were related was the quantitative. A fixed numerical value in drachmas or minas may 'represent' things as widely different in quality as a pair of oxen, a cargo of wheat and a gold drinking-cup."[2]

The first recorded use of paper money was in seventh-century China, but it only gained widespread acceptance in Europe a thousand years later when the Bank of England, founded in 1694, began to issue notes as a receipt for cash. These were originally handwritten and signed by cashiers. In 1855, the first fully printed notes appeared, with the anonymous message "I promise to pay the bearer on demand the sum of ..." If economics is about happiness, then the money system is all about trust—we have to be willing to swap a gold coin for a paper note. It is a kind of mass confidence trick that relies on our group belief to sustain it.

The Master of the Mint from 1701 to 1725 was Isaac Newton, who after suffering some kind of mental and physical breakdown—perhaps brought about by mercury poisoning from his alchemical experiments—had turned his attention from calculating the orbits of planets to even more vexing questions, such as the relative worth of silver and gold.[3] "A pound weight of fine gold," he wrote in one 1717 report, "is worth fifteen pounds weight six ounces seventeen pennyweight & five grains of fine silver, recconing a Guinea at 1£, 1s. 6d. in silver money ... When ships are lading for the East Indies, the demand of silver for exportation raises the price to 5s. 6d. or 5s. 8d. per ounce or above. But I consider not those extraordinary cases."[4] Today, banks rely even more on physics and mathematics graduates to calculate the worth of their exotic products, and convert lead to gold. Money, having freed itself from the physical universe, has become number itself, and finance a strange form of mathematical alchemy.

Newton the physicist believed that matter, the gold and silver of his coins, was made up of "solid, massy, hard, impenetrable, movable particles." The role of God was that of a "prime mover" who set the particles in motion, then stood back and watched them run, as in Figure 3.1 (although Newton the alchemist also made room for a "vital force" that was somehow related to the behavior of elements such as mercury). This particle view of matter was the foundation for the development of nineteenth-century physics. To understand the behavior of a certain substance, it wasn't necessary to model each individual atom or molecule in detail. Instead, scientists could use statistical techniques to deduce the macro-properties by averaging over the micro-properties. The behavior of a gas, for example, could be understood by imagining it as a collection of widely spaced, individual particles that bounced randomly off one another (in liquids and solids, the particles were more closely packed).

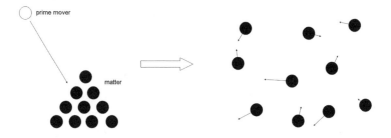

Figure 3.1. According to the Newtonian model, matter was made up of discrete particles that were initially set in motion by a divine force.

For this approach to work, the key requirements were that particles were identical in nature and acted independently of one another. One water molecule was like another, and they didn't get together to form conspiracies. Inspired by the successes of nineteenth-century physics, social scientists attempted to follow in their footsteps by making similar assumptions about human beings. In 1835, the Belgian astronomer and sociologist Lambert Quetelet proposed the idea of *l'homme moyen*, or average man— the human gas particle. Variation around the norm could be understood using statistical tools from astronomy such as the bell curve, otherwise known as the normal distribution, which again assumed that individual variations were independent of one another. By averaging over large numbers of people, economists believed they could deduce laws that governed society. As William Stanley Jevons wrote in 1866, these laws "are to be conceived as theoretically true of the individual; they can only be practically verified as regards the aggregate transactions, productions, and consumptions of a large body of people. But the laws of the aggregate depend of course upon the laws applying to individual cases."[5] The trick was to deal with "the single average individual, the unit of which population is made up."[6]

With these assumptions, Jevons analyzed the behavior of a perfect market. He defined this to be "persons dealing in two or more commodities, whose stocks of those commodities and intentions of exchanging are known to all ... Every individual must be considered as exchanging from a pure regard to his own requirements or private interests, and there must be perfectly free competition, so that any one will exchange with any one else for the slightest apparent advantage."[7] In such a market, which Jevons believed closely approximated real markets, it should be possible to solve for the equilibrium state that would theoretically be obtained if all sellers and buyers were to be simultaneously satisfied. The equations resembled those used by physicists to model the forces on a set of objects, except that here the objects were the "average" producers and consumers, and the forces were their desire to maximize utility.

Of course, a real market was a dynamic thing—there was never a point where all buyers and sellers had everything they wanted, and all trade ground to a halt. However, Jevons pointed out it was "much more easy to determine the point at which a pendulum will come to rest than to calculate the velocity at which it will move when displaced from that point of rest." Similarly, it was "a far more easy task to lay down the conditions under which trade is completed and interchange ceases, than to attempt to ascertain at what rate trade will go on when equilibrium is not attained."[8] The task of neoclassical economics, then, was to solve for this theoretical equilibrium state. By understanding the laws of society, economics would become "a science as exact as many of the physical sciences."[9]

The assumption that the market behaves like a collection of independent, perfectly informed individuals was originally adopted in order to aid computation, but has turned out to be a persistent feature of orthodox economics. In 1965, 100 years after Jevons wrote his *Theory of Political Economy*, Eugene Fama presented his now-famous PhD dissertation on what he called the Efficient Market Hypothesis. Echoing Jevons, Fama imagined "a market where there are large numbers of rational profit maximizers actively competing, with each trying to predict future market values of individual securities, and where important current information is almost freely available to all participants."[10] Fama's hypothesis was that such a market would efficiently allocate resources.

Today, neoclassical economics still assumes the market is made up of free individuals, who interact only to maximize their own utility, and that the economy can be modeled by aggregating over these individuals. For example, economic models typically represent consumers in a country by a single, representative household. The existence of a functioning, regulated market, fed by a perfect flow of information, is also assumed as a given. As economist Kenneth Arrow wrote in 1984, society is "just a convenient label for the totality of individuals."[11] Money may gain its value from the trust a society places in it, but economists have attempted to remove society as much as possible from the picture. But can we really model a bustling human marketplace the same way that physicists model a cloud of gas molecules? How do we incorporate the fact that humans have relationships with one another, and communicate?

This question is one of the subjects of network theory. Instead of seeing a group of people or objects as nothing but a collection of individuals that act independently of one another, network theory focuses instead on the relationships between them. It is about the links between the dots.

JOINING THE DOTS

Physicists—or anyone with a pair of ice skates—have long known that molecules, while they may not form conspiracies, are capable of organizing themselves into connected networks with a huge effect on a material's properties. When water freezes, the process is a little like Figure 3.1 in reverse. In liquid form, the molecules are free to jostle around in a random fashion. Temperature is a measure of the average speed of the molecules, and as the liquid cools, the molecules slow down and begin to align themselves with their neighbors. At first, this is a strictly local phenomenon, but at a critical point—known as the phase transition—large clusters of molecules spontaneously align themselves into the highly ordered network known as a crystal (the word is from the Greek *krystallos* for ice). In most substances, the solid phase is denser than the liquid, but a peculiarity of ice is that the reverse holds, which is why ice conveniently floats on water. This is a property not of the individual molecules, but of the network.

While networks have been around a long time, mathematicians only began to study them in earnest quite recently. In 1959, Paul Erdös and Alfred Rényi explored the properties of randomly connected networks such as the one in Figure 3.2.[12] These consist of individual nodes, connected at random by lines. They found that if there are a large enough number of nodes, say, 1,000 or more, then as random connections are added, most of the connected groups will only consist of two individuals. As more connections are added, larger clusters slowly begin to form. And at a certain threshold—sometimes called a phase transition, after the physics term—the group suddenly gels into a cohesive whole, like water freezing.

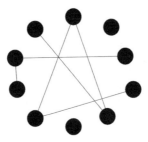

Figure 3.2. In a random network, connections between nodes are made on a random basis.

Random networks have been used to model phenomena such as the spread of disease. Suppose that people (represented by nodes) bump into one another socially (form connections) in a random way. If a disease is only weakly transmissible, it will never become established in the overall population because it won't jump efficiently from one person to another—it won't build enough connections. However, there again exists a certain critical threshold for transmissibility, above which the disease will spread throughout the entire network. That's the difference between a few isolated cases of a disease and a pandemic.

Random networks have the advantage of being mathematically tractable, but they are a rather coarse model of society. Neoclassical theory aside, people don't hang around with each other for purely random reasons—they tend to cluster in groups with shared backgrounds, interests, occupations, or geographical location. Society is not like the random disorder of a gas, or the pure order of a solid, but rather shows a richer and more complex structure—as was graphically illustrated in 1967 by Harvard psychologist Stanley Milgram.

CHAIN MAIL

The year before the *Apollo 8* astronauts took their famous photograph of the earth from space, Milgram launched another experiment that would also make the world look smaller—but on a budget of only $680. He prepared a number of folders, made of thick blue cardboard embossed with "Harvard University" in gold letters, and mailed them out to sixty randomly selected people in Wichita, Kansas. Inside the folder was a letter. It gave information about a target person, and asked the recipient to forward the letter to someone they knew on a first-name basis, who would be likely to know that person. The idea was to find how many steps it would take to find the target—if he or she were ever found at all. The experiment was like sending out a message in a bottle. Milgram was surprised to find that, in some cases at least, the messages reached their targets quite rapidly.

The first target person was the wife of a divinity student living in Cambridge, Massachusetts. After only four days, wrote Milgram, "an instructor at the Episcopal Theological Seminary approached our target person on the street. 'Alice,' he said, thrusting a brown folder toward her, 'this is for you.' ... He had passed it on to an Episcopalian minister in his home town, who sent it to the minister who taught in Cambridge, who gave it to the target person. Altogether, the number of intermediate links between starting person and target amounted to two!"[13]

In another experiment, the target was a Massachusetts stockbroker who worked in Boston. Out of 160 folders sent to starters, forty-four eventually reached their target, after passing through a range of two to ten intermediaries. The median was five, which corresponded to only six mailings to reach a destination.

Thus was born what became known as the small-world phenomenon—the idea that in terms of the network, we are all a short distance apart. *Six Degrees of Separation* was chosen as the title for a 1990 play by John Guare, which also became a film. As one character says, "I read somewhere that everybody on this planet is separated by only six other people. Six degrees of separation. Between us and everybody else on this planet. The president of the United States. A gondolier in Venice. Fill in the names … A Tierra del Fuegan. An Eskimo."[14]

Attractive as the "six degrees" notion is—it's nice to think we're all part of one big family—scientists have recently questioned its accuracy. In the first experiment involving the wife of the divinity student, only 5 percent of Milgram's letters reached their destination; the rest never made it, and were omitted from the results. In the second experiment involving the stockbroker, less than 30 percent reached their target. Perhaps the number six represents not the separation between people, but only how long a chain can become before it gets broken. As psychology professor Judith S. Kleinfeld wrote, the empirical evidence suggests the world is not closely connected, but rather more "like a bowl of lumpy oatmeal," with some of us well connected, and others much less so.[15]

Indeed, another question is why the "six degrees" meme caught on in the first place. One reason is that it appears counterintuitive, and so it sticks in the mind, as do weird coincidences such as acquaintances knowing each other.[16] In any case, both of these issues—the interconnectedness of society, and the spread of memes—are themselves related to the science of networks.

The main problems in analyzing social networks are how to obtain large volumes of data, and how to make sense of it all.

Mailing folders to people in Wichita only gets you so far (to Wichita). Interest in the subject of network theory increased dramatically with the development of two things: the first was fast computers, which enabled simulations of complex systems; the second was a way of connecting those computers. These developments not only helped scientists share information and process data, but also eventually created a powerful example of a global network that was easy to analyze—the World Wide Web.

THE GLOBAL VILLAGE

The basic computer protocol that supports the Internet was born in 1969. It was a project of the Defense Advanced Research Projects Agency, which was founded after the USSR's *Sputnik* launch to help regain the United States' technological edge over the Russians. The network started with a few computers, grew into a communications network for universities in 1983, and was opened to commercial interests in 1995. It then underwent something like a phase transition, spreading rapidly around the world, and becoming a pervasive and indispensable feature of modern life. It is now used by well over a billion people. If you have a computer, it really is a small world. You may not know someone who knows someone who knows the president of the United States, but you can e-mail the White House, or check its web page.

The arrival of the Internet and the World Wide Web meant that scientists could do serious research using enormous computerized databases. Alternatively, they could mess around and have fun. Three fraternity men at Albright College in Pennsylvania chose the latter course, and decided, for reasons best known to themselves, to calculate—in the spirit of *Six Degrees of Separation*—how many steps it takes to link actors with the actor Kevin Bacon. The Internet Movie Database, contains, at the time of writing, about 800,000 actors who have appeared in around 400,000 films.[17] Any actor who has shared the silver screen with Bacon has a Bacon number of 1. At last count, there were about 2,000, including, for example, Tom Hanks, who played the astronaut Jim Lovell in *Apollo 13* (Bacon played his colleague Jack Swigert). Any other actor who has appeared alongside Hanks or anyone with a Bacon number 1 has a Bacon number of 2. The average Bacon number for any actor in the entire database was found to be slightly less than 3. This conclusively proved the film world was small—and helped pass the time. In 1994, the game was featured on the comedian Jon Stewart's talk show on MTV, and its Internet site was chosen by *TIME* magazine as one of their top ten web sites for 1996.[18] The small-world meme went big time.

Interestingly, other databases that had nothing to do with Kevin Bacon also turned out to have small-world structures. Not to be outdone by actors, mathematicians launched into a study of mathematical collaborations. The Mathematical Reviews database contains around 2 million papers, authored by more than 400,000 different mathematicians. The majority of those papers involve two or more authors. The most prolific mathematician of all time was probably Paul Erdös, who wrote or cowrote almost 1,500 papers, including the above-mentioned one on random networks. A mathematician who has collaborated with Erdös on a paper has an Erdös number 1, and so on. The average Erdös number is about 4.7.[19] Furthermore, any two mathematicians can be connected to each other by a path with an average length of about eight collaborative links.[20]

An even larger example of a connected network is the World Wide Web itself, in which sites point to one another through URL links. One 1999 study showed that two randomly chosen sites were only separated by about nineteen clicks.[21] Not as small as Hollywood, but much smaller than one may expect, given that at the time the Web held almost a billion documents (it now holds at least ten times more).

In biology, the Human Genome Project gave researchers access to yet another kind of network—living cells. The nodes in Figure 3.3, for example, represent some of the different proteins responsible for metabolism in yeast. Lines between two nodes mean those proteins interact. Again, such biological networks were found to have a small-world property. Connectedness was a fundamental property, not just of human societies, but also of life itself.

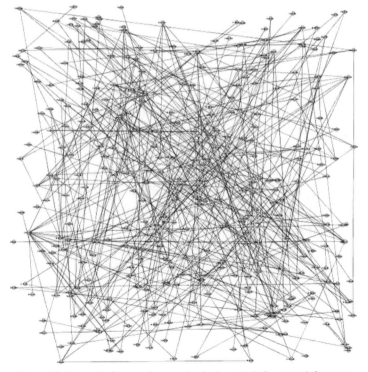

Figure 3.3. Network of interacting proteins in the metabolic network for yeast.

In 1998, sociologist Duncan Watts and mathematician Steven Strogatz published a paper that illustrated the small-world phenomenon in three very different systems: the neural network of a worm, the power grid of the western United States, and film actor collaborations.[22] Such small-world systems are posed somewhere between randomness and order: they show a degree of clustering, so are not completely random, but contain a few long-range connections (see Figure 3.4) that are responsible for the small-world property. Such networks correspond to a society where most people stay at home and only know one another because they are neighbors, but a few travel widely and are on first-name terms with Tierra del Fuegans and Eskimos.

Their research showed that adding long-term connections had a highly nonlinear effect—it only took a small number to drastically shrink a network. One implication was that epidemics might spread much faster than would be evident from mathematical models based on random networks. This fact was demonstrated by the SARS outbreak in 2003. The virus is believed to have originated in Guangdong province in China, but quickly spread to more than two dozen countries as the result of a few random, long-range travel connections. It is debatable whether the world is small in terms of social networks, but for a virus, it is shrinking all the time.

Another intriguing property of many complex networks is that they are scale-free. In any but the simplest network, nodes will have a different number of connections, but in a scale-free network the number closely follows a power-law distribution. As discussed in more detail in Chapter 7 and the Appendix, this implies that most nodes have few connections, while a few nodes have many connections. There is no "normal" number of connections—in other words, no preferred scale.

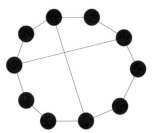

Figure 3.4. In a small-world network, nodes are connected to their nearest neighbors, and in addition there are a few random long-range connections. The latter have the effect of reducing the average number of connecting steps between different nodes.

In order to understand how scale-free networks come about, it is necessary to see the network not as a static thing, but as an evolving, dynamic process. Suppose that a group of children is starting school. Most of the children don't know one another, so they all start with few or no acquaintances. But soon, friendships are struck up, people get to know one another, and groups coalesce. As the school year progresses, a small number of children will have become particularly popular, and will emerge as the social hubs of the in-crowd. Other children are more likely to form some kind of connection with them than others. Social systems therefore have a natural dynamic that tends to siphon connections to a privileged few.

Of course, social ties are hard to measure; what is the difference between a friend, a useful social contact, and a passing acquaintance? A simpler test that can be applied to social networks consisting of more mature people is whether or not they have had sex. One survey based on Swedish data showed the number of sexual contacts is scale-free. The mean number of partners in the sample was seven for women and fifteen for men. However, one woman claimed 100 partners, and one Casanova had 800 partners. In either case, the top 10 percent of sexually active people accounted for nearly half of all sex contacts. As the authors wrote, plausible explanations include "increased skill in acquiring new partners as the number of previous partners grows, varying degrees of attractiveness, and the motivation to have many new partners to sustain self-image ... evidently, in sexual-contact networks, as in other scale-free networks, 'the rich get richer.'"[23]

THE NETWORK ECONOMY

Given that entrepreneurs are often compared with sexual predators—they are always on the lookout for the next score—it is perhaps not surprising that many features of the economy also show signs of being scale-free, or that network theory is finding many applications in the business world.

Traditionally, businesses have modeled themselves after a hierarchical, tree-like structure, as in Figure 3.5. There is a clearly defined flow of command from the top of the organization to the lowest peon at the bottom. The model for this arrangement, which became popular with the Industrial Revolution, can be traced back to Adam Smith. He argued that a business could be made far more efficient if its activity were broken down into many small tasks, with each individual in the company specializing in one task only. In *The Wealth of Nations*, he gave the example of a pin factory, in which "One man draws out the wire, another straights it, a third cuts it, a fourth points it, a fifth grinds it at the top for receiving, the head; to make the head requires two or three distinct operations; to put it on is a peculiar business, to whiten the pins is another ... the important business of making a pin is, in this manner, divided into about eighteen distinct operations."[24] All of this activity would be coordinated from above.

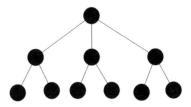

Figure 3.5. A tree network follows a hierarchical structure, in which each node has a low number of connections.

In one of my later jobs, I worked for a company of about 100 people that had an organizational chart displayed at the building entrance, with little photographs by everyone's name. I always found it kind of annoying—it seemed designed to remind everyone of his or her status.

The hierarchical network is well suited to some types of business, such as mass production, or warfare, where a strict top-down system ensures orders are carried out. However, it also tends to be rigid and slow to adapt, and restricts the kind of random, long-range connections that create the small-world effect. Information flows easily from the top down, but signals picked up at the bottom take a long time to reach the boss, if they get there at all. People near the top may get overloaded with information, especially if they are control freaks; those in the lower rungs may suffer a lack of job satisfaction, variety being the spice of life.

Natural systems often incorporate hierarchies, but the flow of information is usually more circular and complex. This may explain why, in recent decades, the top-down business model has increasingly been replaced by a more web-like organization, which better balances the needs for communication and individual autonomy. In the framework of ecologist Eugene Odum (Chapter 1), the business ecology is maturing and becoming more complex and connected.

Network scientists are now often found in the field of business consultancy, advising managers on how to improve the flow of communication inside their companies, and picking over data that before would have been ignored. After the collapse of Enron, for example, the Federal Energy Regulatory Commission posted on their website an archive of about a half million internal Enron e-mail messages. Most were sent between 1999 and 2001, when the company was involved in sophisticated financial scams and was under pressure from regulators. To network researchers, the archive represented a gold mine of data. One thing they found was that much of the important communication wasn't happening through the formal network mapped out in the organizational chart, but rather through informal networks: people who were neighbors, or met in the lunch queue, or were on a sports team, or chatted while smoking cigarettes out by the back entrance (an especially effective networking device—I'm sure some people took up smoking just for this reason). Analysis of the e-mails allowed researchers to discover "who spends time talking to whom, who are the power brokers, who are the hidden individuals who have to know what's going on."[25] Companies are discovering their "corporate culture," and their prospects for success, may be tied up to a surprising extent with the health of such networks.

Many new businesses have been established to navigate and extract information from complex networks. The value of such companies is in turn tied to the network of users they command. Perhaps the best example is Google, which is essentially an advertising company. The influence of a website—and its value to advertisers—is counted in terms of clicks on ads. This was graphically illustrated in August 2006, when Google paid U.S. $900 million for the right to provide search and keyword advertising at MySpace, the social networking site predominately used by teenagers (other companies, such as Wendy's, Adidas, and Honda, simply posed as teenagers and set up their own MySpace profiles).

Other businesses have succeeded by exploiting the connectivity of the network to promote themselves. The archetypal example is the free e-mail service Hotmail, which was started with $300,000 of seed capital in 1996, and sold 18 months later to Microsoft for over a thousand times more. The secret to its success was the message embedded at the end of each e-mail, virally advertising its free service. The more its network of users grew, the more e-mails were sent, and the more advertisements went out.

Advertisers have also taken note that decisions in social networks are frequently the result not just of individual choice, but also of network dynamics. Because some people have more connections and influence than others, firms attempt to target or monitor the trendsetters who act as hubs for the transmission of fads or fashions. Companies also try to influence the government through lobbyists, who are professional networkers. Perhaps the ultimate influence peddlers are the directors of Fortune 1000 companies. One study has shown that these powerful people form a small and highly connected group (otherwise known as an old-boy network), bound together by the approximately 20 percent of directors who serve on more than one board.[26] The companies are legally independent, but they're linked in all kinds of other ways.

Predicting the business network's response to new products or services can be hard. Kodak, for example, was surprised by the speed at which photography switched from film to digital. The transition relied on not just camera technology, but on computers to store and manipulate images, Internet sites to display them, printers to create hardcopies, mobile phones with picture-taking capability, and a community of people who wanted to swap images by e-mail. All of these factors were interrelated—an advance in computer storage technology allowed people to store more images on their computer, which increased the demand for high-resolution digital cameras, and so on.

Firms that rely on external networks of suppliers and subcontractors face a complicated set of challenges. Rather than optimize their own short-term profitability, they have to think of their partners. A network is a team effort, so the art of building and maintaining relationships, along with soft assets such as brand recognition and the ability to attract and recruit talent, are just as important as the bottom line.

Networks also experience a kind of inertia; their evolution is path-dependent and often irreversible, so what happens in the early stages of a product launch can be critical. In 2004, a team led by Duncan Watts performed an experiment at the social network site bolt.com, in which they asked volunteers to rate a set of previously unheard songs by unknown bands. As the researchers increased the level of information users had about each other's decisions, they found that, as Watts put it, "things become more unpredictable ... [Songs] that are popular tend to become more popular still, so that small, possibly random, fluctuations early on can get 'locked in' and generate a large difference in popularity over time."[27]

The entire financial system is now best described as a kind of virtual network of electronic information. Since the Bretton Woods Agreement was abandoned in 1968, currencies have been allowed to float freely against one another. The result has been an explosion in the amount of currency dealing. Every day, around U.S. $2 trillion is shuffled around the international money market—flying through computer networks, bouncing off satellites, relaying through computer terminals—like the neural signals of a giant electronic brain.

One property of such networks, as we are learning, is that they are susceptible to seizure-like failures, such as the ones that periodically afflict the electricity network. In August 2003, for example, a power blackout affecting about 50 million people in the United States and Canada was triggered when a sagging power cable in Ohio brushed against an untrimmed tree. The initial accident caused a pulse that cascaded through the system, growing as it spread. It eventually knocked out 265 power plants. The similarity with financial crashes, where a fall in the New York Stock Exchange can instantly propagate around the globe, is obvious. As network scientist Albert-László Barabási wrote: "Cascading failures are a direct consequence of a network economy, of interdependencies induced by the fact that in a global economy no institution can work alone. Understanding macroeconomic interdependencies in terms of networks can help us to foresee and limit future crises."[28]

WE'RE ALL CONNECTED

The study of particular networks such as the Internet or the transport system is the subject of the new field of network economics.[29] But the importance of networks is so general that it has clear implications for the way in which we model the entire economy. Neoclassical theory is based on a very particular type of network—one in which economic agents have no connection with one another at all, except to buy or sell. As economist Donald N. McCloskey put it, all information comes from "bumping up against constraints. Nobody tells anyone anything."[30] That may be computationally tractable, but it's a poor approximation to reality. If the market were as homogeneous as orthodox theory proposes, there would be no motivation for trade to even occur; if individuals were really unconnected, the market could not function; and if there were no societal trust, there could not even be a shared currency.

The network view of the market is very different:

- Access to information is not the same for all, but rather is biased by the fact that connections are unequally distributed.
- Investors or consumers do not always act independently or rationally to increase their own utility, but are affected by the actions of others. Many consumer fads serve little apparent purpose—as witnessed by the frequent surge of interest in particular toys just before Christmas.
- The response of a particular network depends in a subtle way on its structure. If a network is small-world, then information may propagate very rapidly, while if it is divided into distinct clusters, with few interconnections, then communication will be more controlled. Actions have different effects on different groups.
- Neoclassical theory provides a single, overarching, one-size-fits-all economic dogma. Physicist Leon Lederman wrote, "Unification, the search for a simple and all-encompassing theory, is the Holy Grail [of science]."[31] However, network theory suggests that in social sciences such as economics we need a plurality of theories for different contexts—the market for a particular product, the flow of communication inside a single company, or the best structure for a regulatory framework.
- The neoclassical emphasis on competition only represents half the story, because cooperation is also required in order to survive. As economist J. A. Hobson wrote in 1914: "The presentation of industry as competition with attendant cooperation, instead of as cooperation with attendant competition, has greatly contributed to the popular misunderstanding of

commerce, alike upon its domestic and its international scales."[32] Albert-László Barabási: "A *me* attitude, where the company's immediate financial balance is the only factor, limits network thinking. Not understanding how the actions of one node affect other nodes easily cripples whole segments of the network."[33]

So why do orthodox economists persist in visualizing the economy as a homogeneous collection of unconnected individuals? The main reason is that it makes the economy seem like a predictable machine, which is amenable to mathematical analysis using equations. Abandoning this vision would mean throwing away or completely restructuring 100 years of work (which, as discussed in the following chapters, is more or less what many economists are starting to do). But network theory also suggests another reason for its enduring robustness. Neoclassical economics can itself be seen as a kind of intellectual fashion or meme, which has established itself in society. Studies have shown that people attracted by the subject are more self-interested than usual, and studying it makes them even more self-centered than they were before. For example, students at Cornell University were asked at the start and end of a term whether they would return a lost envelope containing cash. If they studied economics, they became less honest, whereas if they studied astronomy, they became more honest.[34]

A traditional aim of education is to lift people out of their own little worlds and make them think about something bigger than themselves, but economics appears to accomplish the opposite. As economist Neva R. Goodwin notes, "every year, 1.4 million undergraduates in the U.S. take an introductory economics course that teaches that only selfishness is rational."[35] Many of those students go on to hold top jobs in business, government, and international institutions. Our economic paradigm therefore helps create the conditions necessary for its own survival. People who have been trained to see the world in selfish, individualistic terms see neoclassical theory as representing a deep truth about human behavior.

Of course, it isn't necessary to take an economics course to behave selfishly, especially where money is concerned. One 2006 study showed that when subjects were primed to think about money—for example, by seating them in view of a pile of Monopoly cash—it made them act in a more individualistic manner: they were less likely to ask for assistance at solving a problem, or make a donation, or offer to help another person. They preferred "to play alone, work alone, and put more physical distance between themselves and a new acquaintance."[36] With its emphasis on individualism, though, neoclassical economics reinforces and legitimizes this psychological tendency—and in a materialistic world, the dominant economic ideology has a real impact on society.[37]

Since at least the time of the Industrial Revolution, western societies have been on a trend towards increased atomization, and if anything the process has speeded up in recent decades. According to a report based on the General Social Survey, for example, the average number of people with whom Americans can discuss important matters dropped by almost a third in twenty years, from 2.94 people in 1985 to 2.08 in 2004. As the report's authors write, "there appears to have been a large social change in the past two decades. The number of people who have someone to talk to about matters that are important to them has declined dramatically, and the number of alternative discussion partners has shrunk."[38] A healthy degree of self-sufficiency is replaced by excessive isolation and a breakdown in community, as documented in the United States by Robert

Putnam's book *Bowling Alone* (though see "How to be net-worked," below).[39]

This is especially concerning, because a characteristic feature of economically successful societies is a high degree of social capital, which is loosely and fuzzily defined as the collective value embedded in social networks.[40] As with other forms of capital, social capital in the form of mutually beneficial relationships with friends, contacts, and functioning organizations makes it easier to get things done. It is related to the amount of trust people have for one another and for institutions. In poor societies, trust tends to be strong within the extended family and a small radius of close contacts, but is less willingly extended to strangers, banks, the government, or the law.[41] Because things such as credit, economic confidence, and the value of money itself depend on trust, the economy grinds to a halt without it. Societies get caught in a short-term, beggar-thy-neighbor poverty trap, where it is impossible to build or invest anything for the long term. There is a self-reinforcing element to this—it is easier to be trustful when times are prosperous—so escaping poverty may have as much to do with building the right kind of social capital as it does with building other forms of wealth. America's rich social capital is slowly being eroded, which may spell trouble for its economy in the future. An economic mindset that undervalues networks will also tend to destroy them.

The economy is a mix of two effects: the individual and the network. Our choices are neither purely independent nor decided by society, but rather are the result of interplay between the rest of the world and ourselves. The market draws much of its strength from the diversity of its participants, who often react to the same information in very different ways, and influence one another's choices. Network science can give us insights into the structure and behavior of society—and remind us, as

Hobson wrote, that "humanity in all its various aggregations is a social stuff, and ... whatever forms of coalescence it assumes, i.e., a nation, caste, church, party, etc., there will exist a genuinely organic unity ... distinct from and dominant over the life and aim of its members."[42] For, as discussed in the next chapter, the whole can be worth more than the sum of the parts.

TRADING UP

A good demonstration of the power of networks was provided in 2006 by Kyle MacDonald, 26, from Montreal, who traded a red paper clip for a house.

Actually, he put an ad in the barter section of the Craigslist website announcing his intention to trade the paper clip for something better. His first trade was for a fish-shaped pen (I too have a fish-shaped pen, and am kicking myself that I didn't think of bartering it). He then swapped it for, in order: a ceramic knob, a camping stove, a 100-watt generator, a beer keg together with illuminated Budweiser sign, a snowmobile, a trip to the Canadian Rockies, a supply truck, a recording contract, and a year's rent in Phoenix. By this time his quest had turned him into a celebrity, and he had appeared on radio and TV shows. In a move that confused neoclassical economists all over the world, he swapped the rent for an afternoon with Alice Cooper, on the basis that "Alice Cooper is a gold mine of awesomeness and fun." And then gave it up for a snow globe depicting the band Kiss.

Actor Corbin Bernsen (Bacon number: 2), best known for his role in *L.A. Law*, had been following MacDonald's progress and happened to be a snow globes fan—he already owned 6,500 of them. He offered, in exchange for the snow globe, a paid role in one of his films. This was snapped up, not by an aspiring actress, but rather by the town of Kipling, Saskatchewan (population 1,100). Planning to use the role as a prize in a competition, they offered a house, and for good measure they threw in the "keys of the town" and built a sculpture of a red paper clip. MacDonald now plans to swap it all for a decent-sized country.

According to neoclassical theory, there is no way this could have happened—the only utility of a paper clip is to hold pieces of paper together. That is because neoclassical economics has no understanding of networks such as the Internet or media. But how else do people get rich than by exploiting networks to trade what they have for something better, and then swap that in turn? (Of course, the process also works in reverse—someone has to end up holding the paper clip. Or the fish-shaped pen.)

HOW TO BE NETWORKED

It is often said that we live in a narcissistic, self-obsessed age. It is no coincidence that the ideology of neoclassical economics is based on the primacy of the individual. If we are told over and over that society is best served by pursuing our own self-interest, it tends to rub off on our behavior.

However, while we may have fewer close social ties than we used to, in another sense the human species has never been as closely connected as it is today. When the first pioneers opened up the frontiers of North America, the only way to communicate with their homeland was through a slow and sporadic mail system. Even in the 1960s, the expense of long-distance travel and phone calls meant that people easily lost contact with distant friends or relatives. Today, the ubiquity of electronic communication devices—from e-mail to BlackBerries to mobile phones—means the challenge is not to maintain communications with the rest of the world, but rather to keep it at a manageable level. High levels of travel and migration mean social ties often extend across continents.

The shrinking cost of communication has also revolutionized how we get our information. The Christmas Eve broadcast from *Apollo 8* was orchestrated in a top-down fashion by the United States government. It was one of the last times a single government could address a major fraction of the world's population in a prearranged way. Today, we often get our news from online sources, such as blogs or news sites. And when there is a major event, such as a disaster or terrorist strike, the information increasingly comes from people on the spot, who happen to be carrying digital cameras or cell phones connected to the Internet. Stories are coming from the ground up, rather than being imposed from the top down—and instead of being offered a single, "official" interpretation, we are faced with a diversity of often-conflicting viewpoints.

Apollo 8 showed the world as a single picture, but we are now developing a different, more complex view based on a multiplicity of perspectives. One result is that events in other parts of the world take on a greater immediacy. An example was the 2004 tsunami in Asia, which provoked a huge international reaction. Of course, not all disasters get such a response—but maybe the age of narcissism is being replaced by something a little more generous and compassionate.

4 ○ RIGHT VERSUS LEFT
EMERGENT MARKETS

Everything is simpler than you think and at the same time more complex than you imagine.
—Johann Wolfgang von Goethe

On the right hand boys, on the left hand girls.
—Parmenides, *On Nature*

The essence of tyranny is the denial of complexity.
—Jacob Burkhardt

The right hand doesn't know what the left hand is doing.
—Traditional

THE KITCHEN WARS

Economics, according to the neoclassical definition, is the study of how societies allocate scarce resources to produce and distribute goods and services. In the 1960s, this question was being answered in very different ways by the two dominant powers. On the one side was the capitalist, free market United States. According to their system, the most efficient way of distributing goods was for the government to get out of the way and let the market handle it. By contrast, in the communist system, the government set prices. As Nikita Khrushchev, Stalin's successor as leader of the Soviet Union, wrote in his memoirs: "Centralization was the best and most efficient system. [Everything] had to be worked out at the top and supervised from above."[1] The battle for superiority between these systems was fought not just in places like Vietnam, but also in space. The race to the moon was never really about the moon—its utility didn't rest in samples of moon rock. It was about capitalism versus communism, right versus left.

The Soviets were the first to send a satellite into orbit around the earth with the eighteen-kilogram *Sputnik 1*, in October 1957. It did little more than emit a regular shortwave beeping signal. However, the BBC noted, "The rocket which launched it might also be capable of carrying a nuclear weapon thousands of miles. The fact that *Sputnik* is expected to fly over the U.S. seven times a day has also caused unease. There have already been calls for an immediate review of U.S. defenses, given the implications of the technological leap ahead by a political enemy."[2]

Sputnik 1 was followed less than a month later by the larger *Sputnik 2*, which raised the stakes by including a dog, named Laika. A small mixed-breed stray, she was picked up from the streets around Moscow, then put on a rigorous training program to prepare her for her mission. The world was told that she lived about a week aboard her spaceship until her oxygen ran out. In

2002, it was revealed that she actually died within a few hours of launch from panic and overheating.[3] The craft circled the earth 2,570 times before it burned up in the earth's atmosphere.

In December 1957, the Americans retaliated with their own satellite—but the rocket exploded at launch. They eventually succeeded, but the U.S. satellite program remained beset by mishaps. Perhaps sensing they were losing the battle in space, Vice President Richard Nixon attempted to move the argument closer to home—or at least to a replica version of an American home, at a 1959 exhibition in Moscow. This he proudly showed off to a skeptical Khrushchev, and a bevy of reporters.[4]

> **Nixon:** I want to show you this kitchen. It is like those of our houses in California. [Nixon points to dishwasher.]
> **Khrushchev:** We have such things.
> **Nixon:** This is our newest model. This is the kind which is built in thousands of units for direct installations in the houses. In America, we like to make life easier for women ...
> **Khrushchev:** Your capitalistic attitude toward women does not occur under Communism.

The argument in the kitchen continued, the two men sparring for the superiority of their system, and Khrushchev refusing to be impressed.

> **Khrushchev:** It's clear to me that the construction workers didn't manage to finish their work and the exhibit still is not put in order ... This is what America is capable of, and how long has she existed? 300 years? 150 years of independence and this is her level. We

haven't quite reached 42 years, and in another 7 years, we'll be at the level of America, and after that we'll go farther. As we pass you by, we'll wave "hi" to you …

With the household appliance debate resulting in a draw, the action moved back into space. On April 12, 1961, Yuri Gagarin became the first man to get there. The mission, which included an earth orbit, received no publicity until after it was safely completed, perhaps to allow a cover-up if it were unsuccessful. Gagarin immediately became a celebrity and an official spokesman for the benefits of the communist system.

A few weeks later, on May 25, President John F. Kennedy gave perhaps the most famous speech of his career, calling for America to have a man on the moon before the decade was out. It was "time for this nation to take a clearly leading role in space achievement which in many ways may hold the key to our future on earth."

The Russians, meanwhile, continued to advance their program. The next year, cosmonaut Andrian Nikolayev set a new record by spending ninety-six hours in space, circling the earth sixty-four times. At a rally with Khrushchev in Red Square, he called the flight "one more vivid proof of the superiority of socialism over capitalism."

On January 27, 1967, three astronauts died in a capsule fire during the test of *Apollo 1*. A few months later, on April 24, Vladimir Komarov perished when the parachute system failed and he crashed to earth at more than 400 miles per hour.

It was only with *Apollo 8* that the Americans achieved a decisive victory in the space battle of the economic systems. Less than a month later, the Russians canceled their plans for a lunar mission. When *Apollo 11* landed on and returned safely from the moon, newly elected President Nixon saluted it as "the greatest week in the history of the world since the Creation."

In the race to the moon, there was no prize for second place. And communism, at least in the Soviet Union, never quite recovered from the loss. The American astronauts, as they said, had "the right stuff"—and the right stuff won.

RIGHT VERSUS LEFT

The Americans' victory was partly due to their bottom-up approach, which gave freer rein to the astronauts. As Georgi Petrov, head of the Institute of Space Research of the Soviet Academy of Sciences, wrote in *Pravda*, the *Apollo* missions were "distinguished by the fact that the crew apparently plays the main role in controlling the craft."[5] He argued this was inherently unsafe, as compared to the Soviet program that aimed to control the spacecraft mechanically from the ground. However, the complexity of the task meant that the Russians couldn't keep up in the race—just as a centrally planned economy couldn't compete with free markets.

The battle in space was the acting out of a much older debate between economic philosophies. In his 1776 work *The Wealth of Nations*, Adam Smith argued that in a market economy, the price of an asset will naturally be guided towards its "natural price" by market mechanisms. If a particular good is too expensive, then more suppliers will enter the market, and competition will drive the price down. If the price is too low, then suppliers will go broke or leave the market, and the price will go up. By pursuing his own interest, the individual is thus "led by an invisible hand to promote an end which was no part of his intention."[6] The competitive mechanism acted like a constant hand on the tiller of a boat, or a spacecraft. However, Smith still believed some government regulation was necessary, particularly to prevent the formation of monopolies.

While Smith saw the economy in terms of individual investors, acting on their own self-interest, Karl Marx saw it in terms of two great classes—the capitalists, who owned the means of production, and the proletariat, who supplied the labor. *The Communist Manifesto* (1848), written with Friedrich Engels, announced in the first line, "The history of all hitherto existing society is the history of class struggle." Marx believed that capitalists used their position of strength to exploit workers, who were the ultimate source of wealth. Due to what he believed were irrefutable sociological laws, this would eventually lead to revolution, and the formation of a communist society in which goods were equally shared.

Capitalists and communists didn't disagree about everything. One area where they saw eye to eye was the desirability of economic growth. The capitalists pursued growth by harnessing the power of individual greed and the drive for profit. Marx saw this greed as the great weakness of the capitalist system, which would result in its downfall.[7] But the weakness of the Soviet system was its reliance on central planning. Leaders from Stalin on guided the economy with a series of five-year plans. These were reasonably successful in industrializing the economy, but in the 1960s Soviet living standards still trailed far behind that of their American rivals. Khrushchev appeared unimpressed by the American kitchen, but to most Russians, in their cramped and underheated state apartments, it was about as exotic as a lunar module.

The problem was that the economy was too complex for any single person, or bureaucracy, to understand. Suppose, for example, that the Soviet government had wanted to plan the production of nails. They would start by specifying a production quota, based on an estimate of demand. They would then have to arrange the delivery of all the required raw materials, the machinery for fabrication, and the labor. The price and the delivery to stores would also have to be arranged. If any part of the plan failed—say, the demand was underestimated, or a labor shortage was not anticipated—then efficiency would suffer. Since the output of the nail factory was an input for other industries, such as construction, the effect would ripple through the entire economic network.

Furthermore, the factory would react to quotas, rather than the demands of consumers, with sometimes perverse consequences. As a 1964 *TIME* article observed, "Production quotas are nearly always set simply by gross weight, value or units, so that if a nail factory's output is measured by millions of nails, it tends to concentrate on the smallest sizes; if it is computed by weight, it will turn out nothing but big nails; if the quota were in terms of rubles, Russia would have its first Solid Gold Nail Factory."[8] The invisible hand of capitalism was replaced by the clumsy hand of state control. There was no incentive to be efficient, and no flexibility to adapt.

In the pin factory described by Adam Smith, the coordination of the separate tasks was organized within the company, but the price was set by the market and decisions about production levels were made by each producer, rather than by the state. Market demand was therefore an important source of information, rather than just a static quota as in the Soviet system. The competitive system meant that businesses had to perform if they were to survive.

The neoclassical economists went beyond classical economists such as Smith by insisting that the economy can be modeled mathematically, based on the behavior of *l'homme moyen*, the average man. Smith argued in a fuzzy way that competition is a good way to set prices; the neoclassicists tried to prove it using formulas by aggregating over individuals. So in the 1960s, another area where the Americans and the Soviets agreed, was that the economy was a mechanistic, computable system, subject to deterministic laws that averaged over many people.[9] The only argument was over how best to steer it, and calculate its course.

PEBBLES IN THE SAND

The word "calculate" comes from the Latin *calculus* for pebble. One imagines the Pythagoreans arranging pebbles on the ground in the form of the different numbers—the triangular three, the square four, the arrow-shaped dead of the tetractys— as they puzzled over their different properties.

In 1968, as Mission Control in Houston plotted the path of space missions, the Cambridge University mathematician John Conway was going back to basics. On top of large sheets of squared paper, he and his graduate students were to be found shuffling "poker chips, foreign coins, cowrie shells, Go stones or whatever came to hand."[10] They were looking for what John von Neumann had called a "universal constructor"—a simple set of laws that would allow a pattern to reproduce itself, in the same way as a biological organism.

Von Neumann had found a solution, but it was extremely complicated. The one Conway eventually came up with was far simpler, and, in 1970, was publicized by Martin Gardner in *Scientific American* as a mathematical recreation, dubbed the Game of Life. A checkerboard (assumed to extend indefinitely in each direction) begins with an initial configuration of black counters. At each step, every cell is updated according to the state of its eight neighboring cells (those diagonally adjacent are included). If a counter has two or three neighbors, it survives. If it has one or zero neighbors, it dies of loneliness. If it has four or more neighbors, it dies from overcrowding. These deaths are balanced by births in any empty cell that has exactly three neighbors.

Conway and his students originally did their calculations for such cellular automata by hand. Computer simulations are now available on the Internet.[11] The fate of the system depends on the initial condition. It either dies out (no counters left), reaches a stable steady state, enters a periodic regime, or becomes a continuously changing pattern that never repeats. For example, Figure 4.1 shows the first twelve steps for an initial configuration based on the tetractys. After nine iterations, it becomes a periodic pattern, alternating between a horizontal and vertical bar, which Conway called a "blinker."

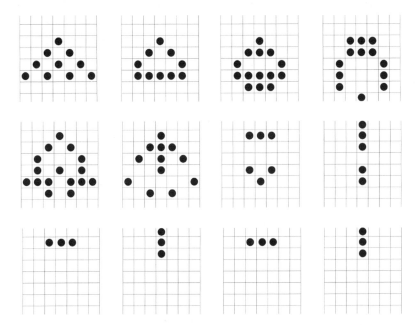

Figure 4.1. First twelve steps of the Game of Life for initial condition based on the tetractys. In the first panel, for example, the black cell at the top of the tetractys has two neighbors, so remains black in the next panel. However, the cells at the two bottom corners have only one neighbor each in the first panel, so they turn white. The pattern eventually evolves into a blinker.

The main interest for Conway and other scientists at the time was to find patterns such as the blinker that repeated themselves indefinitely. But the reason the game caught on with the public— it eventually became a screen saver on many computers—was the way that, with the right initial configuration, the screen would suddenly become alive with an ever-shifting population of weirdly lifelike shapes. How could a simple set of laws lead to such complex behavior?

In the 1970s and 1980s, research continued into the properties of cellular automata based on different sets of rules. The British mathematician Stephen Wolfram classified their behavior in terms of four classes: (i) all activity dies out; (ii) stable or periodic patterns; (iii) random; and (iv) situated on the border between order and pure randomness, with a degree of structure but no enduring pattern. The most interesting were the latter group, which included the Game of Life. Not only were they amusing screen savers, but it turned out they also could be used as what the British mathematician Alan Turing had called a universal computing machine. Properly programmed, they could perform any calculation whatsoever, such as adding or multiplying numbers. In principle, they could do your taxes, or direct a spaceship to the moon. They also showed computational irreducibility, which meant that for an arbitrary initial condition their behavior could not be predicted in advance using any set of equations. Their properties were described as "emergent features" that could only be understood by running the system itself.

The term "emergence" is a rather fuzzy expression that gets used in different ways. The basic idea is that emergent phenomena arise from simpler entities, but cannot be reduced to those entities—there is something novel or surprising about them. In science, the term is often used to describe properties of living organisms, such as consciousness, that seem to go beyond any mechanical explanation. An early exponent of the idea was John Stuart Mill, who wrote in 1843: "All organised bodies are composed of parts, similar to those composing inorganic nature, and which have even themselves existed in an inorganic state; but the phenomena of life, which result from the juxtaposition of those parts in a certain manner, bear no analogy to any of the effects which would be produced by the action of the component substances considered as mere physical agents. To whatever degree we might imagine our knowledge of the properties of the several ingredients of a living body to be extended and perfected, it is certain that no mere summing up of the separate actions of those elements will ever amount to the action of the living body itself."[12] The whole is more than the sum of the parts.

In cellular automata such as the Game of Life, the rules are extremely simple, but they are imposed at a local level. The decision about whether a cell should change color is based on the state of its neighbors, rather than according to any central plan. The rules are therefore simple at a local level, but the behavior at the global level is complex.

But if cells on a computer screen could behave unpredictably, what does that mean for a collection of investors interacting in a marketplace?

BAR-STOOL PREDICTING

As discussed in the previous chapter, neoclassical economics has traditionally viewed the market as a homogeneous collection of independent, equally informed investors, who act rationally to maximize utility. Economists only needed to worry about the behavior of an "average" investor, since all the random differences would come out in the wash. Prices would adjust rationally to external shocks, such as political news, or changes in the weather that affected agricultural crops. However, inspired by experiments with cellular automata, scientists in the 1990s began to investigate the properties of systems in which a number of individual "agents" were free to interact and make their own decisions, as in a market economy.

One of the simplest examples was proposed by Brian Arthur from the Santa Fe Institute.[13] Scientists from the institute, which is famous for its work on complex systems, would often hang out at a bar called El Farol. In Arthur's system, known as the El Farol problem, each week 100 people have to decide whether to go for a drink on a Thursday evening. The catch is that, because it's a small bar, it can get overcrowded. If less than sixty attend, they have fun, but if more than sixty show up, it would have been better to stay at home.

The choice of whether or not to attend therefore comes down to a prediction about what everyone else is doing—but there can be no single perfect strategy. For if everyone adopts the same strategy and decides to attend on the same evening, then they will all lose. The problem, therefore, has a similar characteristic as the liar's paradox—if a strategy is perfect, and everyone adopts it, then it doesn't work. It is also reminiscent of John Maynard Keynes's description of a stock market as a kind of beauty contest, where the aim is not to choose the most beautiful contestant, but rather the one who everyone else thinks is most beautiful. In either case, you're trying to anticipate the decisions of other people.

Arthur simulated the problem by allowing each agent to use one or more different predictive strategies, which are influenced by the behavior of the other agents. For example, they may assume that attendance will be the same as the previous week's, or equal to the long-term average, or a continuation of the trend over the last two weeks, and so on. When the system is run over time, the number of attendees never settles down to a constant number, but rather fluctuates in an apparently random manner. Interestingly, no matter the exact mix of predictors, the mean attendance over time always converges to sixty. Again, local decisions by individual agents result in global properties that are not obvious from the underlying rules. The system has an invisible hand, but it isn't one that can be computed or analytically predicted by analyzing the behavior of an "average" agent. Nor is it stable—some days the bar would be half empty, other days jam-packed.

This agent-based modeling technique was soon adapted to the simulation of "toy" financial markets for some imaginary asset. Each agent had an investment strategy modeled after those used by real traders.[14] For example, "momentum" investors would extrapolate from recent performance, buying if prices were on the way up and selling if prices were going down. "Value" investors would judge whether or not the asset was over-priced according to some specified criteria, and then would buy or sell accordingly. The former tend to make the market unstable by magnifying swings either up or down, while the latter damp out large oscillations by going against trend when prices get out of line with their assessments of underlying value. As in the real world, model investors are also allowed to influence one another, so network effects become important. If the asset price is being driven up by momentum investors, value investors may cave in and join the crowd, pushing prices up even further. Conversely, if prices get extremely low or high, momentum investors may start worrying about value.

Such simulations produced asset price fluctuations that closely resembled real financial data. One problem with neo-classical theory had always been that price fluctuations were more volatile than expected. According to the theory, prices changed smoothly as the market adjusted to external information. In practice, however, sudden swings often seem to come out of nowhere. This volatility is illustrated in Figure 4.2.

Panel (a) of the figure shows a plot of the Standard and Poor's 500 index over a forty-year period from June 1960. The index measures the market capitalization of the top 500 U.S. companies; its apparently relentless march reflects the huge growth in the American economy. However, there has been the odd glitch. Panel (b) shows the daily price changes. On October 19, 1987, otherwise known as Black Monday, the price change was about 25 percent, more than forty times the average change. Panel (c) shows the magnitude of the top 100 ranked price changes, each of which represented a change of a few percent. As discussed further in Chapter 7, these tend to follow a scale-free pattern—most are small, but there is the occasional cataclysmic event. Financial crashes have been a persistent feature of the world economic system, and always seem to come as a surprise—although commentators can usually supply a raft of reasons after the event.

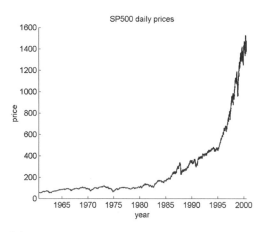

(a)

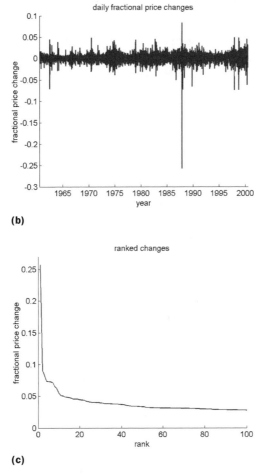

(b)

(c)

Figure 4.2. Panel (a) shows the S&P 500 index for the period June 6, 1960, to June 6, 2000. Panel (b) shows daily fractional price changes. Panel (c) shows the magnitude of the top 100 ranked fractional price movements.

Crashes also happen in the agent-based models, along with scale-free price changes, but they are a property of the system itself, rather than a reaction to any sudden change in the external information. Sudden price changes are therefore an emergent property of the model. They can't be computed from first principles, but rather arise because of local interactions among the different investors. The market is not just reacting in an impartial, unbiased manner to outside events. Like Conway's screen saver, it has a life, and a complexity, of its own.

These experiments therefore refuted the neoclassical idea that the invisible hand of capitalism automatically restores the economy to an optimal state of equilibrium. If each investor pursues his or her own self-interest at a local level, this does not guarantee the net result will be optimal for all of society—the invisible hand has a dangerous case of the shakes. Conversely, a communist state cannot optimize conditions for each individual by controlling the levers of society. The reason in either case is that, according to complexity theory, there is not a direct link between local and global, between micro and macro. Society is what Hobson called "a genuinely organic unity" with characteristics of its own that cannot be reduced to the individual level.

Neoclassical economics and communism are similar in that each thinks of the economy in terms of the average person and aggregates over large numbers to deduce the state of society. But the economy is the emergent product of the interactions of a plurality of agents. A complex system cannot be reduced to its individual components; and because of its complexity, it cannot be easily manipulated or controlled. As a tool for economic policy, neoclassical economics therefore suffers from a similar problem as Marxist theory—which may explain the poor track record of both methods when applied to developing countries.

Like emergence, the word "complexity" has been used by scientists in different ways. By one count, there have been at least thirty-one separate definitions.[15] A popular one is that complexity is at the edge of chaos, between order and randomness. As with class IV cellular automata, such a system can be described by simple rules, and be fully deterministic but still show emergent properties. The difficulty in defining complexity has led to some cynicism about its usefulness as a concept. If scientists can't even agree on a single hard definition, how can they come up with meaningful results?

Complexity is a fuzzy, plural concept that takes on different forms in different contexts. It's hard to pin down, but you can usually recognize it when you see it. Perfect order is boring, perfect randomness is boring, but complex systems are interesting. Like an exciting city, they have enough structure to make a kind of internal sense, and enough unpredictability to produce surprise. In the end, whether or not a system is complex comes down to an aesthetic judgment—it's a right-brain thing.

THE DARK SIDE OF THE BRAIN

Human consciousness—our inner space—has been a subject of study ever since there were philosophers. But it was only in the 1960s that scientists really got their knives out, and separated right from left.

The human brain is divided down the middle into two hemispheres, connected by a large bundle of nerve fibers known as the corpus callosum. The left hemisphere controls the right side of the body, and vice versa. Perhaps because about 90 percent of humans are right-handed—or perhaps because the sun moves clockwise, to the right across the sky—most cultures have come to associate the right side of the body, and especially the right hand (what Aeschylus called "the spear-throwing hand") with strength and masculinity, and the left side with weakness and femininity.[16] The words "dextrous" and "deft" come from the Latin for right, while "sinister" is from the Latin for left. The English word "left" is from the Anglo-Saxon word *lyft*, for weak, while the French version, *gauche*, means crude in English. The poet W. B. Yeats wrote in 1900: "If you wish to be melancholy hold in your left hand an image of the Moon made out of silver, and if you wish to be happy hold in your right hand an image of the Sun made out of gold."[17] To the Pythagoreans, right was on the side of good, left on the side of evil.

It was widely believed until the early 1960s that the left side of the brain, which controlled the dominant right side of the body, was itself the dominant hemisphere, responsible for most of the higher forms of intellect, such as speech and computation. Even small lesions to the left brain could destroy a person's ability to read, while the right side appeared much less sensitive. As the psychologist Roger Sperry noted, the collective evidence "converged to support the picture of a leading, more highly evolved and intellectual left hemisphere and a relatively retarded right hemisphere."[18]

Research into the function of the two hemispheres was hampered by the fact that, in the normal brain, they formed a connected, dynamic partnership. There was no easy way to interrogate the two parts of the brain separately; they were two sides of the same coin. In the 1960s, though, Sperry and others carried out a number of experiments on so-called split-brain patients. These were epileptics who had undergone a radical surgical operation, in which the corpus callosum was severed to prevent seizures from spreading from one hemisphere to another (the ancient Greeks called epileptics *seleniazetai*, after the moon goddess Selene, because it was believed their fits were influenced by the phases of the moon).[19] The operation reduced the magnitude of the seizures, and appeared to have little obvious effect on the personality or cognitive powers of the patients. However, Sperry and his colleagues realized that with these patients the two hemispheres would not be integrated in the normal way, and devised a series of ingenious tests to tease apart their separate roles. For example, by flashing words to one eye but not the other, they could address the two hemispheres separately. The big challenge, they wrote, was "to find out what goes in that silent, mute, speechless minor hemisphere"—the dark side of the brain.[20]

In some respects, their findings confirmed the notion that the left brain was the brighter of the two: it was "highly verbal and mathematical, performing with analytic, symbolic, computerlike, sequential logic," while the right side flunked at even basic math.[21] However, "the so-called subordinate or minor hemisphere, which we had formerly supposed to be illiterate and mentally retarded and thought by some authorities to not even be conscious, was found to be in fact the superior cerebral member when it came to performing certain kinds of mental tasks. The right hemisphere specialities were all, of course, nonverbal, nonmathematical and nonsequential in nature. They were largely spatial and imagistic, of the kind where a single picture or mental image is worth a thousand words." Examples were face recognition, or the detection of patterns. In the context of cellular automata, one could say the logical rules used to define the system are best understood by the left brain, but the emergent behavior that reveals itself in complex, shifting patterns is right-brain.

The scientists found that the two hemispheres seemed to be carrying on a quite separate existence. In some cases, if a split-brain patient had been asked to pick up an object with his left hand, his left brain wouldn't know what it was. The right hand literally didn't know what the left hand was doing. The two hemispheres even seemed to have different personalities. One patient, during Watergate, was asked whether or not he liked Richard Nixon. His left brain said yes, his right brain said no.[22]

The left brain also seemed responsible for our tendency to build mental models for explaining phenomena, while the right brain was more tolerant of ambiguity and uncertainty. In his book *Theatre of the Mind*, Jay Ingram relates a story about a woman patient at a Toronto hospital who had suffered a large hemorrhage on the right side of her brain. Her left side was paralyzed, and her brain couldn't accept that her left arm even belonged to her. The hospital ID on her wrist had a small misspelling, so she concluded that the arm must belong to the person who was in the room before her.

"How do you imagine her arm got onto your body?"

"I don't feel it's really onto my body. It lies on top. It's very heavy, very annoying."

"Did her arm stay behind somehow after she left the hospital?"

"It's the only thing I can suspect. I can't figure out how this happened."

The left side of her brain was struggling to construct a logical, sequential narrative, but because the part of the brain that controlled the arm was damaged, it had no information to go on.

In a way, that's exactly what has happened with neoclassical economics. It tries to explain the economy in a reductionist, logical way, and when it comes across something it can't understand, such as financial crashes, it goes into denial, and prefers to believe its model rather than accept the heavy weight of evidence pressing down on it. As Alan Greenspan, the future chair of the Board of Governors of the U.S. Federal Reserve, said in 1984, when he was head of a private consulting firm, "A surprising problem is that a number of economists are not able to distinguish between the economic models we construct and the real world."[23]

Science's aims—if not always its methods—have long been left-brained in nature. Scientists try to build a logical, sequential narrative by dividing a complex system into its constituent parts. According to the neoclassical economist Frank Knight (1921), "This is the way our minds work; we must divide to conquer. Where a complex situation can be dealt with as a whole—if that ever happens—there is no occasion for 'thought.'"[24] The philosopher Mary Midgley wrote, "during much of the twentieth century the very word 'holistic' has served in some scientific circles simply as a term of abuse."[25] However, holistic phenomena are a fact of life in complex systems, and to ignore them is like cutting off your left hand.

Money is itself a volatile and emotional subject. Words such as greed, generosity, miserliness, and extravagance are all used to describe other people's spending habits. Married couples—not to mention countries—have more arguments over money than any other topic. So it is ironic that the subject has somehow been neutered and stripped of all its psychological and societal implications by the high priests of economic thought in order to make it seem logical.

Adam Smith's invisible hand does exist, but as an emergent property of a complex system. It has a fuzzy tendency to reduce big price discrepancies, but it acts in a rather haphazard way. Commodity producers tend to feel its effects strongly, because it is hard to differentiate their product from the competition. If a farmer charges too much for his wheat, it won't sell at market. As a result, farming tends to be a low-profit activity. Companies that supply the farmer with specialized chemicals and machinery fare better because there are fewer direct competitors. Large stores, too, are in a good position to drive down the prices of their suppliers (they *are* the market). Paradoxically, while commodity prices are strongly affected by competition, and should, according to neoclassical theory, be driven towards equilibrium, they are actually highly unstable, as seen later.

THE JANUS ECONOMY

Just as the left and right hemispheres of a healthy brain work together as part of a dynamic collaboration, so the economy is a mix of individual, local interactions, and larger-scale dynamics. Capitalism emphasizes the individual, while communism emphasizes the plural; but the individual and the plural are two aspects of the same thing. There is a constant flow of information from one to the other, between the left and the right. Indeed, it is exactly this tension that gives the economy the ability to innovate and generate new solutions.

In 1967, Arthur Koestler coined the term "holon" to describe "self-regulating open systems which display both the autonomous properties of wholes and the dependent properties of parts."[26] He saw organisms and societies as being made up of a hierarchical sequence of semi-autonomous holons—cells, organs, bodies, families, tribes, nations—which are in constant interaction through cooperation or competition. Note that the latter is not necessarily the dominant theme; in multi-cellular organisms, competition and growth of cells are highly regulated, unless they're associated with a disease. At each level of the hierarchy there is a dichotomy between the whole and the part. Every holon has a "dual tendency to preserve and assert its individuality as a quasi-autonomous whole; and to function as an integrated part of an (existing or evolving) larger whole." In humans, it is the integrative tendency that results in "flexible adaptations, improvisations, and creative acts which initiate new forms of behaviour." He referred to the dual atomistic/holistic nature of holons as the Janus phenomenon—after the God whose two faces, probably originally representing the sun and the moon, adorned many Roman coins.

Further insight into the Janus phenomenon came from a class of systems that researchers at the Santa Fe Institute called complex adaptive systems.[27] These are made up of individual agents that interact through competition or cooperation, but as the name suggests the population can change and adapt, by learning or by a process of selection. Feedback between the individual agents, the external environment, and the system as a whole mean that everything coevolves in an unpredictable way. The systems tend to become increasingly complex with time, although sudden crashes can also occur, and develop a rich internal order consisting of different hierarchies, or, as Koestler called them, holons.

The archetypal real-world example of a complex adaptive system is an ecosystem, where a degree of natural variation between generations, coupled with selective pressures from the environment and other species, means that successful variants tend to proliferate and establish a niche, thus driving the evolution of the system as a whole. There is a constant flow of information between each individual species, its local habitat, and the rest of the ecosystem. Other examples from human society are the growth of a city, the Internet, and, of course, the economy. The success of a business depends in an intricate way on its ability to compete and cooperate with other firms, and also the state of its employees, its sector, and the overall economy.[28] The argument of top-down regulation versus free individualism is really a false dichotomy, because both are intertwined at every level of the economy: individual people regulate their consumption, companies regulate their expenditure, and societies regulate their financial system.

The most striking thing about complex adaptive systems, and what makes them different from machines, is the way in which they grow and develop. Adaptation occurs at every level of organization, from the most basic to the system's entirety. Complexity research is therefore proving useful in exploring what orthodox economics has always struggled to answer—how the economy learns, innovates, and even develops in the first place. The importance of markets—which are themselves an emergent feature of the economy—is not just their ability to set prices, but also the role they play in this evolutionary process by selecting for businesses that succeed in finding customers.

Institutions such as the London School of Economics now teach courses in complexity, and what Brian Arthur from the Santa Fe Institute dubbed "complexity economics" has become an area of research in its own right.[29] In his 2006 book *The Origin of Wealth*, Eric D. Beinhocker defined the five "big ideas" of complexity economics as dynamics (the economy is an open, dynamic system); agent-based modeling; networks; emergence; and evolution (evolutionary growth generates novelty and complexity).[30] The field has roots in heterodox economics that go back at least to Joseph Schumpeter's theory of "creative destruction," and Friedrich Hayek's 1967 paper "The Theory of Complex Phenomena," but is strongly reliant on the new computational tools that have come out of complex systems research.[31] Rather than try to describe an economy or a particular market using top-down equations, the idea is to build models that simulate the behavior of individual participants. Each agent makes decisions based on incomplete information and a set of preferences, and modifies its behavior according to the actions of other agents in its network, and the system as a whole.

Such agent-based models can be used to simulate a wide variety of real-world systems, from the internal organization of a single company to entire virtual markets. For example, one Australian research program is using an agent-based model of suppliers for the electricity network to understand the causes of "considerable price volatility, inadequate reserves, demand uncertainty and unacceptable levels of greenhouse gas emissions. Traditional energy-economy models are too aggregate, static or stylized to handle these kinds of complexities."[32] Of course, these models can never reproduce the exact behavior of individual people or firms, but it is possible to play around with the model parameters to gain insight into how the real system may react to particular changes, and can be improved (see "Managing complexity" for another example).

In political terms, complexity economics is neither of the left nor the right, but rather freely borrows from each side. The individual and the collective are of equal importance; they are the sun and the moon of the Janus economy. Anyway, the victory of capitalism over communism that began with *Apollo 8* was not as simple, or as permanent, as it seemed. Many third world countries, especially in Latin America, are now turning against the neoclassical model prescribed by first world experts, and are seeking their own solutions to poverty and exploitation.[33] The fastest-growing capitalist economy of all, that of China, is run by a nominally communist government. The old division between left and right is becoming blurred. Another formerly straight line that has lost some of its definition in economic life is the one that separates the sexes. In the next chapter, we discuss the half of the human race that, until quite recently, remained hidden from economic view as surely as the far side of the moon.

MANAGING COMPLEXITY

Agent-based models can be used to model—and improve—particular aspects of businesses. For example, suppose a firm wants to find out why it is having problems delivering its products on time. A model is built in which each aspect of the operation—from assembly lines to warehouses to individual trucks—is represented by an independent software agent with its own set of rules. When the agents are allowed to run freely, the result is a simulation of the entire system, which can be tuned to replicate the real behavior.

The efficiency of the system is an emergent property of the entire complex system, which cannot be determined from reductionist analysis. However, the modeler can adjust the rules of the agents to see the effect on the rest of the system. For example, the assembly line may be set to work more hours, or a truck may be allowed to leave when only half full. Frequently a small change can have an unexpectedly large effect on the rest of the system. The model can be used to tune the network, or detect potential problems that would create bottlenecks.

The company NuTech Solutions used such an agent-based model to simulate the supply chain of Procter & Gamble—known to some 5 billion customers as the maker of Tide, Pampers, Clairol, Crest, and hundreds of other products. The model included a plant, a store distribution center, individual stores, trucks, and so on. By helping to optimize the supply chain (soon renamed a "supply network") the model led to cost savings of some $300 million.

Almost as impressive as the money-saving advantages of the complex-systems approach is the amazing new jargon it offers. The same company advertises one of its programs as employing "millions of fine-grained, locally interacting agents that collectively reason in a self-organizing, 'bottom-up' process akin to processes found in biology and other complex systems . .. [A]gents support reasoning with uncertain data using built-in fuzzy logic techniques. Agent interaction via small-world networks—such as are found in power grids, nervous systems, and social networks (think 'six degrees of separation')—dramatically accelerates the rate of discovering data fragments that usefully connect to yield new inferences. Small-world networks synergize with agent activity heuristics to boost processing in interesting areas and form 'basins of attraction' for relevant data."[34]

I told you it was complex.

HOW TO BE COMPLEX

According to neoclassical economists, the free market optimally allocates scarce resources; according to communists or bureaucrats, the answer is central planning. But of course the situation isn't that simple.

One local (for me) example: my parents used to live in the historical—by our standards—Old Strathcona area of Edmonton, Alberta. In the 1980s, the nearby Whyte Avenue was home to a diverse range of businesses, including a number of independent bookstores and cafés. The nonprofit Old Strathcona Foundation restored buildings, improved streets for pedestrians, and helped build the area's identity.[35] Their success turned Whyte Avenue into a trendy attraction for students, artists, shoppers, and my friends (we used to go there to drink in moderation, often until we fell over). As at Santa Fe's El Farol, though, a crowd could spoil the party. Scale matters.

In the 1990s, new bars and restaurants opened to cater to the growing clientele. Because they were so popular, and generated so much tax revenue, the city turned a blind eye to parking regulations, and allowed these establishments to proliferate. Other kinds of businesses couldn't afford the skyrocketing rent, and many closed. The area became known less as a historical attraction, and more as a place for people to get drunk—often upwards of 20,000 at a time. Local residents protested about the number of bars, and complained of crimes ranging from urination in the streets to assault.

Things came to a head during the summer of 2006, with the Edmonton Oilers' heroic and unlikely progression to the final of the Stanley Cup hockey playoffs. They eventually lost to the Carolina Hurricanes, but after every game, tens of thousands of people would descend to Whyte Avenue. Riots broke out; stores were damaged; it was like Paris in May 1968, but with less politics, and more hockey.

What went wrong? According to neoclassical economics, if bars drive out other kinds of business, that is because they are better serving the customer's needs. But the only reason Whyte Avenue became a destination in the first place was because of nonmarket factors such as the area's historical identity (a valuable resource for future generations), the pedestrian improvements, the relaxation of parking regulations, and so on. The bars also introduced many hidden costs, such as policing, and the consequences of drunk driving (most patrons are no longer local). As economist and expert on cultural heritage Arjo Klamer said: "It is difficult for the economic models to take hold of the sobering reality that traditionally the market has been a destroyer of value of historic sites more than a savior of them."[36]

The immediate solution, as local residents have long argued, is to reduce the number of bars. But part of the problem also goes back to the urban planners who first divided the city into separate zones for business, residences, and entertainment, rather than mixing them up, with the result that people often have to travel a distance to get a drink.

Old Strathcona will survive—it is too lively and robust to be defeated by planners or bar owners. But as Jane Jacobs wrote in 1961, cities are a problem of "organized complexity" that require "dealing simultaneously with a sizeable number of factors which are interrelated into an organic whole."[37] Like a good glass of beer, it's not just about cost or the amount of alcohol.

5 ○ MALE VERSUS FEMALE
WOMEN'S WORK

And Heraclitus rebukes the poet who wrote "Would that strife might perish from among gods and men"; for there would be no melody without high and low, nor living creatures without male and female, which are opposites.
—Aristotle, *Ethica Eudemia*

It (the moon) wanders about the earth, shining at night with borrowed light. She is always gazing earnestly toward the rays of the sun.
—Parmenides, *On Nature*

Women have always been poor, not for two hundred years merely, but from the beginning of time. Women have had less intellectual freedom than the sons of Athenian slaves.
—Virginia Woolf, *A Room of One's Own*

Money can't buy love.
—Traditional

MALE VERSUS FEMALE

On Sunday afternoons, I have of late been attending a session called "Man in the Moon" at my local library for fathers and their babies. Like many of the attendees, I was signed up by my wife. We men all sit on the ground in a circle, infants on laps or in our arms, and sing songs meant, Pythagorean-fashion, to soothe or entertain the young ones. For some songs we stand up and walk around in a circle, do a little turn, walk in the other direction, then all come together in the middle, pushing the kids towards one another. They seem to enjoy coming face-to-face. It's like a choir for fathers, with random interjections from the children—squeals, cries, laughter, incomprehensible chatter, and sudden wails of complaint that are sometimes followed by a rapid escort from the room. Most of the songs have pretty silly lyrics. For example, the session is named after the nursery rhyme:

> The man in the moon
> Came down too soon
> And asked his way to Norwich
> He went by the south
> And burned his mouth
> With supping cold plum porridge

The words don't really stand up to logical analysis—how can you burn your mouth on cold porridge?—but they have stood up to the test of time, since the rhyme has been around for several centuries (it has rhyme, but not reason). Anyway, we're all too occupied with the kids to worry about making sense, or for that matter maintaining any sort of credibility.

The 1960s manifestation of the man on the moon was, of course, Neil Armstrong. When he first put his left foot down on the lunar Sea of Tranquility—the climactic move of an elaborately synchronized dance—he might have felt a little self-conscious, given that he was being watched by over a billion people back on earth. But it's probably safe to say he didn't feel embarrassed. And his words couldn't have been more assertively confident: "That's one small step for man, one giant leap for mankind."

In Western cultures, since the time of the ancient Greeks, the moon has usually been associated with archetypal femininity, as in the Greek goddess Selene and her Roman counterpart Luna; with darkness (it only comes out at night); with dependency (it relies on the sun for its light); with change and transformation (it waxes and wanes and is reborn); with evil (witches and werewolves); with thirteen (the number of complete lunar periods in a year); and with insanity (as in the words "lunacy" or "lunatic"). In Britain, the Lunacy Act of 1842 referred to those who are "afflicted with a period of fatuity in the period following after the full moon."[1]

The *Apollo* missions, in contrast, were very rational, and almost exclusively male—the moon landing really was a step for man, rather than humanity (see "The real facts" below). The *Apollo* missions put an end to the moon's mystique as surely as the birth control pill halted ovulation during women's menstrual cycles, which are named from the Greek *mene* for moon (though the ill-fated *Apollo 13* nearly evened the score). In a very real sense, they represented the conquering of the feminine moon with male technology—and the culmination of a tradition of masculine science that dates back to the ancient Greeks.

Pythagoras allowed women into his group, but the Pythagoreans still associated the female archetype with darkness and evil. Plato described women as originating from morally defective souls in *Timaeus*, and Aristotle excluded them from his Academy. During the Enlightenment, science was seen as an exclusively male pursuit, and nature a passive female entity to be conquered and subdued (male scientists still often speak of scientific discovery in sexual terms[2]). It is an empirical fact that, as Evelyn Fox-Keller notes, modern science was developed "not by humankind but by men."[3]

The social science of economics is no exception—indeed, it appears to be an extreme case. All of the names associated with the development of neoclassical theory are male. Of the sixty-one people to have won a Bank of Sweden Prize in Economics in Memory of Alfred Nobel at the time of writing, zero are women.[4] There is no Marie Curie of economics. The field is everywhere dominated—but especially at the top levels—by guys. To say that it lacks the feminine touch would be an understatement. The butchest of all are the neoclassicists, who economist Donald N. McCloskey likens to a motorcycle gang, "strutting about the camp with clattering matrices and rigorously fixed points, sheathed in leather, repelling affection. They are not going to like being told that they should become more feminine."[5]

Other social sciences, such as sociology and psychology, have no shortage of female representatives. Also, in America, women run around 40 percent of small businesses, and over 85 percent of U.S. corporations have at least one woman on the board. So why is it that women can play a key role in running the economy, and can study related fields, but have had so little influence on our theories of money?

Part of the reason goes back to the Cold War, when the United States Department of Defense pumped funds into all kinds of scientific programs, including mathematical economics, in an attempt to gain technological supremacy over its Soviet rival. In 1965, the Pentagon-affiliated RAND Corporation created a fellowship program in economics at the following universities: Harvard, Stanford, Yale, Chicago, Columbia, Princeton, and California. Ever since, these institutions, along with MIT, win most of the funding battles, publish the leading journals, and decide what gets to enter the canon of economic thought. A whole generation of economists was funded largely by the male-dominated military. It is unsurprising that feminist economics still struggles for funding and attention.

But the lack of a feminine influence in economics is not just a question of funding problems, or statistical under-representation, but also goes to the very core of the neoclassical approach. As McCloskey puts it, male economists "insist on square, fact, logic, science, numbers, cognition, rigor, truth, hardness, positiveness, and the objective with a comical, anxious rigidity of the sort the comedian John Cleese makes fun of." Such male qualities are nowhere better personified than in the neoclassical image of the rational economic man, otherwise known as *Homo economicus*.

HOMO ECONOMICUS

Homo economicus is the fundamental unit—the atomic particle—of neoclassical economics. He is the individual economic agent who acts independently and rationally in order to maximize his own utility (companies are assumed to be small in size and act in the same way as individuals). He was first introduced as a kind of simplifying device and computational aid: it is much easier to predict and aggregate over the behavior of a person who always looks after himself than one who has a complex history and whose actions are influenced by various relationships in which he is embroiled. As feminist critics have pointed out, though, this view of economic life also incorporates a degree of gender bias.

Feminists usually distinguish between sex and gender. The former refers to biological differences, while the latter refers to a fuzzy set of cultural beliefs. For example, economist Julie A. Nelson writes that the characteristics of being "self-interested, autonomous, rational, and free to choose among different actions" are associated in modern western and English-speaking cultures with stereotypical masculinity, while the converse— "people who are dependent, emotional, and subject to decisions made by others or influences from the social or natural environment"—are associated with stereotypical femininity.[6] This, of course, is not to say that our culture cannot consider women rational, or men emotional—the statement is fuzzy, not firm—but it does imply that *Homo economicus* is gendered, and he's a guy.

In neoclassical economics, *Homo economicus* exists only to further his own aims in the marketplace. He is stripped of his history, his emotions, his ability to change his mind, his dependency on others, his altruism, and his love. He never was borne of a mother, or grew up in a family. He shares no allegiances with friends or lovers or associates or a country or the planet or a religion. He doesn't act outside his preference system, or work for no pay, or turn his back on materialism, or devote his life to helping others. All of those qualities and propensities are labeled soft and fuzzy and feminine and are kept in the shadows.

The very idea that an individual can somehow be abstracted from their society in this way, and treated as a single independent entity that can be manipulated in equations, is, according to Nelson, a stereotypically masculine notion: "analytical methods associated with detachment, mathematical reasoning, formality, and abstraction have cultural associations that are positive and masculine," while approaches that emphasize "connectedness, verbal reasoning, informality, and concrete detail" are culturally considered feminine.[7] Neoclassical economics is men analyzing the behavior of a rather corny kind of idealized male world, consisting only of rugged individuals who know what they want and don't let anyone get in their way. It therefore reflects a view of men and women that was common in the Victorian era, but is increasingly at odds with the modern economy.

THE SEXUAL REVOLUTION

In 1873, the British politician Algernon Percy said, "The real fact is that man in the beginning was ordained to rule over woman: and this is an eternal decree which we have no right and no power to alter."[8] Even in the 1960s, the assumption that most transactions in the formal economy were between men would have seemed reasonable. The typical household consisted of a male patriarch who represented his family in financial decisions. His spouse and children were his dependents, and relied on his salary. Studies of labor and wages therefore focused entirely on this male breadwinner, and labor unions fought to guarantee a "family wage" for workers. The activities of women and children were completely off the economic radar. Household activities—even doing the dishes—were assumed to be leisure, and household production was not part of the national accounts.

The cozy image of the nuclear family blew up with the sexual revolution and the feminist movement of the 1960s and 1970s. One contributing factor to these developments was the invention of the birth control pill. Introduced in America in 1963, by 1965 it had become the leading form of contraceptive. For the first time in history, women had control over their own reproduction. They reacted by asserting, not just their sexual freedom, but also other kinds of liberation—particularly in the workplace. They stepped up the fight against labor market discrimination, began to move into occupations that had formerly been the sole preserve of men, and protested for equal rights.

In September 1968, America was shocked when the women's liberation movement staged a rowdy demonstration at the annual Miss America Beauty Pageant in Atlantic City, New Jersey. Hundreds of feminists gathered outside the convention center where the event was held, and performed stunts such as crowning a live sheep Miss America, and tossing "objects of female oppression" such as bras into a Freedom Trash Can. They planned to set it alight, but couldn't get a permit from the police because the protest was taking place on an inflammable boardwalk (even so, feminists were known from then on as "bra burners"). Sixteen feminists snuck into the event, unfurled a sign reading "Women's Liberation," and heckled a speech by the outgoing Miss America until they were thrown out. A couple of stink bombs were set off.

At the time of the moon missions, such feminists were considered by many to be dangerous radicals, who threatened the structure of society and the sanctity of the family. However, the boldness of that 1968 protest attracted many to their cause, and launched the feminist movement into the mainstream.

As shown by Figure 5.1, American society hasn't been the same since. The plot shows the response by Americans to the following yes/no questions, from General Social Surveys:

> Do you approve or disapprove of a married woman earning money in business or industry if she has a husband capable of supporting her?

Do you agree or disagree with this statement? Women should take care of running their homes and leave running the country up to men.

Tell me if you agree or disagree with this statement: Most men are better suited emotionally for politics than are most women.

If your party nominated a woman for president, would you vote for her if she were qualified for the job?

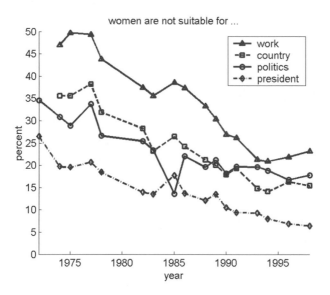

Figure 5.1. Plot showing the changing attitude in the United States to women working, running the country, becoming a politician, or running for president. Source: General Social Surveys.[9]

Since the late 1960s, the proportion of Americans who believe women are not suitable for various types of work has declined enormously. Indeed, dual-income families are now the norm.

The number of people who would oppose a woman becoming the first female president in American history has decreased by a factor of more than four (positive news for Hillary Clinton). The change has been driven by business leaders such as Anita Roddick, founder of the Body Shop, who have shown that women can succeed on their own terms, without having "to be tough-talking or to smoke cigars … Women build alliances, bring people together and, most importantly, they develop networks. Their biggest strength is communication."[10]

This changing attitude towards work and gender represents a true revolution in social values—but one that has not been reflected in the neoclassical model, or the behavior of *Homo economicus*.

HOME ECONOMICS

The feminist movement had two somewhat contradictory effects on the field of economics. It increased the contribution of women to the formal economy, and at the same time drew attention to the value of informal work inside the home.

One of the main feminist objections to orthodox theory is that work within the home—which is still largely performed by women—is not included in national accounts such as GDP. *Homo economicus* doesn't stay home to look after the kids while the wife goes out to work; and the economist Arthur Cecil Pigou noted in 1920, "if a man married his housekeeper or his cook, the national dividend is diminished," because the work formerly done for a price is now done free.[11] This paradox was long treated as a small anomaly in the theory, which didn't merit much attention. In 1988, one textbook ventured: "Many people, particularly leaders of the women's movement, argue that household work should be given a value and included in [GDP]. This is worth thinking about. Would it be a reasonable thing to do? If so, how would one go about valuing household production?"[12]

The same year, New Zealand's Marilyn Waring attempted to answer the question with her book *Counting for Nothing*. She showed that accounting methods such as the GDP missed a huge amount of (largely female) unpaid labor, such as bearing children; bringing them up and educating them; looking after the weak, disabled, sick, or aged; and running the household. It is ironic that economics is named after the Greek for "household rule," but household activities have traditionally been excluded from its area of study.

Because free work is by definition unpaid, its value can only be estimated indirectly. One method is to tally up how much the various household services would cost if supplied by the market. The house can be cleaned by a maid service, a catering company can supply food, and an administrative assistant can take care of the planning. In industrialized countries, unpaid household work, about two-thirds of which is done by women, is estimated to comprise 25–40 percent of the economy. In developing countries, the proportion is even larger.

During recessions, the nonmarket sector tends to expand because people perform tasks such as preparing meals or cleaning the house themselves rather than contracting them out. Therefore, if unpaid work were included in the accounts, it would tend to dampen out the magnitude of the fluctuations in economic cycles—and might remove some of the urgency around maximizing economic growth.

Our economic system also makes no attempt to account for the value of leisure, unless it involves paying someone, which means it tends to be undervalued. Women in industrialized countries still do more than their share of housework, and working mothers in particular are chronically short of time. In

Canada, for example, 30 percent of two-partner families were dual-income in 1967. By 2000, that number had more than doubled to 65.6 percent. Since housework still needs to be performed, the total number of paid and unpaid hours has increased quite dramatically. Unsurprisingly, many working parents find it hard to balance work and family.[13]

Attitudes towards day care are also shaped by the fact that GDP is boosted only when paid carers look after the children while both parents work. From the perspective of maximizing economic growth, parental leave subsidies are counterproductive, not because letting parents spend time with their children is harmful to either party, but because it would subtract from GDP. Since many women now earn more than their husbands—in Canada, the number is around 30 percent—then it may actually make sense for more fathers to look after the kids.[14]

One negative effect of women joining the workforce in increasing numbers is that it has probably contributed to the declining strength of local communities. As Robert Putnam has noted, women have traditionally played a larger role than men in maintaining social ties—between friends, family, and neighbors, or in organizations such as churches (which of course promote a somewhat less tolerant attitude towards me-first individualism).[15] The social dislocation in contemporary western society, discussed in Chapter 3, may reflect an adjustment to a world where women are building careers instead of networks, and men are learning to compensate.

Of course, the value of tasks such as housework, leisure, child rearing, or maintaining social networks is hard to quantify. But as argued in Chapter 2, this does not mean they should be ignored (divorce lawyers are well ahead of economists in this regard). Omitting such unpaid activities from the accounts has real implications. If *Homo economicus* is to represent human wants and needs, then he needs to learn some home economics.

WOMEN'S INDEPENDENCE

As the feminist movement got into swing, some economists attempted to adapt neoclassical theory by extending its methodology to the household. They assumed the difference between male and female roles and expectations was due to innate qualities, and was the natural result of rational choices.[16] The (male) head of the family was assumed to act altruistically for the best interests of his family.

The fact that altruism also appears to exist outside the family remains something of a theoretical challenge to orthodox economists. Some have tried to address it through neo-Darwinist sociobiological theories, which argue that altruism is a disguised form of selfishness.[17] Neo-Darwinists view genes—those sections of DNA that code for particular proteins—as the basic unit of evolution. Because genes are passed on through inheritance, with some modification, they are like quasi-immortal beings. Their only aim in life is to maximize their own chances of survival. Through a kind of invisible hand mechanism, the net effect of all that competition is to produce organisms that are themselves ideally suited for survival. The rational economic man is just a manifestation of his "selfish genes," so any action he takes must increase the chances of survival for his genes in the battle for "survival of the fittest." His independence and competitiveness reflect the true nature of his genes.

This theory claims to explain not only why women will risk their own lives to give birth, or why families will give up other opportunities to look after their children, but also why a Good Samaritan will help a stranger on the street—even strangers share genes, after all. Altruism is therefore nothing but an illusion. As biologist Michael Ghiselin wrote in 1974: "No hint of genuine charity ameliorates our vision of society, once sentimentalism has been laid aside. What passes for co-operation turns out to be a mixture of opportunism and exploitation.... Given a full chance to act in his own interest, nothing but expediency will restrain [a person] from brutalizing, from maiming, from murdering—his brother, his mate, his parent, or his child. Scratch an 'altruist' and watch a 'hypocrite' bleed."[18]

Not only is *Homo economicus* self-centered, he is a murdering psychopath. However, as with much of neoclassical economic thought, there is an element of circularity here. Just as the field of ecology was named after economics, so there is a two-way connection between neo-Darwinist ideas about evolution and theories of economics. Neoclassical economics sees the world in terms of independent, autonomous agents that act to maximize their own utility, measured in terms of financial success. Similarly, the "selfish gene" theory popularized by Richard Dawkins sees the world in terms of independent, autonomous genes that act to maximize their own utility, measured in terms of propagation.[19]

The two theories therefore make the same mistakes. The economy cannot be reduced to individuals; an organism cannot be reduced to genes. People do not act independently, but rather are enmeshed in a complex network—the same goes for genes. An economy is more than the sum of its parts, and so is an organism. Complexity theory shows that such systems cannot be reduced to their elementary components. Selection acts on every level of a system, not just the smallest, so the ability for a group or society to cooperate and work together will make it successful in a way that could never be predicted from a DNA analysis of its individual members. If humanity finds a path towards a sustainable economy that increases our long-term chances of survival, that will say more about our level of social and political organization than the existence of a sustainability gene.

As critics such as the biologist Richard Lewontin and philosopher Mary Midgley have pointed out, the selfish gene theory is as much ideology as science.[20] It is not surprising that it rose to prominence in the 1970s and 1980s during the "no such thing as society" Reagan/Thatcher era.[21] Feminists, too, have often attacked neo-Darwinists for rationalizing sexism. After all, if the theory is taken literally, then rape is just an efficient way of propagating genes.

The problem of altruism disappears if society is viewed not as a collection of *Homo economici* acting to further their self-interest, but rather as a connected network bound by social ties. People help each other, sometimes out of self-interest, but also because they feel compassion, or because they are socially compelled to do so, or because it is their job. Firefighters who enter a burning building to save lives don't do so out of rational self-interest, or as a roundabout way of propagating their genes, but because they feel it is their duty. Loyalty, generosity, cooperation, heroism, a sense of fairness, identification with groups or causes, a willingness to make sacrifices for a greater purpose— these are not aberrations that need to be explained by economists, they are fundamental aspects of human nature.[22] As Adam Smith wrote in *The Theory of Moral Sentiments*: "How selfish soever man may be supposed, there are evidently some principles in his nature which interest him in the fortune of others and render their happiness necessary to him though he derives nothing from it except the pleasure of seeing it."[23]

What needs to be explained is why economic theory doesn't reflect or embrace these basic human qualities—and what are the consequences of that omission. We often worry about the toxic effect on youth of video games, or television violence, but these probably pale in comparison with the toxic effect of a dominant economic ideology that glorifies selfishness.

THE CORPORATION

While *Homo economicus* is a fictional character—really, what kind of person is completely rational and objective and only acts to maximize his utility?—there is a legal entity that has been designed to approach him quite closely in its behavior. That entity is a corporation.

Corporations have a legal status as a kind of person—in the United States, it is known as a "corporate personhood." Their defining features are limited liability and profit maximization. The first means an investor in a corporation is not responsible for the debts or obligations of the corporation. The most she can lose is what she paid for the stock. The second means the corporation is legally bound to make as much money for her as possible. The corporation is therefore a tool for generating wealth while limiting responsibility.

In the early 1800s, when the first corporations were formed, limited liability was intended as a kind of carrot for people to invest in risky enterprises. If a corporation such as the British East India Company failed in its colonialist ventures, the investors would not be on tap to pay creditors. In the United States, the first corporations were special public ventures, such as insurance or canal building. Incorporation was viewed as a special status, and had a limited lifespan—typically twenty to fifty years. As corporations flourished, this was relaxed, and their lifespans became indefinite.

In 1886, the U.S. Supreme Court ruled that a corporation was entitled to the same legal status as a person, with rights including freedom of speech. In 1916, when Henry Ford tried to lower the price of his cars, his stockholders sued. The court ruled the main purpose of a corporation is to maximize the shareholder's profits. As Milton Friedman wrote in 1962: "Few trends could so thoroughly undermine the very foundations of our free society as the acceptance by corporate officials of a social responsibility other than to make as much money for their stockholders as possible."[24]

Unlike real people, corporations act relatively freely of social constraints. They don't get married (apart from corporate merging) or have children. They may be extremely efficient at what they do, but they don't give a damn about anything but themselves. They are rational economic man, writ large.

Feminists such as the writer and activist Naomi Klein have been at the forefront in the battle to curtail the power of corporations.[25] As she wrote in her book *No Logo*, "corporations are much more than purveyors of the products we all want; they are also the most powerful political forces of our time ... corporations like Shell and Wal-Mart bask in budgets bigger than the gross domestic product of most nations." Unlike most nations, however, the concern of corporations for the public weal is somewhat lacking. As Klein describes the situation in so-called export processing zones: "the workday is long—fourteen hours in Sri Lanka, twelve hours in Indonesia, sixteen in Southern China, twelve in the Philippines. The vast majority of the workers are women ... The management is military-style, the supervisors often abusive, the wages below subsistence and the work low-skill and tedious."

In the early 1920s, advertising executive Bruce Barton came up with the idea of giving corporations a soft and human face, telling the president of General Motors, "Institutions have souls, just as men and nations have souls." The main aim of corporations such as Nike or Coca-Cola is to convince the public that they have a personality and stand for some vague quality like freedom or being real. It is ironic that corporations—the ultimate embodiment of rational economic man—find it necessary to dress themselves in warm and fuzzy clothes in order to engage with the public.

BEING OBJECTIVE

Because *Homo economicus* is completely independent—a free agent—he can make his decisions objectively. He is detached not only from other people, but from the world itself. In the particle/wave duality of quantum physics, he is a self-contained particle that interacts with others only through market exchange. He is pure ego. But on what basis does he make his decisions? What drives the rational economic man?

Rather than confront such questions, neoclassical economists have traditionally used the following circular logic: The rational man has a stable set of preferences, which he arrives at independently. He has always had them, and he will have them to the day he dies. Economists often talk about the benefits of choice, but rational economic man doesn't actually have much freedom to choose, because he is a slave to his own preferences. It is impossible for us to know why he has those particular preferences and not other ones—they are a given. The only way we can deduce them is by analyzing his behavior.

Economics has always identified itself with the "hard" sciences, such as physics and chemistry. One way to mimic those sciences is to insist on complete objectivity. The scientist is at all times assumed to be detached and independent of the thing he is studying. The underlying system is assumed to obey deterministic laws that the scientist can reveal.

However, when applied to human beings, a corollary of this "objective" approach is that economic decisions taken by rational economic man are assumed to be immune to any kind of analysis. It is impossible to criticize his preferences, or say that one set of preferences is better, or makes more sense than another. By insisting on objectivity, much of human behavior is simply cordoned off as being subjective and is ignored. The result is that neoclassical economics is fundamentally dualistic—it assumes that rational economic man is independent and objective in asserting his preferences, but the reasons for his preferences are completely subjective and beyond analysis.[26]

Because of its desire to be an objective, mathematical science, neoclassical economics favors abstract models over concrete observations of how people actually behave. Critics have pointed out that this emphasis on the mathematical model serves as a kind of intellectual shield, which allows unsound ideas to hide behind imposing and intimidating formulae. The character flaws of *Homo economicus* are disguised by complicated equations. As Nelson wrote, the mathematics "serves, conveniently, as a protection for the priesthood of economists. Scholars in the humanities who might venture a criticism or want to examine an assumption can often be impressed or intimidated, we economists have discovered, by references to subgame-perfect equilibria or heteroskedasticity."[27] Herman Daly: "How does one say something that is too illogical for words? Usually by burying it in the assumptions of a lot of intimidating, but half-baked mathematics."[28] Mathematical models are essential tools for scientists in any field, but they can easily be abused.

SYSTEMS ECONOMICS

So what would economics look like if women were to take over the economics departments of all the top universities, or if there were as many female economists as there are businesswomen?

The goal of feminist economists is not to simply replace one set of extreme "masculine" assumptions with another set of extreme "feminine" ones. As Nelson writes, the idea is rather to "develop alternatives to such dualistic thinking, seeing the tendency towards binary and 'either/or' conceptions as itself a major cause of problems."[29] The aim is to avoid extremes and take the fuzzy middle path.

Neoclassical economics amounts to a particular mathematical model of human behavior, based on a restrictive set of assumptions. In recent decades, as these assumptions have become increasingly untenable, economists have relaxed them somewhat by allowing agents to have "bounded rationality" (discussed in Chapter 8) or "endogenous preferences" that are subject to a degree of change.[30] However, a persistent theme of feminist economics is that we don't need a single, unified theory at all, but rather a range of theories that capture different aspects of the complex reality. The effect of a particular economic policy depends on all sorts of social, cultural, and historical factors unique to particular places, and can't be summarized by a few pat equations. As economist Paula England wrote, "A story that takes into account the incompleteness of models need not keep searching for the 'best' model. Because models by their nature represent only a partial viewpoint, partiality or bias cannot be eliminated from theories. A greater openness to entertaining alternative perspectives is likely to lead to a multiplicity of perspectives that more adequately captures the complexity and diversity of economic activities."[31]

The call for alternative approaches is echoed by the movement known as post-autistic economics. This approach was founded in 2000 when a group of Sorbonne students submitted a petition to their professors complaining that the closed-off abstraction of neoclassical theory amounts to a kind of economic autism (there is now a post-autistic economics journal and a number of textbooks).[32] As the students wrote: "The instrumental use of mathematics appears necessary. But resort to mathematical formalization when it is not an instrument but rather an end in itself, leads to a true schizophrenia in relation to the real world ... We want a pluralism of approaches, adapted to the complexity of the objects and to the uncertainty surrounding most of the big questions in economics."[33]

The need for alternative models may be met in part by the recent agent-based models (Chapter 4), which come in a wide variety of forms and scales—and are also based on an idea of human behavior very unlike that of traditional economics. To help visualize the difference, imagine that *homo economicus* goes into a bar. He looks at the range of beers for sale. Being something of an expert, he knows his exact preference for each brand. Furthermore, with his remarkable powers to analyze the entire state of the economy into the future, he also knows the pub down the road will have his favorite brand on sale next week. So he orders an orange juice, which is cheaper and will allow him to optimize his utility at a future time, even once interest rates are taken into account. He explains his reasoning to the girl next to him at the bar, and offers to buy her a drink—not knowing that she is a fuzzy, complex agent. She makes a fuzzy calculation that it's time to go.

In agent-based computer models, an agent makes decisions based on observations of what is happening locally, rather than from a global bird's-eye view of the economy. She has limited information, and a limited amount of time. She can be altruistic sometimes (but not always), and she doesn't base every decision on money. She has a fuzzy set of preferences, and isn't rigid in her choices. She relies more on rules of thumb than complicated chains of reasoning, but she can still change her mind, and is open to new information. She is also a social being, influenced by the actions of other agents. Her computer DNA may only consist of some simple code, but she still approximates the behavior of humans of either gender—or for that matter groups, firms, or nations—more closely than does the caricature of *homo economicus*. Furthermore, her behavior can be compared with data from areas such as cognitive science (discussed further in Chapter 8) that deal with how decisions are actually made in real life.

Models of the economy could come to resemble the models that are being developed in that other life science, systems biology. In biological networks, the agents may be proteins and other chemical species at the molecular level (see Figure 3.3); cells in a tumor; organs in a body; or a hybrid mix of these different scales. Modelers draw on a range of techniques including cellular automata, network analysis, fractal mathematics, and traditional equations. The complexity of the system means it is impossible to build a truly accurate model from the bottom up, but the models are still an excellent way to compile and represent information about dynamical behavior, and suggest ways to restore health. Their aims are far more modest than those of grand economic theories, but they are also more realistic and grounded in observation. As one group put it: "For computational modeling to be useful in incompletely understood systems, we must focus not on building the final, perfect model with all parameters precisely determined, but on building incomplete, tentative and falsifiable models in the most expressive and predictive fashion feasible."[34]

Feminist economics involves a shift from a Pythagorean,

reductionist, and mechanistic view of the economy, to one in which the economy is seen as a living thing—organic and inherently creative. Active theorizing is brought into balance with passive observation, and the clear light of rationality with the complexity of real human behavior. Such ideas are still a hard sell in the conservative, male-dominated halls of academe, where the opposition is privileged, well entrenched, and generously funded. As in the 1960s, the feminist battle is not just about ideas, but also power and money. The difference is that today, despite their privileged position, it is the neoclassical economists who are looking like the dangerous radicals with extreme ideas.

By helping to attract more women into the workforce, by drawing attention to the enormous amount of unpaid labor outside the formal economy, and by challenging economic paradigms, feminists have already altered the way we see the world of work in a way that would have seemed impossible in the 1960s. As Heraclitus pointed out: things change.

THE REAL FACTS

The changing role of women in the economy during the last few decades is mirrored by their changing role in space.

On September 14, 1959, *Life* magazine featured the seven male astronauts of the *Mercury* program on its cover. One week later, the cover story was about the "Astronauts' wives: Their inner thoughts, worries." On the cover, the women— permed hair, bright smiles—strike the same pose as their husbands.[35]

The same year, officials at NASA were wondering whether women could make a more active contribution to the space program. Women are on average smaller than men, eat less, and use less oxygen—all useful qualities in an astronaut (or astronautrix, to use *TIME*'s expression).

In 1960–61, NASA put thirteen women pilots through

an arduous training and testing regime to see if they were made of the right stuff. They were known as the Fellow Lady Astronaut Trainees, or FLAT. The women were subjected to the same grueling tests as the men—such as a ride on the Multi-Axis Spin Test Inertia Facility, otherwise known as the Vomit Comet, or being immersed for hours in an isolation tank, which was deemed the closest thing to the emptiness of space.

The women passed the tests, even sometimes outperforming the men, but the program was mysteriously canceled after two years. In July 1962, a House subcommittee was organized to look into the matter. Astronaut John Glenn laid it all out: "I think this gets back to the way our social order is organized, really. It is just a fact. The men go off and fight the wars and fly the airplanes and come back and help design and build and test them. The fact that women are not in this field is a fact of our social order." The subcommittee decided the women had not been discriminated against.[36]

The first member of FLAT was Jerrie Cobb. After the congressional hearings, she went off to the Amazon to work as a missionary pilot. In July 1969, lying in a hammock attached to her plane, she heard over the radio that *Apollo 11* had landed on the moon. She climbed onto the wing, and did a dance of joy, there in the moonlight. "Vaya con Dios," she whispered to the men on the moon. (The local shamans were less impressed—as one explained, they all knew that one of their ancestors, Birdman, had flown to the moon many times.)

In June 1963, only a year after Glenn's House appearance, the cosmonaut Valentina Tereshkova was the first woman in space; astrophysicist Sally Ride was the first American woman in 1983; and in 2006, telecommunications tycoon Anousheh Ansari became the first female "space tourist" to pay her own way into orbit, for a reported $20 million. From the International Space Station, she wrote: "From the side windows in the little cabins and the docking compartment, where I sleep, you see the complete curvature of the Earth against the dark background of the universe. This view is actually my favorite because you see the 'Whole' not the 'Parts' ... I wish the leaders of different nations could do the same and have a world vision first, before a specific vision for their country."[37]

Perhaps it will happen—social facts are sometimes more malleable than they appear.

HOW TO BE FEMINIST

Is there any biological basis for the male domination of neoclassical economics? Is the male brain better suited to the study of abstract equations—just as the male body is better at sprinting 100 yards?

Male and female brains do show physical differences. The "default" human brain in a developing fetus is female. In males, the brain is modified in the womb and just after birth by doses of testosterone. Male brains are about 9 percent larger than female brains, but the latter pack in more of the nerve cell–containing gray matter per unit volume, so the size difference may just reflect the fact that men are on average bigger than women. The corpus callosum, which connects the two hemispheres of the brain, tends to be smaller in men. The female brain also appears to be more affected by fluctuations in hormone levels. As a result, according to psychiatry professor Louann Brizendine, "A woman's neurological reality is not as constant as a man's. His is like a mountain that is worn away by glaciers, weather and the deep tectonic movements of the Earth. Hers is more like the weather itself—constantly changing and hard to predict."[38]

Despite these differences, numerous studies show that men and women have similar intellectual abilities, and there seems no reason why women's brains should prevent them from coming to terms with the subtleties of economic theory, or keep them out of faculty positions. An interesting perspective on the role of gender in science—which also applies to economics—was provided in a 2006 *Nature* article by the biologist Ben Barres. He argued that the reason women are underrepresented in the upper echelons of science was not because of biological factors, or innate ability, but because of discrimination. Barres noted that most scientists are unaware of any such bias, perhaps because of their essential optimism about science: "It seems that the desire to believe in a meritocracy is so powerful that until a person has experienced sufficient career-harming bias themselves they simply do not believe it exists."[39]

What makes Ben Barres an expert on the subject? He used to be Barbara Barres. As a young female student at MIT, a professor once told her that a boyfriend must have solved a tough math problem for her. After changing sex, she heard a scientist say: "Ben Barres gave a great seminar today, but then his work is much better than his sister's."

Barres suggests five remedies for universities, all of which could apply to the training of economists:

- Enhance diversity in the leadership of academic institutions to give a broader perspective.
- Promote female role models, and help women faculty balance career and family responsibilities.
- Speak out against sexism and discrimination.[40]
- Make the selection process for jobs and grants fairer, by including women and minorities in the selection committees.
- Help give young women the confidence required to overcome prejudice.

Of course, if feminist economics catches on, it may be we men who are worrying whether we have what it takes in terms of mental flexibility, or are restricted by our narrow corpus callosum from attaining an integrated view of the world ...

6 ○ AT REST VERSUS IN MOTION
MARKET MOVERS

We are floating in a medium of vast extent, always drifting uncertainly, blown to and fro; whenever we think we have a fixed point to which we can cling and make fast, it shifts and leaves us behind; if we follow it, it eludes our grasp, slips away, and flees eternally before us. Nothing stands still for us. This is our natural state and yet the state most contrary to our inclinations. We burn with desire to find a firm footing, an ultimate, lasting base on which to build a tower rising up to infinity, but our whole foundation cracks and the earth opens into the depth of the abyss.
—Pascal, *Pensées*

We tend to think science has explained everything when it has explained how the moon goes around the earth. But this idea of a clockwise universe has nothing to do with the real world.
—James Yorke

All things change.
—Heraclitus, *fragment 36*

Time is money.
—Traditional

PRICE FIXING

"This is gold, Mr. Bond. All my life I've been in love with its color, its brilliance, its divine heaviness."

The character Goldfinger, in Ian Fleming's 1964 eponymous novel, was not alone. Men and women have long lusted after the yellow metal. Many commodities—from conch shells to salt to beaver pelts—have served as currencies on a local level. But only gold has had truly global appeal. They don't give out beaver pelts at the Olympics. The only thing to come close is silver, but as Chaucer said, silver is to gold as the moon is to the sun: "Sol gold is and Luna silver we threpe."[1] For centuries, the ratio of their prices even held at about thirteen, the number of lunar periods in a solar year.[2]

Pythagoras was said to have a thigh of gold (perhaps referring to a birthmark) that was supposed to be a sign of his divinity. To the Incas, gold was the sweat of the sun, and Latin America probably wouldn't be Latin if the Spanish invaders hadn't found gold there. Shakespeare warned, "All that glitters is not gold." Today, gold is still the substance that traders turn to when markets get roiled by uncertainty, volatility, or insecurity. The riskier the world becomes, the greater it seems is the demand for the stuff. What magical quality does it have that makes it, to many people, the ultimate store of value? What gives it a sense, not just of luxury and glamour, but also solidity and stability? Perhaps it is the unique combination of weight, scarcity, durability, and beauty; or perhaps it has more to do with mythology and gold's association with the yellow sun. Whatever the reason, even if the world financial system falls apart and the survivors are all holed up in cabins with guns and canned food, a gold bar will still be worth its weight in gold.

The reasoning behind the value of gold may be hard to fathom, but the actual determination of the price couldn't be more orderly. Since 1919, the price has been set in a peculiar ritual, known as the London Gold Fix. Twice a day, at 10:30 A.M. and 3:00 P.M., five men representing the city's largest gold traders get together to buy and sell gold bars.

Originally, the meetings were held in a special wood-paneled office at N. M. Rothschild & Sons. The men would sit around a table. Each had a telephone so they could communicate with their trading floors, and would hold in their hand a small Union Jack flag. The auctioneer would announce a starting price, and everyone would declare how many 400-troy-ounce (about 12.44 kg) bars they wanted to buy or sell at that price. If there were more buyers than sellers, the auctioneer would raise the price; if the converse, he would lower it. The traders would then get on the phone and reassess their positions—during which time they would hold up their little flags—and the process would continue until the buyers and sellers were in agreement (to within twenty-five gold bars).

Today, of course, in our age of computers and the Internet, the whole process has been completely modernized. It's still five guys—now representing Scotia-Mocatta (part of the Bank of

Nova Scotia), Barclays Capital, Deutsche Bank, HSBC, and Société Générale—but the meeting is now a teleconference, and instead of holding up little Union Jacks, they just say the word "flag" (progress is relentless). It usually only takes a few minutes. The fix price is used as a benchmark for gold trades, or financial instruments such as option contracts, until the next meeting is held, and then they do it again.

As shown by Figure 6.1, a plot of the postwar price of gold can be divided into two periods, before and after 1968. Pre-1968, the price was stable at U.S. $35 per troy ounce. The reason was the Bretton Woods Agreement, signed in 1944 by the Allied governments, which fixed both the price of gold and the exchange rates of major currencies to the U.S. dollar. The gold price was kept within a narrow band of $35 by direct government intervention in the gold market. Since the United States controlled at the time most of the world's gold (about 60 percent) and could print dollars at will, they could keep the price at a stable level.

In the early 1960s, the growing private market for gold began to show a tendency to lift the price above $35. In order to reassert control, central banks around the world united to form the London Gold Pool, which intervened directly in the London fix by buying or selling gold bars. This worked for a while; however, the private market continued to expand, and by the mid-1960s it had a larger effect on price than production levels. Political pressures were also building. In June 1967, France withdrew from the gold pool to assert its independence from the United States. In November of the same year, Britain devalued the pound from $2.80 to $2.40, thus raising the perceived risk in holding currencies, and the demand for gold. The Tet offensive in Vietnam further tightened the pressure, and set off a wave of buying. Like a caged animal, gold was rattling against its constraints.

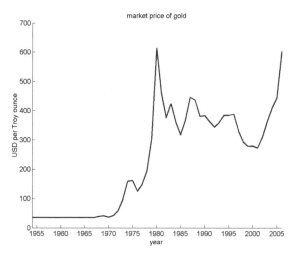

Figure 6.1. The postwar price of gold, in U.S. dollars per troy ounce. Prices are averaged over each year.

The turning point—literally—came in March 1968, with a record turnover of 14,180 gold bars at the London fix. On March 15, after a three-day surge of speculative buying, the fix was suspended for two weeks. When it reopened, the London Gold Pool had been dissolved and efforts to control the price were abandoned.

For a while, a dual standard was adopted, in which the private market was free to determine its own price, while governments continued to trade at $35. The free market soon hit $43, but returned to around $35 by 1970. But the U.S. dollar was losing its luster as a reserve currency. Inflation was picking up, and the United States was running deficits in both balance of payments and trade. More dollars were being printed to fund the war, gold coverage of the currency had decreased to about 22 percent, and the link between dollars and gold was looking weaker by the day.

On August 15, 1971, Nixon reacted by unleashing what became

known as the "Nixon shock"—he unilaterally imposed wage and price controls, an import surcharge, and halted the dollar's direct convertibility to gold. The price of gold would no longer be set by government diktat, but rather by the free market. By November 1971, the price had reached $100; soon after, the Bretton Woods currency system collapsed, and exchange rates between major currencies were allowed to float freely.

Man, it seemed, could control the flight of a spaceship, but not the financial system. An era of stability had been replaced by one of dynamic change. Money was transformed from a stand-in for gold to something more like quicksilver. It lost its association with the sun, and aligned itself instead with the changeable moon.

AT REST VERSUS IN MOTION

If gold is valued for its stability and durability, as well as its beauty, then the same may be said of that substance favored by mathematicians and neoclassical economists—abstract number. One of the appealing qualities of number is that, unlike most things in the world, it doesn't change from day to day. The number two will always be the number two. It doesn't rust or decay or get old, and when multiplied by three, it will always give six. Numbers are something you can count on. They're golden.

To the Pythagoreans, number was the key to understanding the hidden harmonies of the universe. Mathematics governed both music and the motion of the stars and planets—which they believed produced a kind of celestial tune that Pythagoras alone could hear. In the Pythagorean philosophy, the universe wasn't just based on number, it literally *was* number. It was number that made the sun rise and set at regular times, and number that made the planets trace their complex paths across the night sky.

The emphasis on stability and predictability has persisted in science. The ancient Greeks resisted any notion of movement or change, apart from that of the celestial bodies, which were believed to rotate in crystalline spheres. Aristotle divided the universe into two zones: the sun, planets, and stars were divine and eternal, and below them came "that which is passible, mutable, perishable, and subject to death."[3] The dividing line was the orbit of the moon—the sun and planets always have the same form, but the moon waxes and wanes and is always in flux. When the *Apollo 8* astronauts passed around the far side of the moon and lost radio contact with the earth, they entered the realm of the timeless and eternal.

The science of dynamics—of moving things—can really be said to have begun with Galileo's 1638 *Discourse on Two New Sciences*. The two sciences referred to the study of the mechanical properties of objects at rest and the dynamical properties of things that were in motion. Galileo explored the now-familiar concepts of velocity and acceleration—showing, for example, that the speed of a falling object did not remain constant, but increased linearly with time. His experiments were the precursor to Isaac Newton's discovery some thirty years later of the law of gravity, which for the first time linked the motion of falling objects here on earth to the motion of the moon and planets. Neil Armstrong might have been the first man to touch the moon, but Newton was the first to figure out what made it tick.

While the new science of dynamics opened up the study of moving systems, the emphasis was still on finding fixed rules that governed them. The planets may move around the sun, but just as the sun's light doesn't change, so the law of gravity remained constant and immutable. And because the mathematics were complex, scientists often concentrated on systems that were close to equilibrium, or showed regular behavior such as a periodic orbit. As discussed in the next chapter, this made the math considerably simpler. For example, it was much easier to calculate small perturbations to a bridge caused by a modest weight than when the same structure was stressed to breaking point.

In economics, the founders of neoclassical theory adopted a similar approach. As Jevons wrote in 1871, it was "a far more easy task to lay down the conditions under which trade is completed and interchange ceases, than to attempt to ascertain at what rate trade will go on when equilibrium is not attained."[4] And around the same time Jevons was developing his marginal utility theory in England, Léon Walras at Lausanne independently founded what became known as general equilibrium theory, which would become one of the main components of neoclassical theory.

THE GROPING HAND

While Adam Smith saw the marketplace in terms of an invisible hand, Walras thought more in terms of a groping process—or (it sounds better in French) *tâtonnement*. In his book *Elements of Pure Economics*, Walras attempted to determine how prices were set by the market. His model of the market closely resembled the London Gold Fix. He imagined an auctioneer who acted as an intermediary between buyers and sellers. As in the gold fix, the auctioneer would start off with an initial price and then adjust it until buyers and sellers were in agreement. The auctioneer therefore "groped" his way towards the price, rather than determining it in a single step. The final state was the point at which the market cleared—there was no more buying or selling to be done—so the economy was at equilibrium.

In addition to the presence of the auctioneer, Walras assumed the market was perfectly competitive, so prices would be driven down until they equated to the cost of production. In this economy, no one made a profit. Like Jevons, he also assumed market participants would act rationally to maximize their utility, and that they experienced diminishing marginal returns. For consumers, the latter means the utility of some object tends to decrease as more is purchased. For producers, it means production efficiency tends to decrease with units produced—an hour worked in overtime is less productive than the first hour of the day.

Walras of course realized that the economy consists of not just a single commodity, but also a range of products and services, many of which are closely coupled. If the price of wheat goes up, then that will affect the price of bread, which will affect sales in a bakery, which will impact the amount a baker spends on luxury goods, and so on. Walras attempted to capture such effects using a set of equations, to be solved simultaneously. The shortage of data meant there were too many unknowns for even these simplified equations to be solved; however he argued mathematically that equilibrium should in principle exist. He saw this as a rigorous demonstration of Adam Smith's invisible hand, groping its way towards a perfect set of prices.

However, while Walras showed how equilibrium could in principle be attained, it wasn't clear that any such equilibrium point would be feasible, stable, or unique. What would it mean if there were more than one set of prices that would clear the market? The economy also exists in time—consumers and producers are not just thinking about events today; they also have an eye on the future, which is uncertain. What happens when people change their minds?

In the gold fix, for example, suppose the auctioneer starts with a certain price, and a large order for gold comes in. The price rises a little in response. If the group expectation is for a small change in price, then agreement may rapidly be attained. But suppose one of the bankers in the circle interprets the purchase order as a sign of bigger things to come. He raises his price substantially. The other bankers suspect he knows something they don't. To hedge their bets, they raise their prices too. Suddenly the price has shot up to a new level.

Indeed, this kind of volatility happens all the time—as the banker John Morgan said, "The market will fluctuate." On May 18, 2001, for example, the price of gold was $273. In the next session, the price surged to $291.25, a change of 6.7 percent. It then dropped to $284.15, and by June 1 it was at $265.40, 2.8 percent lower than where it started, and a change of almost 10 percent peak-to-trough. Do these prices really represent unique and stable equilibria for the times the fix was held, or is something else at work?

FUTURE PERFECT

The task of proving the Walrasian stability of the economy, in a world that never stays still, was to occupy neoclassical economists for the next hundred years. A more rigorous solution to the general equilibrium problem, which took into account the existence of the future, was finally provided in 1954 by the economists Kenneth Arrow and Gérard Debreu.[5] They showed that a unique set of market-clearing prices would exist. Furthermore, in a result heralded by some as mathematical proof for the superiority of the capitalist system, the resulting price distribution was Pareto optimal, in the sense that no one (such as the government) could change the distribution without making someone else worse off. However, the conditions for this optimal equilibrium included not only things such as rational utility-maximizing behavior, negligible transaction costs, and so on, but an even more demanding requirement: everyone in the economy must be able to compile a list of all the available future states of the world, and figure out the prices in all of those worlds.

For example, the price of wheat will depend on the harvest yield, which is a function of the weather, which different people won't agree on. Farmer A buys the Farmer's Almanac and reads that the weather will be excellent; B assumes the weather will be bad, like the previous year's; C concludes it will be the climate average. Farmers A, B, and C might disagree about the weather, but for the theory to apply, they should concur on what exactly will happen in each scenario to the price of wheat—not just this year, but into the future.

Of course, this assumption is very unrealistic. The economy is just as unpredictable as the weather, and even expert economists rarely agree on what exactly will happen in a particular scenario. Economist A may predict that prices will go up, economist B that they will stay the same, and economist C that the world is on the verge of a major financial meltdown.

In 1968, the American economist Roy Radner managed to weaken the conditions for equilibrium to exist, but still found that everyone in the economy needed to have infinite computational capacity. He concluded that the model "breaks down completely in the face of limits on the ability of agents to compute optimal strategies."[6]

One may imagine that Radner's paper would have led to the abandonment of equilibrium theory. However, the opposite happened: the idea that market forces drove the economy to an optimal equilibrium became increasingly well entrenched as the main result of neoclassical economics.[7] Indeed, the imposing mathematics of the Arrow-Debreu result set the standard for much future economic research. In his 1990 presidential address to the American Economic Association, Debreu said the "acid test" for economic theories was that of "removing all their economic interpretations and letting their mathematical infra-structure stand on its own." In other words, don't bring reality into the argument.

Even today, apart from allowances for effects such as long-term technological growth, mainstream financial theory remains fixated on the idea of equilibrium. For example, governments and major financial institutions continue to model the economy using what are known as computable general equilibrium (CGE) models, which, as the name suggests, assume the economy is drawn towards an equilibrium point.[8] A recent example is the IMF's Global Economic Model. Following the approach of Jevons, it aggregates over consumers and producers, and repre-sents each as a single "average" entity that maximizes its own utility. Different sectors of industry are modeled separately. The model also includes a government that taxes and spends.[9]

The aim of such models is to estimate how the equilibrium will react to effects such as government policy, changes in com-modity prices, and so on. As the *Economist* notes, "When they contemplate big changes ... most governments cannot resist turning to CGE models to forewarn them of the conse-quences."[10] The economist Frank Ackerman wrote: "CGE models have all but conquered the world of American policy analysis. No signs of theoretical uncertainty can be seen; instead, use of the general equilibrium framework is taken as the mark of good science."[11]

Despite their popularity, the accuracy of the models is not much better than random. In the 1990s, for example, general equilibrium models were widely used to assess the economic impact of the North American Free Trade Agreement (NAFTA). A 2005 study by Timothy Kehoe of the University of Minnesota showed "The models drastically underestimated the impact of NAFTA on North American trade, which has exploded over the past decade."[12] The models are very flexible, and so can be adjusted to fit historical data, but they can't predict the future.[13]

Kehoe also observed, "Given the importance of the NAFTA policy debate, it is surprising that no one has carried out such a model evaluation exercise previously." But it's not that surprising. Mainstream economics is always more about the theory than the reality.

So is it plausible for economists to assume the existence of equilibrium in the first place, or are they just groping for stability in an unstable world?

FIXED POINT

On closer analysis, most of the conditions required for equilibrium appear to have been adopted by neoclassical economists in order to satisfy that aim, rather than because they describe the real economy. For example, the preferences of consumers are assumed to be fixed and immutable, at least to a good approximation. As the economist Thorstein Veblen richly put it 100 years ago, it is as if each person were "a lightning calculator of pleasures and pains who oscillates like a homogeneous globule of desire of happiness under the impulse of stimuli that shift him about the area, but leave him intact."[14] But if preferences were really fixed, then advertising agencies would soon go out of business. Instead, the area is highly lucrative, and advertising forms a major component of the budget for building and maintaining market share for products.

Diminishing marginal utility also acts as a kind of stabilizing influence on the economy. While it clearly holds in some cases, it is easy to think of counterexamples. The process of tobacco addiction is one where a small initial exposure leads to increasing demand. People can similarly become addicted to other consumer goods (Imelda Marcos and shoes), or just the act of buying any-thing (it's called consumerism). The assumption that production efficiency decreases with units, meanwhile, is actually rather bizarre. An individual person may become inefficient if she works too many hours, but in a modern economy the main producers are not single people but companies, which typically experience economies of scale as they get more business and grow larger. Ikea doesn't seem to be wearing itself out under the pressure of mak-ing too much flat-pack furniture. Google doesn't call in sick because it can't handle any more websites. For some businesses, such as financial trading, or movie acting, the amount of work involved in a transaction may be almost independent of size. It is no harder for a currency trader to swap a billion dollars than a million, if he has access to the funds; no more testing for an actor to appear in a blockbuster than a low-budget art film.

In the language of dynamics, diminishing marginal utility is an example of negative feedback—the greater the quantity pur-chased or produced, the lower the desire to produce or purchase more. Addiction is an example of positive feedback—con-sumption fuels desire rather than repressing it. Negative feed-back tends to increase stability, while positive feedback reduces it. In reality, the economy consists of both positive and negative feedbacks, and both must be taken into account.

As an example, consider the introduction of a new, innova-tive product to the marketplace. At first, sales are small, but if the product is useful then word will quickly spread. As people buy the product, they'll tell their friends, so the growth rate will increase—positive feedback. After a while, though, the market nears saturation, so the more units are sold, the lower is the potential remaining market—negative feedback. Finally, growth flattens out. The result is an S-shaped curve like the one in Figure 6.2. Many other outcomes are also possible—the company could suddenly go bust, or get bought out, or invent something far better—but the point is negative feedback is only part of the story, since without positive feedback, new products and ideas would never reach the marketplace.[15]

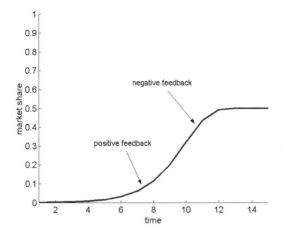

Figure 6.2. Innovations often follow an S-shaped curve as they gain market share. This figure shows a product or technology that starts out with very small market share, grows through positive feedback, then saturates at 50 percent market share. The time points could represent quarters or years.

Radner's 1968 paper showed in a formal way that equilibrium theory only applied to a highly specialized set of conditions that had little to do with the real world. And in the same year, the price of gold was shifting from a stable regime to an unstable one. Equilibrium was cracking under the strain. Stability, it seemed, was the sign of government control, while free markets, which were supposedly the subject of equilibrium theory, were dominated by something rather different—chaos.

BIFURCATION POINT

Neoclassical economists modeled their subject after the elegant results of mathematical physics, the archetypal example being James Clerk Maxwell's equations. These sum up the laws of electromagnetism, including visible light, in a sparse and elegant four lines. However, even as Walras was composing his theory of general equilibrium, Maxwell was questioning the notions of stability in physical systems. In an 1873 essay on free will, he wrote: "Much light may be thrown on some of these questions by consideration of stability and instability. When the state of things is such that an infinitely small variation of the present state will alter only by an infinitely small quantity the state at some future time, the condition of the system, whether it is at rest or in motion, is said to be stable; but when an infinitely small variation in the present state may bring about a finite difference in the state of the system in a finite time, the condition of the system is said to be unstable. It is manifest that the existence of unstable conditions renders impossible the prediction of future events, if our knowledge of the present state is only approximate and not accurate."[16] He believed such instability and amplification of small effects—otherwise known as sensitivity to initial conditions—could explain what is perceived as free will.

Somewhat more alarmingly, in 1890, the French mathematician Henri Poincaré noted sensitivity to initial conditions in a model of three gravitational bodies—implying that even the solar system may be less stable than it appears. Poincaré hypothesized that instability could be a property of many other systems, such as the weather. (His concerns about economics were more basic—replying to a letter from Walras, he warned that the unrealistic assumptions of Walras's theory might make the conclusions "devoid of all interest."[17]) However it wasn't until the 1960s, and the invention of fast computers, that scientists could explore the properties of what are now known as chaotic systems.

In the mythology of ancient Greece, Chaos represented the original formless void from which the deity Gaia was born. Pythagoras associated it with the unlimited, indeterminate aspect of the universe, and the word came to symbolize a dangerous kind of disorder. In mathematics, though, it has a slightly different meaning (first used by mathematician James Yorke), which combines apparent randomness and instability with an underlying pattern.

As an example, consider the S-shaped curve in Figure 6.2. It was generated by a simple mathematical rule: if the fractional market share at time t is denoted x_t, where time is divided into equal steps, then the market share at the next time, step $t+1$, is given by the equation

$$x_{t+1} = rx_t - rx_t^2$$

where r is a constant parameter, here set to 2. For example, if the first point is $x_1 = 0.1$, then

$$x_2 = 2 \times 0.1 - 2 \times 0.1^2 = 0.18$$
$$x_3 = 2 \times 0.18 - 2 \times 0.18^2 = 0.2952$$

and so on. Note that if $x_t = 0.5$, then $x_{t+1} = 2 \times 0.5 - 2 \times 0.5^2 = 0.5$ as well, so there is no change with time and this point represents an equilibrium for this value of r. The equation, known as the logistic map, was first used by the Belgian mathematician Pierre François Verhulst in the 1840s to model population dynamics, but is also used in economics.[18] It is a variant of the equation that Robert Malthus used to predict exponential population growth, but includes a negative feedback term (the one with the minus sign) that represents constraints on growth. For low values of x the first term dominates and positive feedback occurs, but for higher values of x the negative feedback term dominates.

Such equations are called maps because they map the state at one discrete time, t, to the state at the next discrete time, $t+1$. In population dynamics, the time step could represent a generation. In economics, data is often only reported and acted on at regular time intervals, so the time step could represent a quarter or a year.

The behavior of this system depends critically on the value of the parameter r. For the case $r = 2$, the system eventually settles on the value of 0.5, as in Figure 6.2. As r is increased, though, the system becomes more interesting. Rather than settling on a stable point, it bounces back and forth between two or more states. When r is set to 3.7 as in Figure 6.3, the system moves around in an apparently random fashion—not unlike the price of gold, after it was released from its political restraints. The price goes up, overshoots, gets knocked down, recovers, and so on.

Figure 6.4 shows the behavior of the system for four different values of the parameter. For each case, a long simulation was performed, and only the last points are shown, so the graphs represent the long-term behavior. The $r = 2$ case gives a static equilibrium—a straight line at 0.5. At $r = 3.2$, the system oscillates between two points; boom followed by crash followed by boom. At $r = 3.5$, the system alternates periodically between four different states, and at $r = 3.7$ the behavior shows neither rhyme nor reason.

In the early 1970s, the English zoologist Robert May—who was using the logistic map to model fluctuations in fish populations—produced the so-called bifurcation diagram, shown in Figure 6.5. It can be understood by comparing with Figure 6.4. For values of the parameter r between 1 and 3, the map settles on

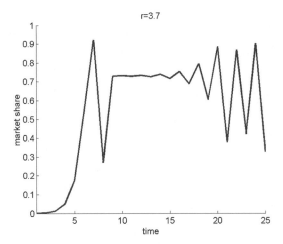

Figure 6.3. Logistic map simulations with parameter *r* set to 3.7. The system grows exponentially at first due to positive feedback, but then never settles on a steady state.

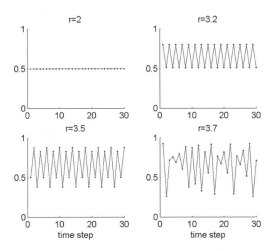

Figure 6.4. Logistic map simulations for different values of the parameter *r*. In each case, a long simulation is performed, and only the last points are shown, so the plots represent the long-term behavior of the system.

a single steady state, shown by the single solid line (see first panel of Figure 6.4). At $r = 3$, which is known as a bifurcation point, this line branches to form two lines. Here the map suddenly changes behavior, and starts to alternate between two states. A similar branching occurs around $r = 3.45$, so the map alternates between four states. Further branching occurs at decreasing intervals, until the map becomes chaotic, as in the last panel of Figure 6.4. The map moves around randomly, and shows sensitivity to initial condition—a small change in the initial point leads to a different evolution with time. Note that the bifurcation diagram has clearly visible windows within the chaotic regime, for example around $r = 3.82$, where the system switches back to periodic behavior.

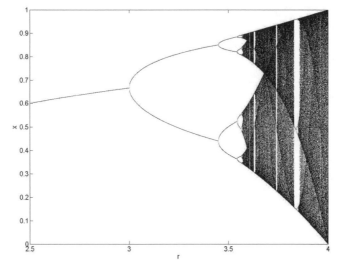

Figure 6.5. Bifurcation diagram for the logistic map. Horizontal axis is the parameter r. A single line represents a single steady state; two lines mean that the system alternates between two values, and so on. The chaotic regions appear as a continuous band.

The logistic map has been studied in detail and has many fascinating properties. Perhaps the most striking is that, despite its name, the logistic map isn't very logical—especially in the contrast between the extreme simplicity of the equation, and the complex behavior shown in Figure 6.5. The logistic map had been in use by scientists since the 1840s, but until the advent of fast computers made long simulations possible, no one could have imagined its richness. The bifurcation diagram can be described as an emergent feature of the system that cannot be predicted from the equation alone.

The logistic map also showed how chaos and randomness could arise naturally in the economy. According to the equilibrium model, all fluctuations in price were due to external events. Every time there was a piece of news, the market would adjust its prices to account for the extra information. But if chaos can appear in simple equations, then it can also appear in the economy—the market can generate its own randomness, rather than having it imposed from outside.

One limitation of maps such as the logistic map is that they can only represent discrete time steps. While this is appropriate for much economic data, which is only reported in regular intervals, such as quarters, the economy viewed as a whole exists in real time. The continuous-time analogues of maps are known as flows. These are described by differential equations, which specify the rate of change of the system variables at any time. An example of a flow is given in Figure 6.6. The system here is usually used as a kind of toy weather model, but exhibits the behavior common in chaotic flows. For low values of the single parameter F, which plays a similar role as r in the logistic map, the system has a steady state. At $F=1$, a bifurcation occurs, and the system enters a regular, periodic cycle. At $F=3$, the cycle has picked up some extra features, and at $F=6$, the system is fully chaotic.

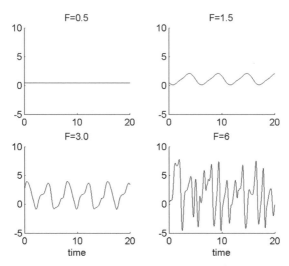

Figure 6.6. Behavior of a flow for different values of the single parameter *F*.
For *F* between 0 and 1, the system has a steady state. A bifurcation then
occurs, and the system enters a steady limit cycle, as shown for *F*=1.5.
At *F*=3, the system is still regular but has picked up more harmonics.
At *F*=6, the system is fully chaotic.

It is less straightforward to produce a bifurcation plot of
flows than of maps, because even a periodic cycle sweeps out a
continuous range of points, rather than producing distinct lines
as with the logistic map. One way to get around the problem is
to interpret the lines in Figure 6.6 in terms of harmonics, as is
done with sound waves. Any sound can be expressed as a sum
of separate harmonics, or frequencies. For example, if you play
middle C on a musical instrument, the tone will contain a dominant frequency corresponding to the note played, plus a number of subharmonics. It is the subharmonics that distinguish a
piano from a viola, or a trumpet from an opera singer.

At *F*=1.5, the system contains only a single base harmonic,
and higher multiples which affect the shape. In Figure 6.7, this

is shown by a single line at the base frequency, plus other lines at its multiples. At $F=3$, the system has also picked up a lower harmonic. Around $F=3.8$ the system becomes chaotic, and contains all frequencies. As with the logistic map, though, there are windows of periodicity inside the chaotic region. Again, the complexity of the figure could never have been predicted from the equations alone.[19]

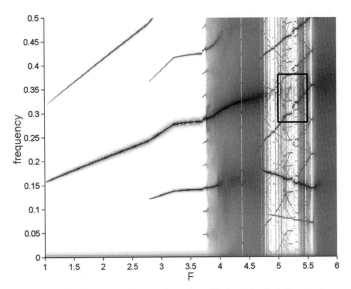

Figure 6.7. Bifurcation diagram for a flow. Horizontal axis is the single parameter F, vertical axis is frequency, grayscale represents the strength of that frequency at each value of F. (The image at the start of the chapter is from a rotated version of the area outlined in black.)

The Pythagorean philosophy was based on the similarity between consonant musical harmonics, and the ratios of numbers encoded by the tetractys. But in a chaotic system, the music is not Pythagorean—it is fuzzy, discordant, and off-tetractys. And so are the markets.

THE DYNAMIC MARKET

The idea that markets achieve a stable equilibrium is attractive from a narrow theoretical perspective. One widely disseminated textbook explains, "An industry is nothing more than a collection of firms; each firm must be in long-run equilibrium. It follows that when a perfectly competitive industry is in long-run equilibrium, all firms in the industry will be selling at a price equal to minimum average total cost—that is they must be in zero-profit equilibrium ... This result plays an important role in the appeal of perfect competition to economists ..."[20] The theory emphasizes negative feedbacks and fixed preferences in order to build a model of an economy at rest, in a perfect and optimal state of equilibrium. As philosopher Philip Mirowski noted, "the neoclassical orthodoxy had a vested interest in neutralizing chaotic descriptions of the economy."[21]

Appealing as the idea of perfect stability may be to economists, the real world does not conform to this picture. Companies are constantly being born, dying, or evolving. Consumers change their minds and their preferences. New business plans or investment strategies appear, proliferate for a while, then lose their prominence as conditions change or better alternatives are invented. The world does not stay still, and there is no such thing as long-run equilibrium. The market is an inherently creative place that is constantly generating new ideas and new possibilities. The strength of capitalism does not lie in the neoclassical idea of stability, but in its ability to unleash this creative energy. Like a chaotic mathematical system, it is capable of producing surprise.

It may appear in our everyday lives that prices are fairly stable—for example, the price of a cup of coffee does not gyrate madly from day to day. But if you look at the price of coffee beans, it is highly volatile. Companies use insurance policies to hedge against fluctuations. Human beings also tend to resist change, so things like the cost of labor will be quite stable, and retailers will try to avoid big price swings. Any apparent stability is less about equilibrium than social inertia, with prices representing a fuzzy consensus on the "going rate." Many items are still subject to huge fluctuations. Companies slash prices in one market to destroy competition, and keep them high in another. Clothing is hugely overpriced one week and on the discount shelves the next. The economy may at times look serene on the surface, but at heart it is chaotic.

Some of this volatility is caused by the mechanics of the market itself—the process of matching buyers and sellers. An investment firm once decided to buy a 1 percent share of a small company I was working for. It was hard to find shareholders willing to sell, so the investment company had to make a series of purchases at progressively higher prices. By the time they were finished, our share price had shot up by a factor of three in one day. It then fell down again by about 30 percent over the next few days, as other investors decided to take advantage of the better price and sell.

We were only a small outfit, but as researchers from the Santa Fe Institute recently showed, even huge firms regularly see their share price buffeted around by a percent or more from apparently inconsequential trades.[22] And when prices of shares or other financial instruments such as loans fall during a crash, the effect is even greater, because it is so hard to find buyers. The market can very quickly seize up. Prices don't adjust in a smooth, continuous fashion, but instead abruptly reconfigure themselves, like the earth's crust during an earthquake.

Within particular industries or supply chains, each business is trying to adjust its operations according to its predictions about future supply and demand. Factories, warehouses, retailers, and suppliers of raw materials all need to coordinate their activities. Because they are all acting on imperfect information, and have a limited ability to see into the future, they make predictive errors, which then impact the others. As John Sterman from the MIT System Dynamics Group has shown, even highly simplified simulations of the business supply chain soon result in chaotic fluctuations. The magnitude of the fluctuations can sometimes be reduced if the chain is made more transparent and delays are reduced, so everyone has a better idea of what is going on, but they never go away.[23]

The market as a whole also experiences longer-scale fluctuations, such as the so-called business cycle. The story is familiar: the economy is going full throttle, businesses and investors get overconfident, credit is easy to find, companies spend a lot of money expanding, their competitors do likewise, soon there is overcapacity, prices come down, factories have to close, some workers lose their jobs so demand drops further, until the economy bottoms out, entrepreneurs buy in at rock-bottom prices, and the cycle starts again. Since economics was invented, the exact causes of the business cycle have been extensively analyzed, but it still remains almost impossible to predict. Some "cycles" are short, others long; some are shallow, others deep. But when the economy is seen in terms of a dynamical system, it becomes clear that such fluctuations do not need to have simple causes, or follow a simple pattern.

There is some evidence to show that the business cycle in the United States has become less extreme in recent decades.[24] Economists working in governments and central banks have become skilled at using interest rates and other policy levers to take the edge off some of the excesses; and improved technology has increased the result of information available to market participants, thus making the market more fluid and quick to adjust. However, one area where neither central banks nor technological developments have managed to reduce volatility is in the behavior of money itself.

With the 1968 collapse of the gold standard, financial deregulation, and the advent of computerized trading systems, foreign exchange markets have grown to a point where they now trade around $2 trillion a day, dwarfing any other aspect of the world economy (for comparison, this figure is about fifteen times the daily world GDP). The vast majority of this activity is for pure speculation, with money sloshing in and out of currencies according to the short-term whims of traders. The result has been a series of monetary crises that have been particularly hard on fragile economies in Latin America, South-East Asia, and Russia—not to mention a general feeling of financial impotence and insecurity that affects everyone from world leaders to factory workers.

It is becoming increasingly evident, at least among those who aren't currency traders or true believers in the optimality of free markets, that it would be nice if this system could calm down a touch. One option is the Tobin tax, which would impose a tax of around 0.1 percent on currency trades, and act as a kind of damper on speculation. The idea was first proposed by the economist James Tobin in the 1970s, and still frequently comes up for debate. A disadvantage of such a tax is that reducing market liquidity may actually increase volatility, because large trades would have a greater effect. However, it would at least generate a lot of money. Another option is to go back to having a Bretton Woods–style reference currency—but not necessarily one based on gold. An example is Special Drawing Rights, which are based on a basket of currencies and are administered by the IMF (see "Down to earth" below for another possibility). Some countries are also forming or joining regional currency blocs such as the Euro (the Mercosur trade bloc in Latin America is also considering a single currency); others such as China just opt out of currency fluctuations altogether, by fixing or otherwise managing their exchange rate.

FUTURE DISCOUNT

After studies of chaotic systems took off in the 1960s, it was soon hypothesized that chaos could explain much of the apparent randomness observed in nature—everything from the unpredictability of the weather, to the upheavals of human history, to the fluctuations of the price of gold. Some speculated that the randomness of the markets might be hiding some deeper order, which could be detected and predicted using the tools of chaos theory. However, the fact that simple equations can produce complex behavior does not imply that complex behavior in nature or the economy can be reduced to simple equations. The number of variables and unknowns in the economy is so huge that it will always defy simplistic analysis.[25] We can build models of the economy to better understand its dynamics and improve our intuition—indeed, these are main functions of mathematical models in any field—but there is no map or flow that will predict the next move for the price of gold or stocks.

The real implication of nonlinear dynamics is the opposite: because of complex feedback effects, many aspects of the economy are inherently unpredictable. Early discoverers of this were the group known as the Club of Rome, who in 1968 built a highly complex dynamical model to forecast the evolution of the world system. It drew attention to mounting environmental problems, but lost credibility by predicting we would run out of key resources like oil by the end of that century.[26] As Alan Greenspan said in 2003, then chair of the Board of Governors of the U.S. Federal Reserve, "Our problem is not the complexity of our models but the far greater complexity of a world economy whose underlying linkages appear to be in a continual state of flux."[27] Attempts to control it can therefore have unexpected, or even perverse, consequences. This doesn't mean governments or policy makers should throw up their hands in despair; but it does mean they have to be what John Sterman calls "systems thinkers," with the humility to acknowledge that all models, including their own mental models, are flawed; and the willingness to "learn about the complex systems in which we are embedded and work effectively to create the world we truly desire."[28]

In nature, the only things that are entirely predictable are inanimate objects, or dead. Living things operate at a point far from equilibrium. The assumptions of neoclassical economists—fixed preferences, diminishing marginal utility, the ability to look into the future—were chosen not because they are a good description of reality, but because they allow the economy to be treated as a static thing, subject to the laws of a rational mechanics. But the economy is very much alive, and kicking. (I'm writing this in August 2007 as the global economy is going through one of its aperiodic fits, this time a credit crunch set off by subprime U.S. housing loans. "Feels like we're on the edge of a panic to me," said a trader in one report. "In our business, psychology is everything and psychology has changed real quick on Wall Street."[29] Meanwhile, Goldman Sachs announced that one of its global equity funds "lost over 30 percent of its value in a week because of problems with its trading strategies created by computer models. In particular, the computers had failed to foresee recent market movements to such a degree that they labelled them a '25-standard deviation event'—something that only happens once every 100,000 years or more."[30])

In the economy, dynamism and creativity are coupled both to short-term danger and to uncertainty about our long-term future.

If we knew the future would be the same as today, there would be no motivation to go out and change it, or to protect ourselves from future events. Neoclassical economics asserts the economy will efficiently allocate resources if we act only out of self-interest, but this only holds true if a number of conditions are met, including equilibrium. The fact that the future will not resemble the present forces us to face up to the consequences of our actions. Our responsibility to the future is not limited to optimizing our own utility, but rather extends also to unborn generations.

A curious feature of most economic models is that they handle the future by discounting it, at a rate related to the interest rate. An expense in a year's time is worth less than one now, and a calamity 100 years from now barely even registers. With a discount rate of 4 percent per annum, for example, an expense of \$100 in 100 years' time counts for only \$1.98 today. It is as if the models are just trying to make the future go away. This may explain why mainstream economists have been the slowest of scientists to acknowledge the true cost of threats such as global warming and environmental destruction.[31] As discussed further in Chapter 10, it isn't very ethical to put the rights of future generations in the discount bin. To build a genuinely sustainable economy, we need to recognize and embrace the dynamic nature of the world, and free ourselves from the dead holds of static dogma.

So what magical ingredient makes the difference between stability and chaos, between a monotonous sameness and unpredictable dynamism? As seen in the next chapter, it all comes down to linear versus nonlinear—or straight versus crooked.

DOWN TO EARTH

The instability of foreign exchange markets makes the idea of a static equilibrium seem quaintly Victorian. Once you reject neoclassical dogma and admit the financial system is dynamic and often highly unstable, it becomes possible to design ways to improve it. One tool that may help bring money down to earth is a global reference currency, known as the Terra, which would replace the gold standard. It would be backed, not just by gold, but also by a basket of commodities such as oil, wheat, and metals, and perhaps other items, such as carbon emission credits. Instead of paying interest, the Terra would actually charge a small fee of about 3 to 4 percent, which would reflect the cost of storing the commodities.

The Terra would be traded just like any other currency, except each note in circulation would be backed by stored goods (the goods themselves wouldn't change hands, only a receipt for them). Its value would therefore be linked to the commodity prices instead of being able to vary of its own accord. Since the price of commodities tends to go up in an inflationary environment, the Terra's value would be protected against inflation, which would help justify the storage fee. The fact that it effectively pays negative interest would prevent hoarding, and (since the discount rate is linked to interest rates) would boost the rights of future generations instead of discounting them. The Terra would also be particularly advantageous to developing countries, since their economies are often linked to commodities anyway.

The Terra would be very different from money as we know it, and, even though it would only serve as a complement to traditional currencies, would change the dynamics of the economy. But money is just an agreed intermediary for economic exchange, and we are allowed to change the rules if they no longer work. After all, Nixon did.[32]

HOW TO BE DYNAMIC

According to orthodox theory, the economy is in a unique state of equilibrium. One implication is that things are the way they are because the current arrangement, insofar as market forces determine it, is in some sense optimal. If an idea or product doesn't catch on, it's because there isn't a market for it. If we aren't all heating our homes with geothermal or solar power, it must be because those technologies are flawed. If the economy as a whole is not fair or sustainable, it's because we don't really want it to be. Instead of teaching us to be active citizens engaged in shaping our destiny, orthodox theory teaches us to be passive consumers, enslaved to the dictates of markets and marketers.

As shown by dynamical systems theory, however, the idea of a perfect, optimal equilibrium in the economy is just an illusion. Dynamical systems are typically drawn to three main patterns of behavior, known as steady state, periodic, and chaotic attractors. A pendulum, for example, will swing about after being perturbed until it comes to rest at a steady state position pointing straight down. If it is lightly pushed in a regular manner, as in an old-fashioned clock, then it will oscillate in a periodic manner. If the force is cranked up above a certain limit, the pendulum will go chaotic, swinging violently around. However, its trajectory still has a certain recognizable pattern to it, known as a chaotic attractor. The systems in Figures 6.4 and 6.6 also show the three types of attractors.

An advantage of the stable attractor, from a mathematical point of view, is that it is easy to calculate. As Jevons pointed out, it is "much more easy to determine the point at which a pendulum will come to rest than to calculate the velocity at which it will move when displaced from that point of rest." However, living things show a persistent tendency to move around, as does the economy, so steady state solutions are of limited use when we try to simulate them. Furthermore, as shown by the bifurcation diagrams above, a small change can make a system abruptly switch from one type of behavior to another. A pendulum swinging in perfect time may suddenly become chaotic if pushed too hard. In human terms, that is like a person who has led a perfectly regular life—waking up each day at the same time, eating the same thing for breakfast, going off to the same job, etc.—suddenly giving it all up to be a professional poker player or to live under a bridge.

An implication for the economy is that *it doesn't have to be this way*.[33] The current economy has not been uniquely determined by fundamental market laws, it does not represent some optimal resting point for the pendulum of human well-being; instead it is the emergent and temporary result of a complex interaction between competing and interacting social forces. Changes in human history or the economy often resemble the switch of a dynamic system from one attractor to another—they happen suddenly, and the resulting pattern looks very different. Viewed in advance, fundamental change often seems impossible, but the reason is that we only think of single changes at a time, instead of the entire system changing at once. From our current perspective, the idea of a sustainable economy may seem like a pipedream. For a start, how can someone who lives in the suburbs get to work without driving a long way in a car? But if we think planning regulations may change to favor increased urban density, more people may work from home, transportation technologies will improve, social attitudes will shift, and so on, then the sustainable economy begins to look more realistic—and even attractive.

7 ○ STRAIGHT VERSUS CROOKED
FRACTAL ECONOMICS

*That which is crooked cannot be made straight: and that which is
wanting cannot be numbered.*
—Ecclesiastes 1:15

*The classical theorists resemble Euclidean geometers in a non-
Euclidean world who, discovering that in experience straight lines
apparently parallel often meet, rebuke the lines for not keeping
straight as the only remedy for the unfortunate collisions which
are occurring. Yet, in truth, there is no remedy except to throw over
the axiom of parallels and to work out a non-Euclidean geometry.*

Something similar is required today in economics.
—John Maynard Keynes

Clouds are not spheres, mountains are not cones, coastlines are not circles, and bark is not smooth, nor does lightning travel in a straight line.
—Benoit Mandelbrot

The track of writing is straight and crooked.
—Heraclitus, *fragment 59*

STRAIGHT VERSUS CROOKED

The *Apollo 8* astronauts were the first humans to look down and take pictures of the earth as a whole—thus confirming to most people that the earth was indeed round. Jim Lovell described the view to ground control: "To give you some idea, Mike, of what we can see: We can—I can pick out the southwest coastline of the Gulf and where Houston should be, and also the mouth of the Mississippi; I can see Baja California and that particular area. I'm using a monocular which we have aboard." Not everyone was convinced by the evidence—the secretary of London's Flat Earth Society, which boasted several hundred members, claimed it was the public being taken for a ride, rather than the astronauts. When informed of his objections, astronaut Frank Borman quipped, "It doesn't look too flat from here, but I don't know; maybe something is wrong with our vision."[1]

While the *Apollo* missions offered direct confirmation of the earth's curvature, the Greek mathematician Eratosthenes had already managed to estimate its diameter back in the third century B.C. On a trip to Syene in southern Egypt on the summer solstice, he stopped at a well and noticed that the noonday sun was reflected straight back from the water at the bottom, imply-ing that the sun was directly overhead. Exactly one year later, back home in Alexandria, he put a stake in the ground and measured the angle that the sun made—about 7.2 degrees, or 1/50 of a full circle. From earlier measurements compiled by Alexander the Great, he knew Alexandria was 5,000 *stadia*, or stadium lengths, north of Syrene. Since the earth was round (Eratosthenes was not a member of the Flat Earth Society), it followed from geometry that the ratio of that distance to the earth's circumference should equal 1/50. His calculation gave a circumference of 250,000 stadia, which equates, depending on interpretation of stadium length, to within a few percent of the equatorial circumference of 40,075 kilometers.

Eratosthenes was also credited with making a detailed sketch of the Nile to Khartoum, and being the first to correctly suggest that its periodic flooding was caused by heavy rains near the source. He developed a grid system—similar to our current longitude/latitude—to locate positions on the earth, and used it to produce a map of the known world (Figure 7.1). The princi-pal axes passed through Rhodes and divided the map into two roughly equal north/south sections. Because the position of any other city could be determined by locating them relative to this linear grid, Eratosthenes' map is known as the first scientific map. Less successful was his estimate for the distance to the moon of 780,000 stadia (around 124,800 kilometers), which was about a factor of three too small.

Geometry was originally used as a method to measure and parcel out land. Its name is from the Greek for earth (*gaia*), and means of measurement (*metron*). The latter, in turn, is from *mens* for moon (the moon is associated with measure-ment in many cultures, probably because its cycles were used to measure time, as in months). One of the founders of geometry

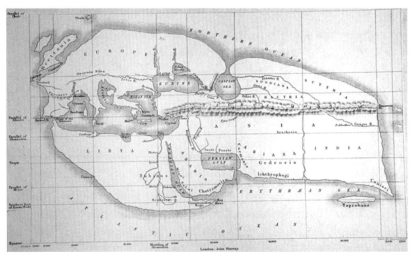

Figure 7.1. A nineteenth-century reconstruction of Eratosthenes' map of the world.[2]

was Pythagoras, who is credited with its first theorems: such as the theorem that the angles of a triangle sum to 180 degrees, and his famous result for right triangles, that the square of the hypotenuse equals the sum of squares of the other two sides.

To the Pythagoreans, the first four integers, which define the rows of the tetractys, also had a geometrical significance. The number one represented a single point; the number two represented a line, which is drawn between two points; three represented a plane figure, like a triangle; and four represented a solid body. Just as the tetractys summed up the basic ratios of musical harmony, so it encoded the foundations of physical space.

Euclid codified all of Greek geometry, including the theorems of Pythagoras, in his *Elements*, which has been called the greatest mathematical textbook of all time. The book derived the properties of geometric objects by assuming only five axioms

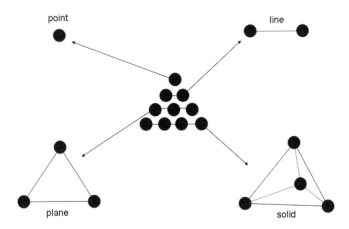

Figure 7.2. The numbers 1, 2, 3, and 4 symbolized the different dimensions of geometrical objects: the zero-dimensional point, the 1-D line, the 2-D plane, and the 3-D solid.

that related to basic defining properties of points, lines, and circles. The first axiom, for example, postulates that it is possible to draw a straight line between any two points.

With its clarity and consistency, *The Elements* introduced a new standard of rigor to mathematics. Its approach of building an entire theory up from a small number of axioms has since served as a kind of template for much scientific thought—including neoclassical economics (Walras, for example, titled his treatise on equilibrium theory *Elements of Pure Economics*). The mathematician B. L. van der Waerden observed that Euclid's book "has exerted a continuous and major influence on human affairs … It is sometimes said that, next to the Bible, *The Elements* may be the most translated, published, and studied of all the books produced in the Western world."[3] It defined the language of science, and therefore changed the way scientists saw and interpreted reality. As Galileo wrote in 1623, the book of the universe "is written in the language of mathematics, and its characters are triangles, circles, and other geometrical figures, without which it is humanly impossible to understand a single word of it; without these one is wandering about in a dark labyrinth."[4]

GOING STRAIGHT

In Euclidean geometry, any figure can be generated by a combination of points and straight lines. A circle can be generated by sweeping a line segment around a fixed point; a cone is generated by sweeping a right triangle around one of the sides adjacent to the right angle.

Furthermore, even a curving line can be made to appear straight, if you look closely enough—just as the earth seems reasonably flat when you are standing on it. The method of calculus, developed in the 1660s by Isaac Newton (and independently by Leibniz), was based on this idea. At any point on a smooth curve, one can define a tangent line to the curve; and zooming in closer and closer, the tangent line and the curve become indistinguishable. The slope of the tangent therefore defines the slope of the curve at that point, and can be used to calculate the instantaneous rate of change of one quantity with respect to another. For the technique to work, the curve must be smooth and without sudden corners, because the tangent is not defined at corner points.

Conversely, a differential equation specifies the rate of change of a variable with time, and can be solved to give a curve such as those in Figure 6.6. Newton originally developed calculus to solve the equations of motion of the moon and planets. Later the *Apollo* team used the same methods to calculate the motion of their spacecraft. As Anders told ground control, while the craft was being propelled towards the moon by its gravitational field, "I think Isaac Newton is doing most of the driving right now."[5]

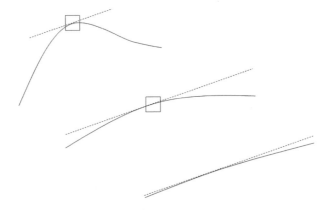

Figure 7.3. Three views of the tangent to a curve, zooming each time into the section enclosed by the box. With each zoom, the curve is better and better approximated by the dashed tangent line. In calculus, the slope of the tangent (i.e. rise over run) is used to calculate the instantaneous rate of change of the vertical coordinate relative to the horizontal coordinate.

Newton's 1687 work *Principia* was the crowning achievement of seventeenth-century science. It introduced the concept of mass, stated the three laws of motion, presented the tools of calculus, and served as the foundation for what Newton called "rational mechanics," which he described as "the science of motions resulting from any forces whatsoever, and of the forces required to produce any motions, accurately proposed and demonstrated."[6] For the first time, the power of geometry and mathematics could be applied in a rigorous manner not just to static objects, but also to ones that moved. The behavior of even the most complicated system could, it seemed, be reduced to a simple set of physical laws, and solved using calculus.

In the following decades, Newton's methods were adopted by scientists from all fields, and applied to everything from electromagnetism to chemistry to astronomy to engineering. As discussed in the preceding chapter, though, the equations were often complicated, and hard to solve by hand. Scientists were therefore forced to work with simplified versions of the equations, in which nonlinearities were removed.

An equation is linear if, when plotted, it gives a straight line. In Figure 7.3, the solid curved line is nonlinear, while the dashed tangent line is given by a linear equation. To convert nonlinear equations to linear ones, mathematicians used a trick similar to that in Figure 7.3: they zoomed in. In particular, they considered only minor perturbations around an equilibrium state. The nonlinear terms then usually shrank in magnitude, and the system could be adequately described by linear equations—it could be flattened.

The resulting linearized systems had a number of advantages. They were well behaved (a prerequisite for chaos is that the equations are nonlinear) and easily solvable using the techniques of the time. They could be decomposed into parts, and each part treated separately—for example, the forces on a bridge could be decomposed into horizontal and vertical components. And they were scalable—if the force on the bridge was doubled, then its deflection should double as well. As with Euclidean geometry, everything could be reduced to the basic elements.

MATHEMATICAL MONSTERS

It was only in the 1960s that scientists began to fully explore the properties of nonlinear systems using computers. But even in the nineteenth century, scientists were aware that not all mathematical objects sat easily with Euclidean geometry, or Newtonian calculus.

In 1861, Karl Weierstrass invented a mathematical abstraction of a curve, for which it was impossible to define a tangent at any point—the curve was all corners. No matter how far you zoomed in, the surface never became flat. In 1904, Helge von Koch proposed another shape, known as the snowflake curve, which was similarly tangent-free. It is generated in an iterative fashion, as shown in Figure 7.4. Starting with a triangle, the middle third of each face is replaced with a triangular extension. This increases the length of the section by a factor 4/3. Every time the process is repeated, the perimeter increases by the same factor. The length of the perimeter therefore goes to infinity, even though the area enclosed is finite. To calculate the tangent for such a curve, you would need to zoom in to find a smooth section as in Figure 7.3—but because of the way the curve is constructed, the sharp corners never go away. It is all knees and elbows. It is infinitely crooked.

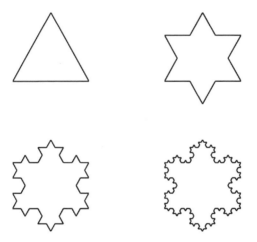

Figure 7.4. The Koch snowflake is the end limit of an infinite number of operations on a triangle, in which the middle third of straight sections are replaced by triangular extensions.

Another geometric object with similarly confounding properties was proposed by Polish mathematician Vaclav Sierpinski in 1916. The Sierpinski gasket, shown in the figure at the start of this chapter, starts with a solid equilateral triangle. This is divided into four smaller triangles, and the central triangle is omitted, leaving a hole in the center. The process is repeated for the three remaining triangles, and so on. At each successive stage, the area decreases by 25 percent, so in the limit it goes to zero. The Sierpinski gasket is like a kind of infinite tetractys, but one with no weight or solidity, only pure form. It is composed from two-dimensional triangles, but has zero area like a one-dimensional line—so what is its dimension?

In 1918, Felix Hausdorff extended the concept of dimensionality to incorporate such objects, based on the idea of scale. If a 1-D line segment is doubled in scale, the new version consists of $2^1 = 2$ copies of itself. If the sides of a 2-D square are doubled in scale, it consists of $2^2 = 4$ copies; and if a 3-D cube is doubled in scale, it consists of $2^3 = 8$ copies. In general, the change in size of a D-dimensional object depends on the change in scale, raised to the power D. In other words, it follows a power law.

Suppose now that we measure the Koch curve using a ruler of fixed length. If we increase the scale by a factor 3, then the measurement will pick up an additional triangular extension, and the total length measured increases by a factor 4/3. By using the same power law, this implies a Hausdorff dimension D of $\log(4)/\log(3)$, or about 1.26. For the Sierpinski gasket, the Hausdorff dimension is about 1.59.[7] Intuitively, this makes sense. The perimeter of the Koch curve is built up from a line, but has infinite length; the Sierpinski gasket starts as a 2-D triangle, but has zero area. In either case, the dimension is somewhere between a 1-D line and a 2-D object.

Instead of having dimension 0, 1, 2, or 3, as in Figure 7.2, these triangle-based figures have a non-integer dimension—they are off-tetractys. They also have a property known as self-similarity, in the sense that they repeat similar features or motifs over a range of scales. Such objects were at the time called pathological—they were mathematical monstrosities, kept in a jar as a freak show for scientists, and not a subject for serious study.[8] They didn't even have a name, until 1975, when the mathematician Benoit Mandelbrot coined the term "fractal" from the Latin *fractus*, meaning broken. Most scientists remained in denial about their existence—as Mark Twain once said, denial isn't a river in Egypt (see "A river in Egypt" below). It turned out that many natural, and economic, systems had "monstrous" characteristics of their own. In fact, they were all over the map.

A LONG WALK BY THE SEASIDE

In 1967, Mandelbrot published what was seen by many as another mathematical curiosity—but one that would eventually relate both geometry and earth measurement to the world of finance. The paper was entitled "How long is the coast of Britain?"

Eratosthenes' map (Figure 7.1) shows Britain as a smoothly contoured blob to the west of Europe. However, more recent maps—or the view from outer space—reveal a complicated shape, full of sudden twists and jagged edges. Since a crooked line is longer than a smooth or straight one, a proper measurement should take that detail into account—and the finer the resolution, the more details appear. The measured length will therefore depend on the resolution.

Indeed, the English scientist Lewis Fry Richardson noticed in the 1920s that countries had very different conceptions of the length of their shared borders. For example, Spain thought its border with Portugal was 987 kilometers, while Portugal thought it was 1,214 kilometers—a difference of 23 percent. Nor has the problem gone away with improved technology. According to the U.K. Ordnance Survey, the length of the British coastline is 17,820 kilometers; according to the CIA World Factbook, it is a mere 12,429 kilometers.[9]

If the thing being measured is reasonably smooth or Euclidean, then the laws of calculus can be used to prove that the measured length will converge on a unique single value. However, as Richardson noted, the measured length of a coastline does not converge, but instead varies in a power-law fashion with the degree of resolution. If one measures the length on the map by dividing the coastline into segments of uniform length ε, and counting the total number N of segments required, then N is proportional to ε^{-D}. The number D depends on the particular geography. (Since the total length is $L = N\varepsilon$, it follows that L is proportional to ε^{1-D}.)

Figure 7.5 shows the result of such a calculation for a map of the British coastline.[10] The data is approximated by a power law with $D = 1.6$ (Mandelbrot found 1.25, but it was for a segment of the west coast only). Note that, as the step length is reduced, the measured length does not converge, but rather goes towards infinity—it is unlimited. If Eratosthenes had arranged for pacers to walk around the coast and count off their steps—which was how distances were calculated at the time—then he would have found the coast was significantly longer than appeared from the map. In fact, assuming the pacers followed every nook and cranny with a step length of one meter, then according to the power law the length would be 6.6 million kilometers, or seventeen times the distance to the moon (in reality, the power law probably won't exactly hold, but the length would still be enormous). At still smaller scales, one would have to take into account the details of individual stones, and then grains of sand. The numbers presented in official surveys are therefore arbitrary and confusing. Geographical features cannot be measured using linear, Euclidean methods.

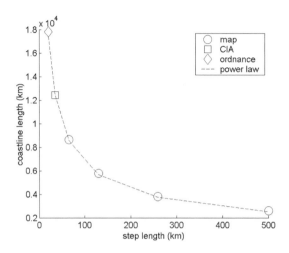

Figure 7.5. Circle symbols show length L of the British coastline measured from a map, using different step lengths for the calculation. The data is approximated by a power law with exponent $D=1.6$ (dashed line). Square symbol shows where the CIA estimate would lie on this curve; diamond shows the Ordnance Survey estimate.

So what is this number D? Mandelbrot realized it could be interpreted as a Hausdorff dimension, which, until then, had been used only in pure mathematics. If a particular feature on a map, say, a road, was a one-dimensional straight line, its length on the map would vary linearly with the scale—a map with twice the scale would show everything twice as long, including the road. The area of a two-dimensional object such as a square city block would vary with the scale to the power 2. The length of a coastline, however, would increase with scale to the power D. So D is a kind of fractal dimension for natural objects.

Power laws are scale-free, in the sense that they maintain the same basic properties regardless of scale. In the case of the coastline, this means if a section is traced, it is hard to tell by looking at it what the scale is. Therefore if you calculate D at large scales or at small, it doesn't change. It represents some fundamental, invariant characteristic, which can be used to classify objects. Richardson, for example, found that the South African coast, which is very smooth, had a D of only 1.02, close to a straight line. Fractals therefore supplied a new way of looking at complex, naturally occurring shapes.

Mandelbrot later described his 1967 paper as a "Trojan horse" with which he could smuggle his evolving ideas about fractal geometry and power laws into the mainstream. His work until then had been scattered in so many different directions, from finance to river discharges to turbulent flow, that few people took it seriously. It also encountered stout resistance from established experts in the fields, to whom "power law" meant getting to decide whose papers were published. The coastline paper, however, appeared to be no more than a diversion, and so excited little opposition from entrenched opinion.

While Mandelbrot's research might have seemed to lack focus, it was actually based on two things: careful observation of data, and the recognition that disparate systems can show similar behavior. The trend in mathematics at the time was to retreat into abstraction and specialization. Mandelbrot later compared mathematics to Antaeus, the son of Gaia, who had to touch the ground from time to time to restore his strength. Just as Hercules killed Antaeus by holding him off the ground, so mathematics would die if it were separated from reality. Geometry was earth measurement—and it needed to be brought back to earth.

Interest in fractals exploded in the 1970s, as scientists used their new tools, high-speed computers, to explore nonlinear systems. The two subjects are linked, because the patterns and statistics generated by nonlinear systems tend to be fractal. An example is the bifurcation diagrams in the preceding chapter: zooming in on certain sections of the bifurcation diagram of the logistic map reveals smaller, self-similar versions. The fact that many of these forms were surprisingly beautiful helped fuel interest among the general public. Perhaps the most famous fractal figure is the Mandelbrot set, a strange bulbous growth that throws off a universe of organic-looking forms, including infinitely many copies of itself at smaller scales. A zoomed view is shown in Figure 7.6. The color of each point in the figure (here converted to grayscale) is determined by performing a simple iterative calculation using the point's coordinates. If the calculation converges to a number below a certain limit, the point belongs in the set and is colored black; otherwise the color reflects the number of iterations required to escape the limit, so is a measure of how close the point is to belonging to the set. The figure can therefore be viewed as representing a fractal, fuzzy set where the shading indicates the degree of membership.

Fractals don't just exist on the computer, but are also found everywhere in nature, from the shape of cauliflowers, to the path traced by a winding river, to the flooding patterns of the Nile, to the branching of blood vessels, to clouds: massive cloud formations viewed from a satellite have a similar appearance to wisps of cumulus viewed from an airplane window. Of course, these patterns had always been around, but it was only the invention of fractal geometry that gave scientists a language to describe them.

While fractals were catching on everywhere else, though, there was one area that wasn't buying into it—economics. Mandelbrot's fractal theory was in large part motivated by his study of financial data. An intriguing feature of many financial charts is that they show a degree of self-similarity, in the sense that plots of price changes have similar statistical properties whether the fluctuations are daily, weekly, monthly, or yearly (traders say it is hard to tell the time scale for a graph of price changes just by looking at the shape of the squiggle). They also do not vary

Figure 7.6. A zoomed view of the Mandelbrot set.[11] The set proper
consists of the black points, while the grayscale of the other points can be
interpreted as a degree of fuzzy membership. The two black, bulbous shapes—
the large above and the small below—are distorted copies of the complete
set. The boundary of the Mandelbrot set—its "coastline"—is so complex
that its dimension is 2, the same as the plane.

in a smooth, continuous fashion, but rather are punctuated by
sudden surges or plunges. From the point of view of classical
mathematics, they are extremely poorly behaved and their
roughness doesn't go away when you zoom in. Yet as with fractals, their self-similarity reveals a different kind of order.

Despite Mandelbrot's background in economics—he taught
the subject at Harvard in the early 1960s—his observations that
financial data showed fractal properties did not go down well. In
fact, he found himself "about as welcome in the established

church of economics as a heretical Arian at the Council of Nicene."[12] The reason was that his conclusions struck at the very heart of orthodox theory.

INFINITE VARIATION

Since the nineteenth century, the economy had been viewed as an essentially static system, which when perturbed from the outside by external events, automatically self-adjusts to get back to its optimal equilibrium. Of course there is a constant supply of news to be assimilated, so the market never quite settles, but at any single moment it is nearly in a state of perfect balance.

Since news is random and unexpected, it follows that price fluctuations, too, should be random—like the toss of a dice, or a draw from a pack of cards. The market was therefore unpredictable. No one could say whether its next move would be up or down. However, as Louis Bachelier argued in his 1900 dissertation *Theorié de la Spéculation*, it was still possible to control the odds. If one assumed price changes were the result of many independent fluctuations, each with the same probability distribution, then they should follow the familiar normal, or bell curve, distribution.

Bachelier's work was initially controversial, but as discussed in the next chapter it gained widespread acceptance in the 1960s when analysis showed random changes in market prices outweighed any systematic effects. The good news was that mathematicians and physicists had already constructed sophisticated techniques for dealing with randomness, so it was just a question of applying these methods to the economy. There followed a slew of techniques for what became known as financial engineering. The Capital Asset Pricing Model was a method for determining valuations; Modern Portfolio Theory was an asset allocation technique; the Black-Scholes formula allowed investors to price options. These methods were rapidly adopted by banks and other businesses, and soon formed the backbone of our financial system—if you have a pension fund it is no doubt based on them. They also had one thing in common: they assumed price fluctuations were normally distributed.

It followed that the tendency for an asset price to fluctuate could be described by a single number, the variance (discussed further in Chapter 9), which gave a typical scale or size for "normal" fluctuations. Since risky assets, such as commodities, tend to fluctuate a lot, while non-risky assets, such as cash, are stable, the variance could serve as a proxy for risk. To apply the Black-Scholes formula to a particular asset, it was only necessary to calculate the variance in that asset from its recent price fluctuations, input the number along with other known parameters, and out came the price.

As Mandelbrot showed, however, there was a problem in how to define "recent." Gold prices were stable up until the late 1960s, and then went on a ten-year rocket ride. At which point was there enough data to calculate the variance? Similarly, the variance of the Standard & Poor 500 index in Figure 4.2 for a particular time frame depends critically on whether or not it includes the stock market crash of October 1987. The variance is not a fixed or stable quantity—its calculation depends on how far back the financial analyst decides to go. Just as the U.K. Ordnance Survey and the CIA disagree on the length of Britain's coast, so two analysts can disagree on an asset's variance.

One approach was simply to write off such surges or crashes as exceptional events that said nothing about the real economy. (An alternative was the time-honored technique of denial— when economists Andy Lo and Craig MacKinlay presented some data in 1984 that violated a simple variance test, they were informed by a senior economist in the audience that they must have made a programming error.[13]) But Mandelbrot's fractal analysis revealed that these events were an intrinsic feature of financial systems—in which case risks (or rewards) could be far higher than conventional models assumed.

WALKING ON THE MOON

Financial institutions are in the business of calculating and managing risk. If a bank loans money to a certain customer, it needs to know the risk of default. If an insurance company sells home coverage in Florida, it needs to know the risk of a hurricane. If a broker sells an option that hedges against a fall in the dollar/yen exchange rate, then she needs to know the odds of that happening. And they don't just care about the typical variation in recent years—they also have to worry about the probability of major events, because those are the ones that can knock them out. Orthodox tools based on a normal distribution therefore fail exactly where they are most needed, at the extremes.

The scars left on the records by financial crashes are rather like craters on the moon. As *Apollo 8* astronaut Anders observed, the moon "has been bombarded through the eons with numerous small asteroids and meteoroids, pock marking the surface every square inch ... Only the very newest feature is of any sharp definition to them, and eventually they get eroded down by the constant bombardment of small meteorites."[14]

Craters have a fractal, scale-invariant property (what is the scale of the picture below?). If you were walking on the surface of the moon, surveying the location of a future space colony, you might only be aware of the smaller craters, which are still well defined. You would therefore conclude that the chances of a colony being wiped out by a giant meteorite would be negligible. But if you then

Figure 7.7. The large but indistinct crater in the middle is Korolev.
See notes for its size.[15]

lifted yourself off the surface, to get a better perspective, you would become aware of much larger craters from eons past.

The question of the size of a typical crater is therefore similar to the question of a coastline's length. With coastlines, the more you zoom in, the more detail appears, and the longer they seem. With craters, the farther you zoom out, the more you become aware of the large events—which statistically speaking are likely to have happened a long time ago.

Another example is earthquakes. I have been living in Vancouver for a couple of years, and so far I haven't noticed so much as a tremble. But if I talk to people who have been here a bit longer, they tell me about the magnitude 5.5 earthquake of 1996, which was centered east of Seattle and was also felt here. Some can even remember the magnitude 7.3 event of 1946, centered under Vancouver Island. If it happened today, it would do billions of dollars in damage. And according to historical records, around 1700 there was a massive quake of magnitude 8 or more.[16]

Because things like meteorite impacts, earthquakes, or financial crashes are scale-free over a huge range, there is always the possibility of an earth-shattering event. Going back in the historical records is like lifting yourself above the moon—you start to see the big features, those huge events that only happen very occasionally. Anyone remember the crash of 1929?

Using variance as a proxy for risk in financial models is like measuring the risk of an earthquake in Vancouver based on recent evidence. As the author and former trader Nassim Nicholas Taleb wrote, the lessons learned from financial crises "are ignored in what is taught to 150,000 business school students worldwide."[17] If you believe the economy is optimal, it's impossible to learn from past mistakes. Since banks and other financial institutions base their reserves on such models, this has real implications for the health and stability of the world financial system (and your pension).

One solution is to tweak the existing methods so as to better account for risk. New valuation tools, going by names such as GARCH (for "generalized autoregressive conditional heteroskedasticity"), include extra parameters to account for the fact that variance is not stable. However the results are highly sensitive to the choices of parameters, and whether or not events such as the 1987 crash are included in the data. And by staying with concepts such as variance, they avoid the real problem, which is that financial data is not well modeled by the normal distribution.

Traders tend to use simpler models for volatility forecasting, based on patterns in financial data. New techniques of fractal market analysis are also being incorporated into their toolbox. One approach is to generate fractal shapes that resemble price charts. These can then be used to "stress test" portfolios, by simulating how they react to extreme events. If assets that are expected to be highly vulnerable to a crash are combined with assets that are more resistant, then the overall robustness of the portfolio can be improved.[18]

The advantage of such methods is that they do not assume the markets are "normal" so are more realistic than orthodox techniques. As seen in Figure 4.2, and discussed further in Chapter 9, fractal distributions like the power law are a much better match to most financial data than the bell curve. However, like GARCH, the models are sensitive to small changes in parameters, and they still can't look into the future. The basic problem is that the squiggle of a stock market index is an emergent property of the entire world economy, which cannot be captured by a single equation, or set of equations.

The knowledge that we cannot precisely predict future events, or even the risk of future events, is highly useful information in itself. It implies that we should take a conservative attitude towards risk, and build a protective degree of redundancy into our financial system, while also being open to new ideas or technologies that have the potential for sudden growth. In the words of Alan Greenspan, "given our inevitably incomplete knowledge about key structural aspects of our ever-changing economy and the sometimes asymmetric costs or benefits of particular outcomes," the best way forward is "a risk-management approach" that considers "not only the most likely future path for the economy but also the distribution of possible outcomes about that path."[19] (Experience at managing complex economies, as opposed to theorizing about them, often seems to turn people into fractal/dynamic/complex systems experts.[20])

The inverse question to the risk of financial disaster is the possibility of outlandish financial success—the biotech company that invents or accidentally discovers a blockbuster drug, the rash entrepreneurial gamble that pays a million to one. Again, these are events that don't register in the "normal" economy of mainstream theory, exactly because they are statistically unlikely. And yet it is just such extraordinary events that define the economy. What are the chances that a small hamburger restaurant could grow into a global fast-food chain? Or that a new author will produce a huge best seller? We just don't know. That's why such events always come as a surprise—and also why it is worth investing in small biotech companies, or even writing books, despite the apparently poor odds.

CROOKED MONEY

The theory of fractals and nonlinear systems has helped improve our technical understanding of risk, but its real contribution to economics is deeper, and lies in the way it has forced us to see the economy, or society itself, as something far more wild and complex than a simple linear system. Mainstream economics acknowledges the unpredictability of day-to-day market movements, but it is still based, as Thomas Homer-Dixon writes, on the belief that the main track of the economy is "linear, predictable, and reversible . . . An alternative theory would recognize that the economy is intimately connected with nature and its energy flows . . . and [is] often neither predictable nor controllable."[21] The economy is crooked, not straight; and mainstream economists are like flat-earthers who keep saying the world is flat despite all the evidence to the contrary.

In the 1980s, for example, a popular theory among economists was the quantity theory of money, which links inflation to money supply. It is based on the formula $MV=PQ$, where M is the money supply, V is the velocity of circulation (i.e. the rate at which money changes hands), P is the average price level, and Q is the amount of goods and services purchased. The left-hand side represents the flow of money through the economy—if $100 changes hands ten times in a month, then it represents $1,000 in total transactions. The right-hand side PQ is just the gross domestic product, so the equation says that GDP equals money times velocity.

The equation has a clear analogue in physics, where an object's momentum is equal to its mass times its velocity. Double the mass, and the object has twice as much momentum. The equation is linear, because a plot of momentum versus mass gives a straight line.

Reasoning along similarly straight lines, economists in the 1980s argued that V and Q would remain constant, so if the amount of money M doubles, then the prices P would also double. Ronald Reagan in the United States and Margaret Thatcher in Britain therefore tried to control inflation using money supply. In either case the results were not as hoped. In Britain, inflation hit 18 percent at one point. The problem is that the equation looks linear, but it isn't really, because the terms are not constant or independent. Inflation in Britain at the time was being driven by factors such as increased value-added taxes and ballooning public-sector wage deals, and couldn't be controlled by something as simple as twisting the knob of money supply.

In fact a major contributor to inflation is expectations of

future inflation—a factory worker who thinks his expenses will go up next year will demand a higher pay settlement, which in turn drives up prices of the factory's goods, which increases inflation. This in turn affects expectations at the individual, company, country, and global levels. When this positive feedback loop gets out of control, the result can be hyperinflation and a loss of faith in the value of money that effectively breaks the economy, as happened in Germany in the 1920s, or Latin America in the 1970s and 1980s. The economy is a nonlinear, fractal system, where the smallest scales are linked to the largest, and the decisions of the central bank are affected by the gut instincts of the people on the street.

Another example of linear thinking is the uncritical acceptance among many mainstream economists of the benefits of free trade and globalization. The assumption is that we are all the same under economic law—the neoclassical version of Euclid's *Elements*—so national or local boundaries just get in the way. The aim is therefore to reduce the rich fractal structure of the world economy to a kind of uniform blancmange. Every city should look the same, with the same stores and the same access to the same consumer goods. On the other hand, each country should specialize only in what it can produce cheaply, and should import the rest.

Such policies are based on the nineteenth-century theory of comparative advantage, which was developed, and made sense, in an era of low capital mobility.[22] However, when it is possible for an American company to own a factory in Southeast Asia, or the other way round, the only parties to have a comparative advantage are large corporations. Countries are therefore motivated to lower their environmental and social standards in order to attract business and cheap labor. Poorer nations become increasingly reliant on a small number of exports, and vulnerable to price swings. Corporations meanwhile exploit their position, according to John Ralston Saul, by "selling at the cheapest possible price in unstable markets with the aim of destroying smaller competitors; selling at the highest possible price in other areas, where there are already the elements of oligopolistic combines in place."[23] The net effect is that regions and nations find it increasingly difficult to organize around local social and political needs (of course, corporations are very effective at policing their own boundaries—just try strolling into head office without the proper paperwork). Reducing barriers to trade between nations obviously has huge benefits, such as encouraging competition and forcing industries to modernize; but the flip side is becoming increasingly obvious.

As discussed in Chapter 4, a complex adaptive system, such as an ecosystem, tends to develop a fractal hierarchy with organization over many different scales (see "How to be fractal"). An advantage of such a structure is that failure in one area need not propagate through the entire system. In the human body, if you develop a disease in a specific organ, it often remains localized. One of the reasons cancer is so deadly is because it does not respect such boundaries; cancerous cells from the breast or prostate or skin can metastatize and form a tumor elsewhere in the body.

Viewed in this way, the local and national boundaries, which adherents of globalization see as obstacles to efficiency, can actually serve an important purpose. Those random-looking lines on the map, both straight and crooked, make the world economy stronger, as well as more interesting. That may not seem very neat or logical—but, as discussed in the next chapter, neither is the economy.

A RIVER IN EGYPT

Scientists since Eratosthenes—along with farmers and entire civilizations that relied on its floods for irrigation—have long been fascinated by the irregular rhythm of the Nile River. Ancient Egyptians organized their calendar around three seasons, which related to the state of the river: the flood, *akhet*; the time when the land reemerged, *peret*; and the time of low water and harvest, *shomu*. The flooding was critical for the agricultural harvest, but both the timing and the magnitude were highly unpredictable.

In the early twentieth century, when the river's 4,160-mile length was part of the British Empire, the hydrologist Harold Edwin Hurst investigated its flood patterns as part of the Aswan Dam project. He had at his disposal an 847-year record, maintained by the Egyptians, of overflows for the years A.D. 622 to A.D. 1469. Although the overflow was wild and erratic, there was some method to the madness. The system had memory, so a good flood tended to be followed the next year by another good flood. Bad years also tended to cluster together. Traces of this memory persisted over many years. This had real consequences: without taking it into account, dam builders could grossly underestimate the likelihood of a breach.

Benoit Mandelbrot encountered Hurst's results in 1963, when he was teaching economics at Harvard University. He was immediately struck by their resemblance to the cotton price data he had been studying, which was equally wild, and again had a long-range memory so that crashes had repercussions that lasted over many decades. Similar memory or persistence has since been detected in a wide range of financial data. This contradicts the orthodox theory that price movements are independent of history, but is consistent with the fractal view that each part reflects the structure of the whole—and that apparently unrelated phenomena, such as the floods of a river and the price of a stock, can turn out to be mysteriously linked.

HOW TO BE FRACTAL

Viewed as part of the world ecology, our economy is like a metabolic process that converts food and resources into energy and structure. Just as many natural systems show self-similarity over a wide range of scales, so does the economy.

Starting at the smallest scale, each cell absorbs food and other substances and expels waste products through the cell wall. A molecule known as adenosine triphosphate (ATP) facilitates molecular reactions, such as the fabrication of proteins and DNA, by supplying the necessary energy, acting as a kind of cellular money. In a single day, a person typically goes through a staggering 60 kilograms of ATP, which is constantly recycled in the body's equivalent of a currency market.[24] For comparison, the ratio of ATP use to food intake is even greater than the ratio of currency trading to global GDP (see "Down to earth" in Chapter 6), although, of course, it is highly regulated and not susceptible to crashes.

At the next level, cells exist within organs, such as the liver or stomach or skin, which have a specific function within the overall metabolism of the body. Individual bodies, in turn, exist within a household that consists of one or more people, plus superstructure, including clothing, house, car, and so on. Professionally, people are organized into companies, which have their own internal structure. The collection of companies and households makes up the local and national economies, which are embedded in the world system. The size distribution of companies follows a roughly scale-free distribution, with many smaller outfits, and only a few multinationals at the top.[25]

A consequence of this fractal structure is that decisions made at any level propagate, in a nonlinear way, up and down the system. For example, decisions about the food you eat affect your metabolism at the cellular level, but they also affect the overall economy by providing a market for certain producers. Macroeconomic phenomena both affect and are affected by the mental expectations of the person on the street. This rich structure means that control is not easily exerted from the top down, since the response may be crooked rather than straight.

Institutions such as the World Bank and the International Monetary Fund have traditionally behaved like diet coaches for developing countries—whenever there is a problem, they jump in with a ten-step guide to financial health that rarely seems to work. Of course there is a place for such schemes, but new approaches to fighting poverty tend to emphasize small-scale, local solutions. The Peruvian economist Hernando de Soto, for example, champions property rights for barrio dwellers, while Bangladesh's Muhammad Yunus won a Nobel Peace Prize in 2006 for his development of microfinance schemes that target loans at small-scale entrepreneurs rather than enormous state institutions. They may not fix the government's debt problems, but they do help put resources where they are really needed—in people's stomachs.

8 ○ LIGHT VERSUS DARKNESS
GREEN

Detail from the Great Seal on the reverse side of the U.S. one-dollar bill.

And I will bring the blind by a way that they knew not; I will lead them in paths that they have not known: I will make darkness light before them, and crooked things straight.
—Isaiah 42:16

Socrates is the prototype of the theoretical optimist who with his belief in the explicability of the nature of things, attributes to

*knowledge and perception the power of a universal panacea, and
in error sees evil itself.*
—Nietzsche, *The Birth of Tragedy*

When the Moon's in the full, then wit's in the wane.
—William Rowley, Thomas Dekker, and John Ford, *The Witch
of Edmonton*

Money doesn't grow on trees.
—Traditional

DARK SIDE OF THE EARTH

Due to a fluke of the solar system's formation, the moon's rotation around its own axis is perfectly in phase with its rotation
around the earth. Its orientation relative to us is therefore
fixed—we always see the same face. We call the other side the
dark side, though of course it too gets its share of sunlight.

What the moon was trying to hide had always been a great
mystery—an unsightly blemish? A colony of aliens? An antenna?
We first had a peek at the unknown when the Russian satellite
Luna 3 orbited the moon in 1959 and took some blurry snaps.
Most of the larger features were therefore given Russian names,
such as Gagarin and Korolev (shown in Figure 7.7).

The *Apollo 8* astronauts were the first to fly around the far
side, out of sight of the earth, which gave a special poignancy to
their Christmas Eve reading of Genesis: "And God saw the light,
that it was good: and God divided the light from the darkness."
While they were there, they too took the liberty of naming a few
geographical features. Some craters were named after NASA scientists and personnel. Another was called Apollo. A mountain
became Mount Marilyn, for Jim Lovell's wife. Three craters on

the very edge of the dark side were referred to as Anders, Borman, and Lovell.

However, the public affairs officer in Houston butted into the television broadcast of the mission to point out that the naming was not official: "This is *Apollo* Control, Houston. 72 hours, 24 minutes into this mission. In this lull, perhaps we can clarify some of the names you heard being given to craters during that television pass ... you distinctly heard Lovell—Anders and Lovell talk about craters named for themselves. Incidentally, this is perhaps a pardonable bit of geologist personality creeping into it. Historically they have been named for discovering geologists or observers."[1] Afterwards, the names were submitted to the international body responsible, and they all got changed.

It has traditionally been the prerogative of explorers to name what they find. America was given the name of Italian explorer Amerigo Vespucci (his first name was probably used because Vespa means wasp in Italian). Victorian explorers often named geographical features after important people back home (such as Victoria). It can be annoying to find out the name of a famous local landmark has no significance other than belonging to some distant relation or drinking buddy of the explorer. George Vancouver named Mount Rainier in Washington State after his friend Admiral Peter Rainier in 1792, despite the fact that Rainier never actually made the trip to see it.

In the latter part of the nineteenth century, when neoclassical economics was being formulated, it wasn't necessary to go to the moon to name a mountain—you could just go to Africa. The scramble between the Americans and Russians to be the first on the moon recalled the earlier struggle between great European powers to colonize what the Victorians called the "dark continent." Apart from southern Asia, Africa was the only major part of the globe not to have come under European control. It offered the raw resources required by industrial economies—such as cotton, rubber, gold, diamonds, minerals, and, of course, labor—as well as fresh markets for industrial produce.

The path of imperialism in Africa was paved by figures such as the businessman Cecil Rhodes, whose fortune later funded numerous Rhodes scholars, and explorer David Livingstone, who went missing for several years while attempting to determine the source of the Nile. In October 1871, the journalist Henry Morton Stanley finally managed to track him down, with the famous words "Dr. Livingstone, I presume?"

The motivation for exploring Africa was not just economic. It was also about filling in the voids in the map. In the eighteenth century, Enlightenment thinkers such as Jean-Jacques Rousseau, David Hume, and Voltaire, along with scientists such as Newton, had shined the light of reason on much of nature and society. But if there was one part of the world that remained in the shadows, it was Africa. Very little was known about the interior. The blankness of the maps became a metaphor for the unknown—what Joseph Conrad called the heart of darkness. It also became tied up with Victorian ideas about race, which put African people on the lower rung of evolution, well below Victorian scientists. As the U.S. politician Alexander Stephens put it in 1861, "As a race the African is inferior to the white man; subordination to the white man is his normal condition. Therefore our system, which regards the African as an inferior, rests upon a great law of nature."[2]

The only way to conquer this darkness was to explore it and put it on the map. Colonization was equated, at least in the minds of the colonizers, with the drive for enlightenment. The continent was a lure for adventurers. Joseph Conrad wrote of the attraction aroused in him as a young boy by those empty maps: "Regions unknown! My imagination could depict to itself there worthy, adventurous and devoted men, nibbling at the edges, attacking from the north and south and east and west, conquering a bit of truth here and a bit of truth there, and sometimes swallowed up by the mystery their hearts were so persistently set on unveiling."[3] (The Victorian scientist Francis Galton, who explored and mapped Southwestern Africa for the Royal Geographical Society, was so taken by the physique of one African woman that he decided to map her as well, making "a series of observations upon her figure in every direction … I worked out the results by trigonometry and logarithms."[4])

The process of colonization, once begun, was incredibly rapid. Between 1871 and 1900, 95 percent of Africa was carved up and divided among the European powers, with no regard to existing ethnic or social boundaries. Britain, France, Germany, and Belgium were the biggest gainers. Africa was finally on the European map. Of course, the locals had long managed to get along fine without place names such as Lake Victoria, and the continent was never really dark. From space, it apparently looks quite green, apart from the northern desert regions.

The Victorians were also conquering their fear of the dark in another way—with the incandescent lightbulb, first publicly demonstrated by Thomas Edison in 1879. Claims for its invention were also made by Joseph Wilson Swan in England, Heinrich Göbel in Germany, and others (thus raising the question of how many Victorians it took to screw in a lightbulb). In 1888, the physicist Nikola Tesla presented his "system of alternating currents and transformers," which allowed the efficient distribution of electric current over large distances, and the wiring-up of the planet. Never again, it seemed, would the world be hidden in darkness.

LIGHT VERSUS DARKNESS

Since long before the lightbulb, science has been in the business of illumination. As the classical scholar Francis M. Cornford observed, the Pythagoreans believed "Light is the medium of truth and knowledge; it reveals the knowable aspect of Nature—the forms, surfaces, limits of objects that are confounded in the unlimited darkness of night."[5] Aristoxenus wrote, "Pythagoras went to Babylon and learnt from Zaratas [the prophet Zoroaster] that Light and Darkness were the male and female principles from which the world was created."[6]

Plato's "allegory of the cave" in *The Republic* compared mankind to prison dwellers watching shadows on a wall, who could only apprehend the true nature of reality, and the source of all that is good, by breaking free of their chains of ignorance and escaping into the light: "in the world of knowledge the idea of good appears last of all, and is seen only with an effort; and, when seen, is also inferred to be the universal author of all things beautiful and right, parent of light and of the lord of light in this visible world, and the immediate source of reason and truth in the intellectual ... this is the power upon which he who would act rationally, either in public or private life must have his eye fixed."[7] In Plato's utopian society, the guardian class would be "brought from darkness to light" through education in arts such as mathematics, astronomy, and dialectic—along with some selective breeding.

The astronomer Johannes Kepler described how he had to "grope in the darkness of my ignorance until I found the door which lets in the light of truth."[8] Newton's epitaph, penned by Alexander Pope, reads: "Nature, and Nature's Laws lay hid in Night / God said, Let Newton be! And All was Light." Rational science acted as a kind of beacon for society, and a driver of progress. (And, of course, still does. In 2003, Rick Tumlinson, the founder of the Space Frontier Association, attempted to excite the U.S. Senate about space exploration by saying that "America needs a shining light. The world needs a shining light. Space can be the place where that light can hang for all to see ... Within my lifetime I want to be able to cast my eyes upwards and see a string of pearls in the night above the Earth as the first orbital community of Alpha Town celebrates its first quarter century, while glittering lights shimmer at the South Pole of the Moon.")

In the 1870s, while imperialist powers were thrusting their way into Africa, and engineers were stringing up the first lights, neoclassical economists were shining the lightbulb of reason in a different direction—towards the murky workings of the economy.

In *Theory of Political Economy*, William Stanley Jevons laid out the basic principles and axioms of his "mechanics of utility and self interest" which would allow a scientific understanding of the market. One of them was "every person will choose the greater apparent good"; in other words, man acts rationally to maximize his own utility. The idea was based on the "hedonistic calculus" of Jeremy Bentham, who wrote, "Nature has placed mankind under the governance of two sovereign masters—pain and pleasure ... The principle of utility recognises this subjection, and assumes it for the foundation of that system, the object of which is to rear the fabric of felicity by the hands of reason and of law. Systems which attempt to question it deal in sounds instead of sense, in caprice instead of reason, in darkness instead of light."[9] Not only was man rational, but to assume otherwise was to be irrational.

By equating their theory of utility with rational behavior, both in *homo economicus* and the theory itself, the neoclassical economists therefore aligned themselves with Enlightenment ideals of science and reason. Jevons believed the principles of economics were "as sure and demonstrative as that of kinematics or statics, nay, almost as self-evident as are the elements of Euclid, when the real meaning of the formulae is fully seized." In 1897, Vilfredo Pareto compared neoclassical economics to the rational mechanics of Newton: "Rational mechanics gives us a first approximation to the theory of the equilibrium and of the movements of bodies. In the same way the theories of Jevons, Walras, Marshall, Irving Fisher, and others present us with a first approximation to the full theory of economic phenomena ... The problem of pure economics bears a striking likeness to that of rational mechanics."[10] It therefore followed that economics could emulate the success of physicists and engineers and explorers, and join in the march of progress.

RATIONAL MAN

In order for a science to prove it is completely objective and based on impartial truth rather than mere opinion, it must be able to make accurate, verifiable predictions. Otherwise, scientists argue, theories are no better than stories—they are just more shadows on the wall. The assumption that economic man was rational was therefore a useful one for neoclassical economists to make. It is generally easier to predict the response to some incentive of a rational person than a crazy one; and if everyone were to behave in a totally chaotic and random fashion, there wouldn't be any economic laws to discover.

Not all economists found it rational to assume economic man was entirely rational. The American economist Thorstein Veblen observed that the theory demanded mankind to be "clearsighted and farsighted in its appreciation of future sensuous gains and losses ... Such a theory can take account of conduct only in so far as it is rational conduct, guided by deliberate and exhaustively intelligent choice."[11] In his 1899 *Theory of the*

Leisure Class, Veblen provided plenty of examples of behavior that seemed less than rational, such as gambling or conspicuous consumption.

However, one of the great strengths of the rationality assumption was that it was impossible to completely disprove. It may seem to an impartial observer that a person who spends a major part of his or her income on lottery tickets, despite the poor odds, is behaving irrationally. However, the "hedonistic calculus" only requires that the person is acting to satisfy his or her fixed preferences. If those preferences include buying losing lottery tickets, then the behavior is rational. By this circular argument, of course, everything is rational, so long as people are consistent (the theory did not allow for flux or change).

Another challenge to the establishment of economic theory as a serious, rational, prediction-based science was raised in 1900 by Louis Bachelier in his PhD dissertation on the Paris Exchange, or Bourse. After following the activities of the traders, he was led to the conclusion that its behavior was essentially random, and so it was "impossible to hope for mathematical forecasting." Although he went on to argue that it was still possible to calculate the odds using the laws of chance, the idea that the economy would always elude rational prediction was not well received. It was like surrendering to the forces of darkness, or saying Africa could not be mapped. Bachelier's thesis was awarded a mediocre grade, and his theory was banished into the shadows of economic thought for the next sixty years.

Bachelier's work was revived in the 1950s, when a series of experiments showed markets did move in an apparently random fashion—which explained the poor track record of most economic forecasters. And it finally moved into the mainstream following another famous PhD thesis, that of Eugene Fama in 1965. The reason we could not predict the economy, Fama argued, was not because the market was irrational—it was because it was too rational.

RATIONAL ECONOMY

In his thesis, Fama defined an efficient market as a place where "there are large numbers of rational profit maximizers actively competing, with each trying to predict future market values of individual securities, and where important current information is almost freely available to all participants." In such a market, he argued, "competition among the many intelligent participants leads to a situation where ... the actual price of a security will be a good estimate of its intrinsic value." Any deviations will be small and random, so "actual prices of securities will wander randomly about their intrinsic values." It followed that an efficient market was unpredictable—no investor could exploit price discrepancies based on fundamental analysis or any other method.

Fama and Bachelier, therefore, said very similar things. The difference was that Bachelier saw the market as impenetrable to the light of reason, while Fama saw it as being itself the light of reason (another difference was that Bachelier spent his life in obscurity, while Fama immediately became famous). The market was the sum total of its "many intelligent participants," so its collective wisdom was greater than that of any one person.

Fama's thesis was based on empirical evidence, which showed that economic forecasters were consistently unable to predict market movements. Attempts to choose winning stocks by analyzing the attributes of different companies were a waste of time because, he argued, all the necessary information had already been priced in by the market. And the work of the chartist, who looks for patterns in historical data, was "like that of the astrologer ... of no real value in stock market analysis." (Of course, this hasn't stopped both chartists and astrologers from running investment funds.[12])

As the *Economist* wrote in 2006, "The [efficient market] hypothesis has been hugely influential in the world of finance, becoming a building block for other theories on subjects from portfolio selection to option pricing."[13] Again, not everyone has found it rational to assume the market is rational. John Maynard Keynes argued in the 1930s that market bubbles and crashes were due to changes in the psychological state of investors, which moved asset prices away from their "intrinsic values." But the beauty of the efficient market hypothesis—which made it a great masterstroke of neoclassical economics—was that it neutralized the criticism that economics was not a predictive science. Other sciences, such as chemistry and physics, had to justify themselves by making testable predictions, but economists had handed themselves a pass card. And like the assumption of investor rationality, efficiency was very difficult to disprove.

To show the theory was wrong, one would have to demonstrate that asset prices were out of line with intrinsic values—for example, that the price of gold was too high. If the analysis was correct, then the price of gold should revert to its long-term intrinsic value. However, it was obvious that investors were unable to make such predictions in a consistent way. No one could out-predict the market.

The efficient market hypothesis soon became an article of near-religious devotion for mainstream economists (Warren Buffet sarcastically compared it to "holy scripture").[14] It provided a kind of closed, hermetically sealed box in which neoclassical theory could flourish. Because investors were rational, and markets were fair, and there was perfect competition, and prices had a stable equilibrium that reflected their intrinsic value, it naturally followed that any deviation from that value would be small and random. Lack of predictability was not a problem, but merely confirmed the validity of the assumptions, and the infinite wisdom of the market, which was as omnipotent and benevolent as the all-seeing eye adorning the U.S. one-dollar bill (see figure at start of chapter).[15] But are investors always rational—and is the market always right?

STOP MAKING SENSE

In the 1970s, the Israeli psychologists Daniel Kahneman and Amos Tversky tested the neoclassical model of rational behavior using techniques from cognitive psychology. They soon found a number of decision-making situations where people tend to act less than rationally.[16] For example, they showed we have an asymmetric attitude towards loss and gain: we fear the former more than we value the latter. We therefore bias our decisions towards loss-avoidance rather than potential gains, and often miss out on good opportunities. We also dislike change, which explains why investors often become inordinately attached to shares which do nothing but go downhill. Kahneman was later awarded the 2002 Bank of Sweden Prize for his work with Tversky (who died in 1996), but at the time their work was hugely controversial. Kahneman relates meeting a well-known American philosopher at a party: after Kahneman started to explain his ideas, the philosopher turned his back, saying, "I am not really interested in the psychology of stupidity."[17] (I imagine he then tripped over and spilled his drink over someone's shirt.)

The work of Kahneman and Tversky helped spawn the field of behavioral economics. A mix of psychology, sociology, anthropology, neuroscience, and finance, it has given economists a much more realistic idea of how people actually make decisions where money is involved. It appears people do, on the whole, behave rationally when given a narrow and clear range of alternatives. For example, if someone is given their pick between three comparable products, and one is obviously a better deal, then they are likely to respond to that price incentive. However, it is equally easy to come up with examples where choices are influenced by other factors. If someone is asked to choose between three versions—low, medium, and high—of a certain product, there is a tendency to choose medium, because it seems neither cheap nor extravagant. This may explain why gas pumps often offer three grades of fuel—it increases the chances of people choosing medium over the basic grade.

In most real-life situations the choices we face are not so simple, but rather are highly complex. Shall I move cities for another job, or stay where I am? Shall I rent a small apartment in the city, or buy a larger home in the suburbs? Such choices often depend more on rules of thumb and emotional factors than on reasoned appraisal. Studies of patients who are neurologically incapable of processing emotional information show that, for most people, judgments are made "not only by evaluating the consequences ... but also and even sometimes primarily at a gut or emotional level."[18]

The framing and the timing of financial events make a big difference to the way we perceive them. Neuroscientists, using brain scans, have revealed that different parts of the brain are active when a subject is offered an immediate or a delayed reward—and the part favoring immediate rewards usually wins.[19] This is one reason many people fail to plan properly (or rationally) for their retirement. Our emotions—and therefore our decisions—can also be influenced by more direct means. In one experiment involving controlled simulations of investment strategies, researchers in 2005 found the attitude of student volunteers towards risk changed if they were first given a nasal spray containing oxytocin. This hormone, which is normally released during activities such as breastfeeding, orgasm, or close social bonding, has the effect of making people more trusting and therefore willing to take financial risks.[20] (Traders also no doubt behave differently when exposed, nasally or otherwise, to other mood-altering substances.)

Economic theory may be based on rational behavior, but many areas of the actual economy, such as sales, marketing, and advertising, operate on the idea that people are to a degree irrational and can be influenced by psychology, social networks, and so on. The point of many sales techniques is to stop people from thinking rationally—if you're selling a camera, you don't overexplain the features, you let the customer hold it in their hands. Companies try to make their products exciting and emotionally appealing, which helps differentiate them from the competition. As the cognitive neuropsychologist David Lewis observes, "When we make a decision to buy something the emotional response is critical. We may then intellectually justify it but if you read the brain activity you would see it is more emotional than logical and generated in the oldest part of the brain."[21]

Neuroscience aside, there is no particular reason to believe the economy is best described as rational. Economists increasingly talk about "bounded rationality," but even that seems too weak an expression.[22] For most people, the subject of money is charged with emotion. People get killed for it, they marry for it, they spend their lives chasing it, they hoard it, they lose it, and they enjoy it. Nations form alliances or go to war over it. Money has a life and a power of its own, which often subverts rather than obeys reason. The assumption of rationality was perhaps an understandable simplification when putting a theory together back in the 1870s—but the desire to cling on to it for more than 100 years probably says more about emotional factors such as "fear of loss" or "resistance to change" than human behavior.

The use of the term "efficient" (i.e. rational in aggregate) to describe markets is also open for debate. As seen in the next chapter, it is not possible to assume, as Fama did, that markets are perfect, or that everyone has equal access to information. The main problem with efficient market theory, though, is its notion of "intrinsic value." The theory was born out of the neoclassical belief that the economy has some kind of stable equilibrium—a unique set of prices that perfectly matches buyers and sellers. As discussed in Chapter 6, for a dynamical system such as the economy, there is no requirement that an equilibrium point even exist. The stable point was a mathematical convenience, modeled by nineteenth-century economists after the physics of their time.

Viewed in this way, it seems bizarre that unpredictability could somehow be taken as a sign of efficiency and rationality. A deranged psychotic carrying a gun may be unpredictable, but no one would take that as a sign of rational behavior. The weather is unpredictable, but scientists don't interpret sudden rainstorms or droughts as signs of an efficient atmosphere. The reason investors cannot accurately predict fluctuations in the price of gold is not because they can't determine the substance's intrinsic value, it's because a unique intrinsic value doesn't exist. The price of an asset reflects the market's fuzzy consensus about its future value, which is highly variable and prone to all sorts of forces, including irrational ones.

One area where advanced mathematical techniques have been enthusiastically adopted is in the proprietary statistical algorithms used by quantitative traders (who are often mathematicians or physicists by training) at banks or hedge funds. Analysts scour financial data for subtle but persistent (for a while) patterns that, according to efficient market theory, should not exist, and use them to devise clever trading strategies. These methods can be very successful—as evidenced by the income of mathematician turned hedge-fund manager Jim Simons, who made $1.7 billion in 2006—but are risky and need to be backed by a large amount of money.[23] For the rest of us, the strongest pattern in the data is that the market tends to go up, which is why a buy-and-hold strategy is so hard to beat.

The true genius of the efficient market hypothesis—and the reason for its enduring popularity with economists—was the way it co-opted the words "rational" and "efficient," which are repeated like mantras in much economic theory. By granting these attributes to free markets, neoclassical economists both explained the benefits of modern capitalism and vicariously took credit for them. The equations showed why free markets were so good at setting prices and creating wealth. They also rationalized away problems such as the unequal distribution of riches. Because free markets were rational and efficient, it followed that everything companies or individuals did was in the best interest of society—even if it didn't look that way. The efficient economy became a kind of deity, interpreted to the masses by the economist-priests. Anything that impeded its workings, such as government regulation or unions or anti-globalization protests, was by definition inefficient and irrational. And if third world countries, or some portions of society, couldn't adjust, it was because there was something wrong with them.[24] To use Bentham's expression, they dealt "in caprice instead of reason, in darkness instead of light."

BRIGHT LIGHTS

The connection between economic and industrial progress, and the progress from dark to light, is more than just metaphoric. The

Industrial Revolution began with the development of coal-driven steam engines. These found their first major application in mining—they helped dig up their own fuel—but they were soon being put to diverse uses in weaving, milling, transportation, and powering the industrial machine. The rapid industrialization of countries such as the United States in the early twentieth century was on the back of electricity networks. More recently, studies have shown that electricity consumption tracks economic growth to the point where it can almost be used as a proxy for GDP. Figure 8.1 shows that the threefold increase in U.S. electricity consumption since 1968 closely matches the similar growth in GDP. In many developing countries, the GDP is impossible to measure directly, but it can still be inferred from power use.

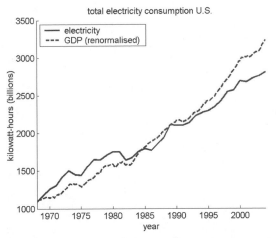

Figure 8.1. Total electricity consumption in the United States. Also shown is the GDP, renormalized so the lines agree at 1968 for purposes of comparison.

While the world has grown brighter, it has not done so in a uniform way. Figure 8.2 is a composite picture showing a view of the earth at night from space, taken in November 2000. The

Apollo 8 astronauts would have had a similar view, but there would have been about a third as much light, which gives an idea of the enormous economic growth since that time. The added horizontal line corresponds to the axis through Rhodes in Eratosthenes' map (Figure 7.1), and now divides Africa from Europe. Note that, while Africa may be on the European map, it hasn't tapped into the European power supply. The brightest area in Africa is the portion of the Nile River downstream from the Aswan Dam.

Figure 8.2. Composite picture of earth at night from orbiting DMSP satellites, November 2000. The horizontal line added to the picture corresponds to the axis through Rhodes in Eratosthenes' map.[25]

Although industrialization has brought huge benefits to society, at least in developed countries, its unpleasant side effects have also long been obvious. Not all Victorians were enamored with the sight of steam-driven trains barrelling through their countryside, or the emphasis on competition, or the unequal distribution of wealth. In *The Condition of the Working Class in England* (1845), Friedrich Engels wrote, "It is utterly indifferent to the English bourgeois whether his working-men starve or not, if only he makes money. All the conditions of life are measured by money, and what brings no money is nonsense, unpractical, idealistic bosh."[26] John Stuart Mill wrote in 1848, "I confess I am not charmed with the ideal of life held out by those who think that the normal state of human beings is that of struggling to get on; that the trampling, crushing, elbowing, and treading on each other's heels, which form the existing type of social life, are the most desirable lot of human kind, or anything but the disagreeable symptoms of one of the phases of industrial progress."

Because capitalist societies as a whole were getting so much richer, such statements were usually written off as the moaning of those who didn't like, or couldn't keep up with, a progressive, competitive world. In the 1960s, though, the burgeoning environmental movement uttered a much more profound heresy against the church of capitalism. They said that the purpose of man was not just to combat and dominate the "darkness" of nature—we also had a responsibility to protect and nourish it. If we neglected that duty, then we would pay a price—for the fabric of life is "on one hand delicate and destructible, on the other miraculously tough and resilient, and capable of striking back in unexpected ways." Progress had a shadow side.

Rachel Carson's 1962 book *Silent Spring* warned the world of the unpredictable—and often deadly—effects of pesticides and other chemicals on plants, animals, and humans. She was an established writer as well as a scientist, and her metaphor of a silent spring grabbed the imagination and the emotions of the public. "There was once a town in the heart of America where all life seemed to live in harmony with its surroundings...Then a strange blight crept over the area and everything began to change ... On the mornings that had once throbbed with the dawn chorus of scores of bird voices there was now no sound; only silence lay over the fields and woods and marsh."

Her book was perceived as a threat by the chemical industry, and provoked a massive backlash. She was described as unqualified, a Communist, and a "hysterical woman." A spokesman for the chemical industry, Dr. Robert White-Stevens, called her "a fanatic defender of the cult of the balance of nature," and warned, "If man were to follow the teachings of Miss Carson, we would return to the Dark Ages, and the insects and diseases and vermin would once again inherit the earth."[27]

In retrospect, it now seems it was the critics who were being hysterical and over the top. At the time, chemical pesticides were used in a profligate and indiscriminate fashion, with no concern for the possible consequences. *Silent Spring* alerted everyone to the fact that chemicals that kill pests are biologically active substances, which have complex effects on other forms of life. One of Carson's main targets was DDT, or dichlorodiphenyl-trichloroethane, which was the poster child of the chemical industry. First synthesized in 1874, it was used extensively during World War II to control insect populations that carried typhus and malaria, as well as to dust soldiers for lice. It was credited with the elimination of malaria in Europe and North America, thus saving millions of lives. But it kills or weakens many species other than the pests it targets—and because the chemical doesn't break down quickly, it persists in the environment and tends to accumulate in organisms higher up the food chain. Largely as a response to Carson's book, DDT was banned in many developed countries in the 1970s (though Carson herself only called for restrictions rather than an outright ban). It is still used in some countries to control malaria, but in far lower concentrations than would earlier have been deemed acceptable.

The reason *Silent Spring* was so controversial was that it turned the utopian vision of technological and economic progress on its head—and questioned the rationality, not just of individual people making financial decisions, but also of markets and society as a whole. According to theory, the market was rational and efficient, and everything that happened outside the market was an externality. Carson's book, however, put the market into context with the larger ecosystem. Everything we did had an effect on the environment—and because the "web of life" was a complex system, we couldn't predict or control the effects. Rather than being the light of reason, the market was a bit of a lout, its technology "as crude a weapon as the cave man's club."

GREEN POWER

Carson's book—assisted to some degree by the clumsy attempts of chemical companies to suppress it—became a runaway best seller, and, along with works such as E. F. Schumacher's *Small Is Beautiful*, helped establish the environmental movement and the field of green economics. The most basic principle of green economics is that, as discussed in Chapter 1, the human race cannot be viewed as somehow distinct from the world ecosystem. A consequence is that an economy's efficiency must not be measured solely in terms of its activity or production. American farmers, for example, appear to be highly efficient in terms of their output per person. But if you take into account the enormous amount of energy input required to produce their fertilizers and pesticides, they are among the least productive in the world.[28] According to a study by Peter Tyedmers of the University of Dalhousie, the fossil fuel energy used by many commercial fisheries exceeds the nutritional value of the fish by a factor of ten.[29] The fact that people and industries are burning a lot of energy isn't necessarily a sign of progress.

Green economics is concerned with many of the same things that worried some Victorian observers of the industrial revolution, such as environmental damage, harsh social inequalities, and the side effects of technology. Chemicals boost food productivity and help to feed humanity, but they also accumulate in the environment and have long-lasting, harmful effects. Genetic engineering may produce more "efficient" plant species for agriculture, but the risks are hard to quantify and the motivations often seem to have more to do with corporate greed than improving the food supply. Nuclear power will help keep the lights on as fossil fuels run low, but brings with it a waste disposal problem that makes the world less safe (though see "Nuclear sunshine" below).

A main problem with technological progress is the way it does not benefit all sectors of humanity equally. This is graphically obvious from Figure 8.2. Half the world powers ahead, lights ablaze, sucking in nonrenewable resources, while third world countries still live in the shadows, despite the earnest ministrations of institutions such as the World Bank. The American Black Power activist Malcolm X had a point when he said in 1965, "the system of capitalism needs some blood to suck."[30] The inherently dualistic vision of neoclassical economics is reflected in a world where the benefits of the rational economy congregate in rich countries, while "externalities" such as poverty and environmental devastation congregate in the rest.

Unlike neoclassical economics, green economics is highly diverse and has not converged on a single, reductionist worldview.

It is openly political, and incorporates aspects of ecology, feminism, antiglobalization, green politics, antiracism, the peace movement, conservation, and so on. It does not separate subjects such as poverty and technology into different boxes, but rather attempts to treat them in an integrated fashion. After all, it isn't very efficient for the environment or for society if resources such as energy are distributed in a grossly unequal manner; or if a large fraction of the world's population is malnourished while rich countries struggle with the problem of childhood obesity; or if sexual inequality in underdeveloped countries contributes to an explosive birth rate.

While mainstream economics is obsessed with the appearance of rationality, green economics isn't afraid to allow a little emotion into the mix. Carson's book was a best seller not just because it made a carefully reasoned argument against the excessive use of pesticides, but also because it was both frightening and inspiring. James Lovelock's Gaia theory is powerful because it engages with our gut feelings—if the earth is alive, it demands a different response than a lump of rock. According to green economics, the economy is an organic entity, not a deterministic machine; and to fully participate in its evolution, and make the right collective decisions, we have to be rational, but we also need to be emotionally engaged.

Another defining feature of green economics is its practicality. It isn't trying to make the world perfect by dogmatically applying abstract economic theories; instead it is trying to improve matters, one step at a time, by redesigning industrial processes or the layout of cities or the flow of traffic in a transportation system. The thing we celebrate and admire most about the Victorian era is its spirit of ingenuity and invention: the bridges of Isambard Kingdom Brunel, the lightbulb, the London sewer system, photography. That spirit of inventiveness is now to be found in places like the Rocky Mountain Institute in Colorado, set up by physicist Amory Lovins and his wife L. Hunter Sheldon to develop and promote sustainable technologies; or the Natural Capital Institute in California, which conducts research in areas from socially responsible investing to water management; or in the international effort to develop hydrogen-powered fuel cell cars. As Mathis Wackernagel of the Global Footprint Network said, the aim of building a sustainable infrastructure is similar to that of an engineer building a bridge: "they build the safety factors into the bridge and say, we want to make sure this bridge will work for decades to come. And in the same way, we can apply these kind of principles to cities and say, are we making cities future-friendly? Are we preparing them to live on lower footprints with a higher quality of life?"[31]

Anthropologists say that the best way to understand a society is through its stories. The neoclassical story that the economy is the efficient product of rational *homo economici* who guide it to a state of optimal equilibrium, is a Pythagorean fantasy. It is being replaced by a more humble perspective, which states that we live in an interconnected world, where progress is a double-edged sword, and our actions can have unforeseen consequences. It acknowledges that we can't always predict the effects of our technologies on complex natural systems, but we can still aim to move our society in the right direction. In order to see the world better, perhaps we need to turn down the lights.

NUCLEAR SUNSHINE

Ernest Rutherford, who is known as the father of nuclear physics, said in 1933, "Anyone who expects a source of power from the transformation of these atoms is talking moonshine."[32] The promise of a new energy source was, he believed, like the idea that the moon produces its own light—a case of false appearances. Only two decades later, though, the first nuclear power plants were coming online and supplying electricity. In 1954, the chairman of the U.S. Atomic Energy Commission, Lewis L. Strauss, promised that one day nuclear power would be "too cheap to meter."[33]

That prediction has not come true either. Instead, the nuclear industry has been struggling for decades. One problem is social: for some reason, we tend to be very afraid of radiation, despite the fact that we are surrounded by it (most radiation is naturally occurring). We feel no such immediate and visceral fear for the harmful side effects of other energy sources, such as carbon dioxide pollution. Other reasons are the difficulty of storing nuclear waste, and the threat of terrorism. These concerns appeared to be justified by the 1986 Chernobyl disaster, which spread radioactive material over Europe and resulted in twenty-eight deaths from acute radiation exposure. But are atoms really that dangerous?

One supporter of nuclear energy is James Lovelock, founder of Gaia theory. In *The Revenge of Gaia*, he points out that at the peak of the Cold War in 1962, the two superpowers tested hydrogen bombs that released an amount of radioactivity equivalent to two Chernobyl disasters per week, for an entire year. Anyone who was alive at the time has traces of the radiation in his or her bones. Yet life expectancy has increased, and there is no evidence of a surge in cancers or other diseases that can be traced to that time.

In fact, many cancers are the result not of pesticides or radiation, but of something a little less sinister or mysterious: oxygen. Unlike plants, our bodies obtain energy by combining food with oxygen—we essentially burn the food in a controlled manner. Every cell contains organelles known as mitochondria, which release the energy in the form of ATP molecules (see "How to be fractal" in Chapter 7). The mitochondria also release toxic by-products, known as free radicals, which are highly reactive and tend to damage anything they come in contact with, including DNA. Most of the damage is repaired by cellular enzymes, but over the course of a lifetime the chance events pile up, and DNA-mutated cancer cells develop.

Relying on nuclear energy for a power source may look like playing with fire. But we're doing that all the time in our own bodies. Nuclear energy has many drawbacks, but so do the alternatives. The best approach is probably to adopt a mix of power sources—and use less energy of any type.

HOW TO BE GREEN

A basic tenet of green economics is that progress has a shadow side, and even the most innocuous inventions can have harmful consequences. An obvious example is nuclear energy, which can be used to power a city, or flatten it. But even the environmental movement has its shadow. It sometimes seems dominated more by individualistic fears of contamination by chemicals or radiation than genuine concern about society or the environment. This is especially true now that companies have learned to exploit green credentials as a marketing tool.

Rachel Carson's book drew attention to the dangers of chemicals such as DDT. However, in most developed countries, the main threat to birds is not pesticides, but rather land use and cats. The over-zealous banning of DDT helped spread malaria and cost human lives. And while organic food may contain less harmful chemicals, it uses about as much land and energy to produce as the industrial version. Buying organic produce is not necessarily the same thing as helping the planet.

It also isn't clear that organic food and "sustainable" energy between them will power the current population of more than six billion people. They would have been a really good idea back around the time of the Industrial Revolution, but we're past that point now. These confusions have made it easy for neoclassical economists, or other skeptics, to write off green concerns as irrational.[34] The argument over the two therefore comes down to who owns the words "rational" and "efficient."

Rationality and efficiency are not ends in themselves, but rather are relative to a set of ideas about the world—rational according to what assumptions? Efficient for what end? The basic principles of environmentalism—that we belong to a larger ecosystem, that our actions have complex consequences, that we should respect and protect the environment—are fundamentally different from those of neoclassical economics, which are concerned only with short-term individual utility. (Of course, this does not mean that the two are always incompatible—having a healthy planet is good for our utility too.)

Being green is obviously more complicated than being selfish—just as being a grown-up carries more responsibility than being a child. Perhaps the best way forward is to emphasize not the light of reason, but the darkness of humility. The human race has grown to a size where our activities are on the same scale as the planet's own processes. We have taken over most of the available land for farming, we have plundered the oceans, and we are warming the atmosphere. The earth has been around for billions of years, and suddenly we are messing with the way it works. We're way out of our depth. So it's time to stick to basics: less stuff, less travel, smaller families. It may be bad for the economy—but in terms of ecology, it's rational and efficient.

9 ○ SQUARE VERSUS OBLONG

BREAKING THE MIRROR

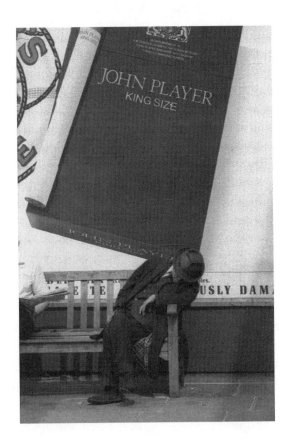

Economic science has been affected by what one calls "modernist values." Just like a Mondrian painting, we think in terms of squares—square thinking, you could call it. We want to be very precise and mechanistic in thinking about the world. This has led

to the demoralization of the economic imagination. We have left values and morals out of our discipline.
—Arjo Klamer

Time is a child playing dice; the kingly power is a child's.
—Heraclitus, *fragment 52*

"The forecast," said Mr. Oliver, turning the pages till he found it, "says: Variable winds; fair average temperature; rain at times." ... There was a fecklessness, a lack of symmetry and order in the clouds, as they thinned and thickened. Was it their own law, or no law, they obeyed?
—Virginia Woolf, *Between the Acts*

Money is power.
—Traditional

SQUARE VERSUS OBLONG

What does it mean to be square?

To the Pythagoreans, numbers were symbolized by arrangements of dots or pebbles. The square numbers were therefore those—like four, nine, and sixteen—that corresponded to squares. These were also associated with the "masculine" odd numbers, because they can be expressed as the sum of consecutive odd numbers. For example, the first few squares can be written:

$$1 + 3 = 4 = 2^2$$
$$1 + 3 + 5 = 9 = 3^2$$
$$1 + 3 + 5 + 7 = 16 = 4^2$$
$$1 + 3 + 5 + 7 + 9 = 25 = 5^2$$

The proof of the above is based on the idea that a square can be extended by adding an L-shaped line of pebbles to the original, as in Figure 9.1 (the Greeks used the term "gnomon," or carpenter's square). The number of pebbles required at each step is the next odd number.

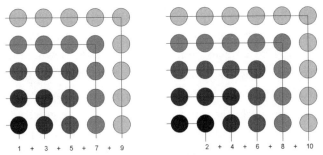

1 + 3 + 5 + 7 + 9   2 + 4 + 6 + 8 + 10

Figure 9.1. The sequence of square numbers can be formed by adding L-shaped lines (gnomons) of pebbles at each step. Starting from the bottom left corner, the square 4 is formed by adding 3 pebbles to 1; 9 is formed by adding 5 pebbles to 4; and so on. Oblong numbers are formed by rectangles in which the ratio of the sides is not 1. The first oblong number is 2 (right panel). As additional gnomons are added, the ratio of the two sides changes at each step—1:2, 2:3, and so on.

As Aristotle pointed out in *Categories*, squares differ from oblongs because, as they grow in this way from the inside out, the ratio of their two sides remains fixed at unity.[1] For example, the oblong number two can be represented by one row of two, with a ratio of 1:2. When a gnomon is added, the ratio changes at each step, as seen in the right panel. Squares are therefore fixed and limited, while oblongs are unstable and plural.

Because the length of each side is identical, a square can be specified by that single dimension, just as a circle can be specified by a diameter. Squares therefore embody a sense of equality, elegance, and mirror-like symmetry. This may explain their ongoing appeal, both to artists and scientists. We are all drawn to symmetry. Studies have shown that we judge a person's beauty in part by the degree of symmetry in their features (though sex hormones such as testosterone appear to be something of a symmetry-breaker in the human body, so men on average tend to have slightly larger right testicles, and women slightly larger left breasts). Scientists, too, have long sought out the symmetries of nature. The astronomer Johannes Kepler, on discovering that the path of planets was not perfectly circular, spent months trying to find a way to "square" the ovals. Isaac Newton finished the task by showing it was not the shape of the orbit that mattered, but rather the form of the underlying principle; and nothing is more perfectly symmetrical than the law of gravity, which says the gravitational force decreases with the square of distance. Modern "theories of everything," such as string theory, are similarly based on a quest for underlying symmetries in the patterns of nature. When the physicist Wolfgang Pauli heard of symmetry being violated in certain subatomic particles—they weren't that square—he exclaimed, "I cannot believe God is a weak left-hander."[2]

Perhaps because of associations with carpentry we say that something is square if it is balanced and well aligned. The Leaning Tower of Pisa, for example, is not quite square. Dice that are fair are known as square or straight; if they have been tampered with in some way, say, by shaving a side or bevelling an edge, they are called crooked. A square deal is one that is fair and honest, and Aristotle used the term "four-square" to describe a "good man."[3] You can eat a square meal, or square a story with the facts, or look someone squarely in the eye.

In the 1920s, the invention of jazz music gave the word a new meaning. When a traditional piece of music was to be performed in standard 4/4 time, the conductor would indicate this by framing a square symbol with his fingers. Perhaps because jazz musicians found 4/4 straight and boring they began to call that kind of music "square." This sense of the word didn't enter the popular vernacular until the 1960s, when it came to mean anyone who was conventional, orthodox, or generally unhip— as when NASA administrator Thomas O. Paine called the *Apollo 8* mission "the triumph of the squares."[4]

As the economist Arjo Klamer noted, economists, too, "think in terms of squares ... We want to be very precise and mechanistic in thinking about the world." The squareness of modern economics can be traced back to the original T square wielded by its founders, such as William Stanley Jevons. When Jevons read Adam Smith's *The Wealth of Nations*, he was struck by Smith's constant references to quantities and measures and equalities and proportions. Even though Smith didn't employ equations, Jevons argued it would be a small step to translate Smith's thoughts into the more precise language of mathematics: "Now every use of the word *equal* or *equality* implies the existence of a mathematical equation; an equation is simply an equality; and every use of the word proportion implies a ratio expressible in the form of an equation."[5]

The utilitarian philosophy of Jeremy Bentham was similarly based on quantitative concepts. To estimate the net effect of some action, he instructed the reader to "Sum up all the values of all the pleasures on the one side, and those of all the pains on the other. The balance, if it be on the side of pleasure, will give the good tendency of the act upon the whole, with respect to the interests of that individual person; if on the side of pain, the bad tendency of it upon the whole."[6] The aim of neoclassical economics was to show how to achieve the equilibrium set of prices which would exactly balance the pain of producers in producing goods, and the pleasure of consumers using them— that would make things all square.

In order that the economy achieve this aim, Jevons wrote, "It is also essential that the ratio of exchange between any two persons should be known to all the others ... Every individual must be considered as exchanging from a pure regard to his own requirements or private interests, and there must be perfectly free competition, so that any one will exchange with any one else for the slightest apparent advantage." Everyone had to be on the straight and level; all trades had to be open and honest and fair. There were to be no secrets or shady dealings or withholding of information. This was an economy without shadows. Because no individual participant had an advantage over any other, Jevons argued the behavior of the market as a whole could be reduced to "the single average individual, the unit of which population is made up."[7]

Apart from minor allowances for market distortions, such as "asymmetric information," where, for example, sellers know more than buyers because they own the object being sold, the emphasis on fairness and balance persists in economic theory.[8] Eugene Fama, for example, defined his efficient market as a place where "important current information is almost freely available to all participants." That includes both individual investors and firms themselves. But is that a good model of reality? Is the market really square?

THE MARKET SQUARE

In the 1870s, the assumption that all economic agents are more or less identical and have equal access to information was useful in order to mathematicize the economy, in accordance with the Pythagorean notion that "number is all." It would be impossible to model each person or firm individually, let alone their myriad interactions, so the only alternative was to restrict the model to the "average person" and hope that differences between individuals would be small and cancel each other out. The utility of an ounce of gold might vary somewhat from person to person, but what counted was the utility to *l'homme moyen*.

The economists felt justified in making this assumption because of its success in the area of mathematical physics. To model a gas, consisting of an ensemble of molecules, it wasn't necessary to model each molecule in detail, but only to average over all molecules using a statistical approach. Scientists had also developed tools such as the bell curve, or normal distribution, to model small deviations from average behavior.

As shown by Figure 9.2, the bell curve has the same attractive properties (in a mathematical sense) as the square. It is symmetrical about the mean, and like the square, it is specified by only one dimension, usually expressed as the standard deviation (or variance, which is standard deviation squared). If a bell curve is used to describe fluctuations in the price of an asset, for example, then the risk in holding the asset can be expressed by just the standard deviation, and 95 percent of the fluctuations should be smaller than twice that number. The bell curve is therefore a way of reducing the plurality of past fluctuations to one single quantity.

Furthermore, if many different fluctuations are added together—says we are interested in the variation in a basket of assets—then the total also follows a normal distribution. Just as a square remains a square when gnomons are added, so the normal distribution grows without losing its shape.

While the normal distribution may be square, though, it doesn't quite square with the data—as was discovered by the Italian economist Vilfredo Pareto. In 1870, Pareto obtained his engineering degree with a thesis on *The Fundamental Principles of Equilibrium in Solid Bodies*. He went on to apply the same

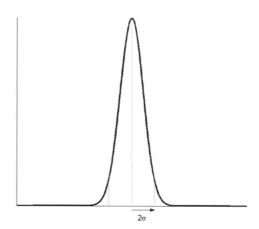

Figure 9.2. The bell curve, or normal distribution, is symmetric around the mean, and its width is specified by the standard deviation ó. Approximately 95 percent of events fall within two standard deviations of the mean.

mechanical techniques to the economy, and introduced the concept of Pareto optimality. However, he is perhaps best known for his purely empirical observation that income tends to scale according to a power-law distribution.[9] Rather than being symmetrically distributed around a mean, income was sharply tilted. For example, in the Italy of his time, he estimated that 80 percent of the wealth was concentrated in the hands of only 20 percent of the population. (See the Appendix for further discussion of normal and power-law distributions.)

This law, he wrote, "can be compared in some respects to Kepler's law in astronomy; we still lack a theory that may make this law of distribution rational in the way in which the theory of universal gravitation has made Kepler's law rational." Similar power-law distributions in a variety of contexts were discovered by the twentieth-century American George Zipf, such as the frequency of words in texts. Perhaps because they defied rational explanation, or because they were inconsistent with the normal distribution, power laws were not viewed seriously by social scientists for many years (which, as Mandelbrot wrote, may help account "for the striking backwardness of their fields"[10]).

This began to change only in the 1960s, when new areas of mathematics such as nonlinear dynamics, fractals, network theory, and complexity revealed the ubiquity of scale-free behavior and power laws. The world, it seems, isn't quite square—and neither is the market.

WINNER TAKE ALL

As an illustration of the decidedly funky way the economy works, Figure 9.3 compares three different distributions. Panel (a) shows the wealth of the top 100 Americans, from the 2005 *Forbes* list.[11] The wealthiest person on the list was Bill Gates, from Microsoft, at $51 billion, followed by the investor Warren Buffet at $40 billion, and Paul Allen (ex-Microsoft) at $22.5 billion. Note the skewedness of the numbers. Allen may be rich compared to, say, a small third world country, but next to his former colleague Bill Gates you can see that he is struggling.

The second panel shows sales over the first six months from books released in the United States in 2001 or 2002 (sales usually decline rapidly after six months).[12] The top seller was *Skipping Christmas*, by John Grisham. Again, book sales are highly skewed, so that best sellers account for most of the total sales. It is amazing to note that in 1994, only five authors—John Grisham, Tom Clancy, Danielle Steel, Michael Crichton, and Stephen King—accounted for 70 percent of fiction sales in the United States. As far as the accountants of the big publishing firms were concerned, there wasn't really much need for the other approximately 100,000 authors to have shown up (though of course it is still possible to make money by catering to niche markets, especially for online booksellers such as Amazon that can stock many obscure titles[13]).

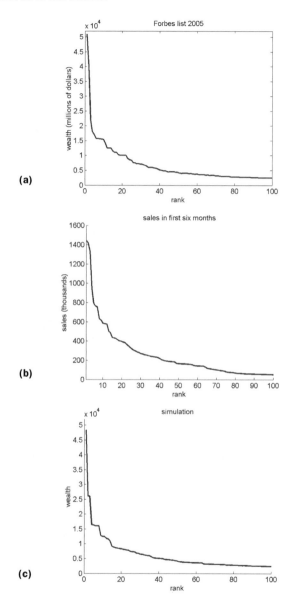

Figure 9.3. Panel (a) shows total wealth, in ranked order, of the richest 100 Americans. Panel (b) shows sales of the top 100 books in the United States for 2001/2002. Panel (c) shows a computer simulation of a hypothetical market, which is described in the text. A similar rank plot for a normal distribution would be symmetrical around the median, instead of highly skewed towards a few winners.

Whether it comes to amassing wealth or selling books, the field is dominated by a few people at the top. This is a signature of systems that follow a power-law distribution, rather than the bell curve. It also seems reasonable when you realize the economy is a complex network with positive feedbacks that tend to enhance differences.

To illustrate how easily such distributions can be made to occur, panel (c) of Figure 9.3 shows the results of a simple computer simulation, in which a large number of "investors" start with $1,000. They each invest their money in a hypothetical market, with a random rate of return ranging from a maximum gain in any one year of 50 percent, to a maximum loss of the same amount, with an average return of zero. The figure shows the total wealth of the top-ranked investors after twenty years. It has a very similar character to the real-life distributions, with a few investors enjoying most of the success, though here it is purely a result of luck.[14]

In this simulation, all investors started off with exactly the same initial funds, and the rules were entirely fair, with everyone having the same chances to make or lose money. The market appears square, but the end result is highly skewed. The reason is that, although each investor starts with the same odds, this changes as the game progresses. Returns are proportional to the amount invested, so an investor who makes a lot in the early stages has a chance of adding to it substantially. She may instead lose, but someone who did less well at the beginning doesn't even have the opportunity. This acts as a positive feedback, which tends to accentuate differences. Instead of clustering symmetrically around the median value, which would be the case for a normal distribution, earnings diverge. It's winner take all.

In the real world, feedback loops are far more complex, and the rules aren't quite so fair. Investors are part of a connected network, and some have more connections than others. It is probably safe to say that Warren Buffet knows more about what is going on in the market than even the best-informed day trader, let alone a disinterested pensioner. There is also a lock-in effect, which allows the protection of early gains. Being first into a market may bring substantial advantages. Many people know who the first man on the moon was—but who was the last?[15] And again there is an element of chance. Bill Gates and Paul Allen may be terrific software designers and business visionaries, but they were also in the right place at the right time when IBM was looking for an operating system for personal computers.

In the case of book sales, these depend in part on the quality of the book, but also on many other factors, such as marketing and publicity. An author who scores with success on one book will be allocated a higher marketing budget for his next book, is more likely to be reviewed in newspapers, and so on. If a film is based on the book, sales will soar even higher. Authors at the bottom of the list, meanwhile, struggle to get their works distributed, even if they are of higher quality than the ones at the top. I enjoy the works of authors such as John Grisham and Michael Crichton as much as the next person, or million people, but it would be a very boring library that consisted only of their books.

One exception to the rule that sales tend to decay after six months was *Beyond Good and Evil* by Friedrich Nietzsche. Following poor sales for his other works, he decided to self-publish, with the aim of selling 300 copies to break even. By June 1887, after more than six months, he had shifted only 141. However, since 1900, after his death, the book has never been out of print. A library sometimes needs the worst sellers as well as the best sellers, to have long-term utility.

Perhaps the most extreme examples of the nonsquare, winner-take-all society are entertainment businesses such as acting or sports. Movie stars or athletes at the top of their professions all earn amazing salaries, while those who don't quite qualify may be lucky to serve them at a restaurant. The neoclassical dogma of diminishing returns is completely wrong—success begets success and wealth begets wealth.

ONE LAW FOR THE RICH

The skewed distribution of wealth applies not just within particular industries or countries, but also holds on a global level. Figure 9.4 shows how net worth—defined as the value of physical and financial assets less debts—was distributed around the world's adult population in the year 2000, according to a recent U.N. survey. The median net worth, with currencies adjusted for purchasing parity with the U.S. dollar, was about $8,400 (shown as a circle symbol). To qualify for the top 1 percent of the global population, you needed a little more than half a million dollars. Most neoclassical economists with a senior faculty position at a major U.S. university—the gatekeepers of orthodox theory—would be in that category, which may explain some of their enthusiasm for the current system. The richest 2 percent of the population, who are concentrated in North America or Europe, owned more than half of the world's financial assets, while the poorest half of the population owned about 1 percent of the wealth.[16] (Somewhat ironically, the richest countries also have the largest number of people who are heavily in debt, so have negative net worth.)

Note that the figure does not include the world's richest billionaires—to accommodate them, the vertical scale would have to increase by a factor of 100,000. It may therefore seem that the billionaires live in a completely different world. However, a better way to view distributions over such a large range is to use a

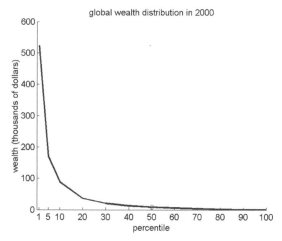

Figure 9.4. Distribution of the world's financial assets in the year 2000. Bottom axis is percentile. The median wealth (i.e. half the people have more, half have less) is indicated by the circle symbol at the fiftieth percentile. The top one percentile owns $523,264 or more.

logarithmic scale, as in Figure 9.5, which includes both the *Forbes* list of billionaires, and the U.N. list of nonbillionaires. The logarithmic axes are expressed in powers of ten, so $10^0 = 1$, $10^1 = 10$, $10^2 = 100$, and so on. The dashed line shows a fractal power law with exponent -0.67. A feature of power-law distributions is that they appear as a straight line in the logarithmic scale. The power law is a good fit for anyone with wealth over $100,000, at which point there is a transition that is not obvious in Figure 9.4 to a somewhat less skewed distribution for those with under the median wealth.[17] There really is one law for the rich and powerful—a power law—and one for the rest. The multimillionaires who are too poor to qualify for the *Forbes* list, but too few in number to register in the U.N. survey are missing from the data; however, results for individual countries such as the United States or the United Kingdom appear consistent with the power law.[18] From this figure, the extreme inequality of wealth begins to seem less an anomaly and more a built-in emergent feature of the overall economy—or at least the current rich country economy. Billionaires such as Warren Buffet and Bill Gates may appear to have little in common apart from being rich, but their level of wealth can be anticipated, more or less, just by extrapolating the trend to the top-ranked few.

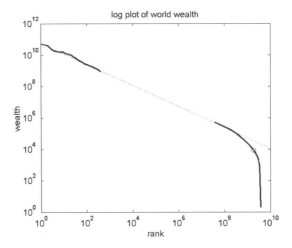

Figure 9.5. Plot of wealth (in dollars) versus rank in the world economy, with logarithmic scale. The top left data is the *Forbes* list of the 400 richest people, the lower right data is from the U.N. survey representing the other estimated 3.7 billion adults. The median wealth is indicated by a circle symbol. The dashed line represents a power law with exponent −0.67, which appears as a straight line in the logarithmic scale.

The degree of inequality—i.e. the slope of the line—has increased substantially in recent decades. In the United States, the spoils of increased productivity have accrued to the top 10 percent of workers, while the median salary has lagged behind.[19] In the 1960s, the top 1 percent of Americans earned about 8 percent of all income. That has nearly doubled to 15 percent.[20] A typical chief executive in the United States now earns around 300 times the average wage—an increase by a factor of ten since the 1970s.[21] Professional investors make even greater sums. As the *Economist* magazine noted the same year, "every measure shows that, over the past quarter century, those at the top have done better than those in the middle, who in turn have outpaced those at the bottom. The gains of productivity growth have become increasingly skewed."[22]

The inequalities in many developing countries are equally glaring. São Paulo, in Brazil, has one of the world's largest private fleets of helicopters. These are used to ferry the ultrarich to work, so they can avoid traffic and carjackings. One popular model seats up to seven and costs $1.5 million, or about 350 times the average annual income.[23] In China, the high-tech economies of coastal cities such as Shanghai contrasts sharply with the rural economies of the interior, where most of the people live. During the period 2002–03, when the Chinese economy was booming at a rate of almost 10 percent annually, the real income of the poorest 10 percent actually fell.[24] Globalization has enhanced the general trend towards income disparity by giving those at the top the opportunity to exert their influence on an international scale. The power law is pulling the world apart.

As discussed in Chapter 2, income differences have a greater effect on happiness than income itself. One usually compares one's salary with that of people who are in the next highest range. The scale-free nature of wealth means, however, that the next highest range always has a lot more. If you buy a vacation home by the lake as a status symbol, then you'll soon meet someone who has one twice as large—which kind of destroys the purpose. The consequences for the poor are far worse than a hurt ego. Even in rich countries, such as America, not everyone has benefited greatly from economic expansion. John F.

Kennedy once said, "A rising tide raises all boats." Unfortunately, as Hurricane Katrina showed in 2005, not everyone has a boat.

The highly unsquare distribution of wealth among individuals is matched by the variation in the size of firms. Because neoclassical economics views the economy as a level playing field, it treats individual people and large businesses in much the same way. It is assumed that for any particular product there are a large number of firms who are competing to make exactly the same thing, with the only variable being price.[25] The fair and square competition between them means the price is driven towards its equilibrium value, which should reflect the cost of production. In a power-law world, however, it doesn't make sense to talk about average producers any more than it does to talk about an average length for the coastline of Britain, or the average size of a moon crater, or the average financial crash. The economy consists of a few dominant players, who wield tremendous power, and a large number of much weaker contenders.[26] Large companies can control markets, hook networks of consumers into their products, and buy out or eliminate the competition. That's how they stay big.

It is ironic that neoclassical economics was formulated at a time when some of today's largest firms were just getting into their stride in the biggest market of all, the United States. Perhaps unaware of the theory of diminishing returns, they instead exploited economies of scale to expand their reach. The more they produced, the more they could invest in machinery and marketing, and the faster they could grow. The final decades of the nineteenth century saw the arrival on the national or international stage of companies such as American Telephone and Telegraph, Campbell Soup, Eastman Kodak, Heinz, Procter & Gamble, Quaker Oats, Singer, and Westinghouse. Growth was further supported by the rapid spread across the continent of telegraph communications, railways, the electrical grid, and, of course, people. America itself exploited economies of scale and pulled ahead of the European competition.

Today, the largest corporations dominate not just other businesses, but entire countries. Sometimes their scale benefits the rest of society, for example through enormous research and development budgets. But, while they may have the legal status of individuals, their size and power gives them access to lawmakers that no real person would enjoy. They routinely force governments to change tax laws, or demand incentive packages for new factories. If the corporations don't get what they want, they just move their operations on to another country that is more pliable. The economy has never before been so oblong.

SQUARING THE STORY

The idea that money begets money, and that the rich and powerful enjoy unfair advantages, goes against what we are taught— or like to believe—about the capitalist system. The development of capitalism in nineteenth-century Europe overthrew the traditional class-based hierarchy, and opened up the possibility of success to a much greater range of people. The American dream has always been about fighting your way to the top from a humble background. Marx, however, argued it would all end in tears, with conflict between the laborers at the bottom and the fat-cat capitalists, who owned the means of production, at the top. So was Marx right?

One reason the lumpen proletariat have yet to overthrow the system is that, in developed countries, there are many laws that attempt to correct disparities in wealth and power. Progressive taxation takes from the rich and gives to the poor. Antitrust legislation prevents companies from fixing prices or overly abusing their power. These are innovations of government, not the market, so according to neoclassical theory, they are inefficient. Different attitudes towards government regulations and taxes may explain why some countries are noticeably more skewed than others. For example, the richest 10 percent of the U.S. population controls 70 percent of that country's wealth. However, the corresponding group in Germany holds only 44 percent of wealth, and in Japan the number is 39 percent. The power law is a tendency, but it isn't destiny.

Another reason is that people believe in social mobility. In a dynamic capitalistic society, everyone gets a shot at the prize, in principle at least. Americans are especially optimistic in this regard, with 80 percent still believing the American dream is within anyone's grasp. That sense of optimism undoubtedly helps to power the American economy. However, sociological studies have shown that social mobility in the United States is actually lower than in Canada or much of Europe.[27] The importance of social networks means it is a definite advantage to be born into a well-connected family and go to a good school; and a look at the *Forbes* list shows that quite a few made the bulk of their money directly from family businesses or inheritances (Bill Gates and Warren Buffet bucked that trend by devoting the bulk of their wealth to unprofitable, nonmarket activities, such as curing malaria in African countries). Even if the faces at the top get rotated from time to time, that's not much use if your chances of getting there yourself are effectively zero.

Some economists and scientists have argued that social inequalities are a natural result of differences between individuals, and represent an efficient outcome. This idea dates back to the Social Darwinists of the nineteenth century, who compared economic survival to the law of the jungle: the strong survive, and the weak are eliminated, all for the good of the system. As Herbert

Spencer wrote in his 1851 *Social Statics*, "It seems hard that widows and orphans should be left to struggle for life or death. Nevertheless, when regarded not separately, but in connection with the interests of a universal humanity, these harsh fatalities are seen to be full of the highest beneficence—the same beneficence which brings to early graves the children of diseased parents." Charity would only prevent society from "excreting its unhealthy, imbecile, slow, vacillating, faithless members." It followed that any attempt by individuals or the government to interfere in the process would lead to a weakening of the human stock.

More recently, as discussed in Chapter 5, the selfish gene theory from biology has been evoked to rationalize economic inequalities. The argument goes that genes have been involved in a battle for survival through billions of years of evolution, so only the best survive and pass on their good qualities to the host organism. Similarly, individuals in the economy are involved in a competitive struggle in which the weak are eliminated and the strong succeed. As the codiscoverer of DNA James Watson (always good for a provocative quote) put it: "Maybe one of the reasons for this growing inequality of income may in some sense be a reflection of some people being more strong and healthy than others. Some people, no matter how much schooling you give them, will never really be up to what is now considered a necessary degree of effective intelligence."[28] Presumably, the reason that five of the ten richest Americans in 2005 are all members of the Walton family of Wal-Mart has something to do with their DNA.

Such arguments resemble the Victorian rationalization of colonization based on then-trendy ideas about races; or the Victorian belief that women are less intelligent because their average head size is smaller. It is true that people have different abilities, but to assume the reason some people are billionaires and others live on a dollar a day comes down to genetics is ridiculous. The emphasis on selfishness and competition is also excessive. Nature provides as many examples of cooperation as competitive, winner-take-all behavior. Ants or honeybees aren't exactly hardened individualists, and ecosystems rely on myriad cooperative interactions between species. Competition may help drive the evolution of the system, but cooperation is the glue that holds it together.

Social inequalities say more about the dynamics of money and our economic system than human qualities or biology. The huge discrepancies in wealth are vivid proof that our current economy is not a very efficient way of allocating resources, especially when those resources are human beings. Genetics doesn't explain how the Waltons got rich, any more than it explains why "they can't find the money to secure health coverage for their own workers and their families" (as John Kerry complained in 2006).[29]

Of course, inequalities are easier to tolerate when the economy is growing, and inflation and unemployment are low, since this creates a general feeling of optimism, and a sense that the future may be better than today. If each person's lot seems to be improving, it distracts them from comparisons with their neighbors—which is one reason politicians don't like the idea of a nongrowing, steady state economy. But even in rich countries with healthy economies, people still need to feel they are being given a fair shake of the dice.

The human desire for justice has been demonstrated graphically by researchers at Princeton University. Neuroscientist Jonathan Cohen and his colleagues set up an experiment based on the so-called Ultimatum Game. Two subjects are offered ten dollars, but are told that one must decide how to split the money, and the other has to decide whether to accept the offer. If the offer is rejected, all the money is returned, so they both lose. Neoclassical theory would imply that any offer would be accepted, no matter how low—if you receive only five cents out of the ten dollars, it is still better than nothing. However, the game has been performed in many countries around the world, and the results consistently show that people reject an offer that is overly cheap, just to stop the other person making an unfair profit. Most offers are near to five dollars, and the typical minimum acceptable offer is around three dollars. In the Princeton experiment, the subjects were having their brains scanned at the time by an MRI machine. When someone was given a cheap offer, say, two dollars, the part of their brain responsible for reasoning lit up, but so did the bilateral anterior insula, which is associated with anger and disgust—emotions they were willing to pay to express.[30]

Around the world, the income disparity between those at the top and those at the bottom is continuing to grow at a time when poor people have increasing knowledge of rich lifestyles through television and the Internet. It's not hard to imagine that mounting anger will soon lead them to reject the offer they have been given, in a way that will cause real social problems even in the richest countries. Politicians and corporations therefore work very hard to foster the impression of fairness—and so do mainstream economists.

A LEVEL PLAYING FIELD

The entire thrust of neoclassical thought is to argue that the free market economy is an efficient system that will optimize utility for all mankind, if only government will get out of the way. It therefore departs from classical economists such as Adam Smith, who recognized the importance of governments for regulating markets and preventing monopolies. It emphasizes individual freedom over group values—on the political spectrum, it stands firmly on the right. Neoclassical economics pretends to be objective and apolitical, but it is actually profoundly political. Saying that politics should be kept out of the market is itself a political stance—and one that serves the rich. As Karl Marx said, "The ruling ideas of every age are always the ideas of the ruling class."

This ideology is evident in the drive towards free trade and globalization, and the belief that all countries are best served by the same set of economic principles. After the 2000 meeting of the World Bank was disrupted by thousands of protesters, its then-president James Wolfensohn gave a speech at a symposium in Aspen, where he defined globalization for his audience as well as "for the critics, for the people in the streets," as "a practical methodology for empowering the poor to improve their lives."[31] However, the data is in, and it does not always match the theory. As Thomas Homer-Dixon observes, "During the decades from 1970 to 2000—the very decades when globalization surged ahead and free markets penetrated every nook and cranny on the planet—economic crises became more common, the income gap between rich and poor stayed wide, and, perhaps most surprisingly, the growth of average income per person declined."[32]

We are all becoming increasingly connected, through travel, the Internet, and telecommunications, and this rewiring of the global brain has enormously powerful and beneficial effects; indeed it represents a continuation and fruition of that moment in 1968 when we first saw ourselves as one world from outer space. However, this type of connectivity is very different from the economic doctrine that aims to effectively erase national and regional boundaries, and reduce the multiplicity of local markets into one uniform market.

The problem is that markets do not give the nice, equal, "normal" distribution of consumers and producers that was originally envisaged, but instead siphon money towards the most powerful players. The larger the market, the larger the effect. This is hard to understand for economists who have been educated that the world is ruled by the bell curve—unfettered capitalism bears no relation to the models used to approximate it—but it comes easily to those who have been exposed to the new branches of mathematics developed since the 1960s. International corporations don't have unlimited power to fix prices, but they can shape markets and control their suppliers. They can also imprint their brands on the mind of anyone in the world who watches TV or drives by a billboard. Nowhere is the balance between producer and consumer more distorted than in the barrage of advertising aimed at preschool children, who hardly meet the neoclassical definition of rational, informed investors.

In practice, markets seem to work best when they are complemented and balanced by regulations and nonmarket initiatives. Most developed countries end up supporting centrist political parties and are against untrammeled capitalism, at least in their own country. Complex labor, environmental, and safety regulations, together with a social safety net, protect us against market excess. Company laws devised by government economists encourage competition while preventing the formation of monopolies. A degree of squareness at the individual level is sacrificed for squareness at the societal level, and the power law is controlled by other kinds of law. The Swedish prime minister Göran Persson said in 2006, "The market is a good slave, but a terrible master."[33] In other words, the market is great to have around, exciting and energetic, but occasionally it needs to be brought back to earth.

The science of economics was founded at a time when capitalism promised to cure social ills. Adam Smith's invisible hand was a force for democracy, aimed at removing the privileges of the powerful. But it has turned into the opposite. So is economics still on the side of the good? We consider this question in the final chapter.

SALARY CAPS

Since social inequality is a main economic determinant of happiness, it seems that, if the aim of economics were really to improve happiness, this would be a good place to start. It is hard to see how it promotes world happiness, or a just economy, if much of the human race is struggling to survive while a billionaire, such as casino magnate Sheldon Adelson (Forbes.com's top earner for 2005), can pull in a million dollars an hour; or a third of city dwellers live in slums while the ultrarich pay $30,000 a night for a megasuite at the Four Seasons New York.[34] If life is a casino, then the odds aren't square but crooked.

One possible solution, as the ecological economist Herman Daly has argued, would be to impose bounds on wealth, both upper and lower, with the two differing, say, by a factor of ten.[35] The idea dates back at least to the Jubilee year of the Old Testament, in which wealth was redistributed. Three centuries ago, Jonathan Swift wrote, "In all well-instituted commonwealths, care has been taken to limit men's possessions ... when bounds are set to men's desires after they have acquired as much as the laws will permit them, their private interest is at an end, and they have nothing to do but to take care of the public."[36]

Neoclassical economists would argue that such bounds would act as a disincentive for the most productive citizens. But this assumes two things: that the richest people are the most productive, and that they are motivated only by money. Both are debatable. Success depends on many things apart from raw talent, and people who are successful at their occupation often appear more driven by the joy of their work than by amassing personal wealth. Neoclassical economics started off as a kind of enlightened democratic movement that aimed to make as many people as happy as possible. However, it has turned into the opposite—a way of justifying the power of elites.

Bounds on salaries appear to work quite well in some occupations, such as professional sports. The National Football League in the United States adopted a salary cap in 1994. In 2006, the most any team could spend on all its players was $102 million. Modified cap systems are also used in the National Basketball Association (since 1984), and more recently the National Hockey League (since 2005). The caps were introduced to limit ticket prices, but also to foster competition and stop large-market teams from building dynasties. Companies and institutions outside the world of sports have also adopted internal salary caps. In the U.S. military, a general makes approximately ten times as much as a private. One of the most successful architecture firms in the world is headed by Richard Rogers, who draws no more than six times the salary of his lowest-paid architect. For comparison, the median net worth of a world citizen is about 6 million times smaller than that of the richest person.

We'll never get rid of injustice and inequality, economic or otherwise, but we can at least tone it down a bit (even billionaires must be worried about social unrest). The first step is to recognize that the system isn't square. Sports leagues know the importance of a level playing field (or court, or rink). Perhaps the adoption of similar caps in other industries would make the economy as a whole a little fairer—or at least more entertaining for the majority of participants.

HOW TO BE POWERFUL

The typical American chief executive today earns about 300 times the average wage, a factor of ten more than in the 1970s—even though a company's success is the emergent result of many contributions from all its employees, combined with the luck of the market, rather than just the person at the top.[37] According to neoclassical economics, it all comes down to supply and demand. People get paid what they are worth, and some happen to be worth a lot more than others. But does it make sense for CEOs to walk away with billions of dollars—even after they are fired for bad performance?[38]

In his 2005 letter to shareholders, Warren Buffet explained how the compensation process works: "Huge severance payments, lavish perks and outsized payments for ho-hum performance often occur because comp committees have become slaves to comparative data. The drill is simple: Three or so directors—not chosen by chance—are bombarded for a few hours before a board meeting with pay statistics that perpetually ratchet upwards. Additionally, the committee is told about new perks that other managers are receiving. In this manner, outlandish 'goodies' are showered upon CEOs simply because of a corporate version of the argument we all used when children: 'But, Mom, all the other kids have one.' When comp committees follow this 'logic,' yesterday's most egregious excess becomes today's baseline."[39]

As with everything to do with money, compensation is a social process that depends on a lot more than abstract economic theory. The pay awarded to CEOs depends greatly on the particular country, with America leading the pack. Executive compensation is about half as high in Europe, and lower still in Japan. Part of the reason may be because many Americans (including compensation committees) have bought into the idea that wealth is an accurate reflection of ability, so it's all square. Napoleon Bonaparte wrote, "Religion is what keeps the poor from murdering the rich." Today, the religion is called neoclassical economics. Maybe it's time for shareholders to exert more of their power, and bring executive compensation back to earth. Attitudes do appear to be changing: according to a 2007 poll, "Large majorities of people in the U.S. and in Europe want higher taxation for the rich and even pay caps for corporate executives to counter what they believe are unjustified rewards and the negative effects of globalisation," according to the *Financial Times*.[40]

Of course, lower salaries for executives won't make the rest of us feel richer or more powerful. In general, the most effective way to do that is to choose as our own psychological and financial baseline not those who have more than we do, but rather those who have less. After all, in a scale-free world where the poor outnumber the rich, you can bet that whatever it is you want, not all the kids have one.

10○ GOOD VERSUS EVIL
DOING GOOD

Utopia could be the answer to some of your problems: let me explain.

You utilitarians, you too love everything useful *only as a vehicle of your inclinations—you too really find the noise of its wheels intolerable?*
—Nietzsche, *Beyond Good and Evil*

Money is the root of all evil.
—Traditional

Money is the root of all good.
—Ayn Rand

Good and evil are one.
—Heraclitus, *fragment 57*

UTOPIA

Mankind has always been attracted by the idea of utopia—a perfect society that will cure all ills. The word was first used by Thomas More, the Roman Catholic saint, in his 1516 book *Utopia*. More described a mythical island where everyone worked for the common good, and poverty, misery, and immoral behavior were banished. The name was a pun on the Greek words *ou topia* (no place) and *eu topia* (good place), and so meant a good place that doesn't exist.

More's book was based in part on Plato's accounts of the mythical island Atlantis. Francis Bacon's 1627 *The New Atlantis* gave us a scientifically advanced utopia where the residents could control the growth of plants and animals to improve the food supply, much as today's genetic engineers strive to do. In the 1960s, there was, for a while, a belief that science and technology could solve the world's problems and create an Atlantis here on earth. As *TIME* magazine wrote in 1968, "the moon flight of *Apollo 8* shows how that Utopian tomorrow could come about."[1]

Perhaps the original utopia of western society was that of the Pythagoreans. They believed the soul could be purified by aligning oneself with a certain set of principles, represented by the first column of their table of opposites. The Pythagoreans attempted to establish a society based on their ideas, and for some decades were quite successful. Their commune grew in size and power, and soon exerted considerable influence over Croton and the surrounding area. As always with utopian visions, though, it turned out there was a downside. The townspeople turned against the secretive and elitist group. Members of the group were attacked and killed; Pythagoras managed to escape, and probably died in exile.

Neoclassical economics, too, was born out of a utopian vision. Like Newton and Pythagoras, William Stanley Jevons had more than a theoretical interest in money—he actually helped mint the stuff. In 1854, he broke off his studies in chemistry and botany at University College London to take up a position as assayer at the newly formed Australian mint. His father's business had recently collapsed, and perhaps he needed to help the family finances. His work there included weighing and measuring the coins.

Even then, his ambitions were much greater than to work at a bank. He wrote later that he wanted to be "... powerfully good, that is to be good, not towards one, or a dozen, or a hundred, but towards a nation or the world."[2] His aim was to find a scientific way for society to maximize its utility, defined by Bentham as a sum of pleasures and pains "which will give the general good tendency ... [or] the general evil tendency."[3] The way to do this, Jevons believed, was to show how money could be used to further a just and efficient society.

Philosophers such as Bentham and Adam Smith had brought the enlightenment values of truth, fairness, and rationality to the economy. But Jevons went a step further by using mathematical models. As he wrote, "if Economics is to be a real science at all, it must not deal merely with analogies; it must reason by real equations, like all the other sciences which have reached at all a systematic character." Good, he believed, could be calculated mathematically. But to write the equations, it was necessary to make some assumptions about human behavior.

As seen in earlier chapters, neoclassical economics embodies a mathematical model that was originally built on a number of axioms. The main ones are:

- Economics is about the allocation of scarce resources.
- Utility can be measured or ranked numerically.
- Consumers and producers in the economy can be modeled as a collection of self-interested individuals.

- Each individual has fixed preferences.
- Individuals act rationally to further their own utility.
- Competition drives prices towards a fixed equilibrium.
- The economy is linear in the sense that global behavior can be determined by summing or aggregating over individuals.
- Markets are fair, and individuals have equal access to information.

Based on these axioms, and some additional assumptions, economists claimed to show that:

- Free markets drive the economy to a Pareto-optimal equilibrium that cannot be modified without making someone worse off.

Of course, no one would maintain that the axioms are exactly true, and, as discussed further below, economists have experimented with relaxing some of them in recent decades; but the assumption has generally been that they are good enough to form a basis for demonstrating optimality, at least to a close approximation. The axioms have also shaped many of our ideas about money and the economy. As the *Economist* wrote in 2005, "The goal of a well-run company may be to make profits for its shareholders, but merely in doing that—provided it faces competition in its markets, behaves honestly, and obeys the law—the company, without even trying, is doing good works ... The standard of living people in the West enjoy today is due to little else but the selfish pursuit of profit."[4] Given a square market, neoclassical economics is a recipe for producing the nearest thing to utopia.

It is no accident that the character of these axioms—square, linear, fixed—bears a striking relation to the Pythagorean list of opposites that so shaped the foundations of Western science.

The neoclassical economists were basing their new science on the "rational mechanics" of Newton, and the successes of mathematical physics. In the 1960s, the *Apollo* program—named after the god they claimed was the father of Pythagoras—was in many ways the ultimate realization of the Pythagorean project to understand and control the universe through number. But the peak of a trend often coincides with a turning point, a change in direction, an acknowledgment of previously repressed forces. When the *Apollo* astronauts flew to the moon, they looked out the window and saw something even more amazing—the living earth.

Back at home, scientists were already turning their attention inwards, from grand programs to explore space to the dynamics of complex physical and biological systems. Almost simultaneously, several new branches of mathematics appeared—complexity, chaos, fractals, network theory, fuzzy logic. One thing they had in common—apart from a tendency to exploit the new power of desktop computers—was they were all related to the "evil" side of the Pythagorean list. The systems studied were plural, crooked, and in motion. They showed emergent properties that did not yield to a reductionist approach. Scientists had to rely on graphs and figures, rather than mathematical proofs, to explore their properties.

Perhaps unsurprisingly, these evildoers were met with uniform hostility by the scientific old guard. Their work was criticized as being full of pretty pictures, but low on hard results. Some of this criticism was warranted, as theories such as the "butterfly effect" or the "small world phenomenon" were overhyped; but after forty years, none of these areas of study has gone away, and they are addressing problems that couldn't even be expressed in traditional mathematics. It is an empirical fact, for example, that complex systems show emergent properties that defy a bottom-up, reductionist approach; or that nonlinear systems do not necessarily tend towards equilibrium; or that changes can be sudden and unpredictable rather than smooth and gradual.

Other areas of science, such as ecology and systems biology, have actively embraced techniques from nonlinear dynamics, network theory, and complexity, but economics lags behind. Neoclassical economists are still trying to prove the validity of their arguments with "real equations," but they are using the equations of the nineteenth century. Apart from the trading algorithms used by some hedge funds or banks, new mathematical methods have had amazingly little impact. As economist Steve Keen wrote in 2001, most economists are trained only in simple linear equations, and are isolated "from much of what is new and interesting in mathematical theory and practice, let alone from what scientists in other sciences are doing."[5] This is especially strange given that the economy is so obviously nonlinear, networked, and complex (Pareto spotted power-law distributions before biologists did); and, furthermore, directly impacts the lives of billions of people (so you would expect the field to adopt best practices).

The problem doesn't just exist in the university, but permeates society. Most business leaders or politicians are advised by university-trained economists, or pick up on economic ideas espoused by the orthodox experts. As Keynes wrote, "Practical men who believe themselves to be quite exempt from any intellectual influences, are usually the slaves of some defunct economist."[6] The equations do more than model the economy, they help to shape it.

But slowly a new type, or types, of economics is emerging. They view the economy as a dynamic, evolving, organic system that never achieves equilibrium, but rather is in a constant state of flux. Feminists, environmentalists, and ecologists are moving away from a male-biased, or even human-biased, perspective to a global view that puts the economy into context as just one part of the living planet. In the late 1960s there was a pulse of energy—Herman Daly and Eugene Odum's work in ecological economics, Lotfi Zadeh's fuzzy logic, John Conway's experiments with his Game of Life, Benoit Mandelbrot's fractal mathematics, James Lovelock's Gaia theory, to name a few of its manifestations—that formed part of an entire social and scientific revolution. As with silver-based photography, the latent picture takes a while to develop; but despite much resistance, the ideas and images are finally working their way down to the street, and changing the way we think about the coins in our pocket.

AXIOMS OF EVIL

Like the Pythagoreans, neoclassical economists attempt to reduce the world to number—to find good in an equation. The axioms of neoclassical economics actually have less to do with the nature of the economy than with the demands of a particular type of numerical model. This can be seen by comparing them with the insights (or basic assumptions) of the new sciences and movements.

"Economics is about the allocation of scarce resources." This is based on the idea that the human economy is a static, closed system that converts a fixed amount of wealth from one form to another.[7] Our obsession with conquering scarcity means that we invent it even where it doesn't exist. In the United States, the richest society ever to inhabit the planet, a survey from the American Psychological Association showed that money is still the "number one cause of stress."[8] As Henry David Thoreau asked in *Walden*: "Why should we live with such hurry and waste of life? We are determined to be starved before we are hungry." A better definition, consistent with ecological economics, would be to say economics is about a number of goals, including: allocating and distributing resources, whether they are scarce or not; helping to produce a fair and prosperous society; and maintaining a suitable overall scale for the economy.

"Utility can be measured or ranked numerically." This axiom allows economists to assign a number to every pleasure or pain. In practice, though, happiness is a fuzzy concept that is not easily broken down into a sum of pleasures and pains. Economists therefore work the other way—they assume the price paid for a product reflects its utility. In this circular logic, money is a kind of proxy for utility—you can trade it for happiness. It therefore begins to take on a value of its own. Our obsession with money is like the Pythagorean obsession with number. But not everything can be reduced to dollars and cents.

"Consumers and producers in the economy can be modeled as a collection of self-interested individuals." Economist Francis Edgeworth wrote in 1881, "The first principle of economics is that every agent is actuated only by self-interest."[9] People do, of course, behave selfishly at times. They also feel love and duty and all kinds of other emotions and responsibilities that often overcome self-interest. They are part of a connected social network. As J. A. Hobson wrote, "No graver injury has been inflicted on the mind of man, in the name of science, than the prepotence which [economics] assigned to the competitive and combative aspects of industrial life."[10]

"Each individual has fixed preferences." The assumption that *Homo economicus* is constant and steady rather than changeable is useful for reductionist mathematical models and theories because it is very hard to track shifts in fashion or taste, at the level of either groups or individuals. Yet the reality is that our tastes are always changing and evolving. The economy is not static, but rather is a fluid, complex, ever-shifting system. If preferences were really fixed, then advertising would be redundant, and we could watch television shows without being bombarded by commercials telling us what to prefer.

"Individuals act rationally to further their own utility." This axiom is hard to prove—what's rational?—so can only be assumed. Neoclassical economists thus equate financial benefits not just with utility, but also with the force of reason. The economy as a whole is imbued with a kind of bracing Victorian rationality and efficiency. While economists have traditionally taken that position, no one else seems to agree. In literature, money is often portrayed as provoking all kinds of irrational behavior, from passion to murder. It's emotional stuff: that's one of the reasons we like it.

"Competition drives the economy towards an equilibrium set of prices." This assumes the economy is essentially static, and the forces of competition act to maintain prices at their optimal point. Changes in prices are due only to external perturbations, just as a bridge is perturbed by traffic or a strong wind. However, nonlinear dynamics shows that static equilibrium is a special property of certain systems dominated by negative feedback. The real economy, in contrast, is full of positive feedbacks—such as fads that ripple through the investor network—that drive the system away from equilibrium. A perusal of price changes in commodities such as gold show that stability is a sign of price-fixing, not free markets.

"The economy is linear in the sense that global behavior can be determined by summing or aggregating over individuals." Neoclassical economists model the economy as an aggregate of individual producers and consumers, so the whole is equal to the sum of its parts. But the fractal, dynamic nature of social networks means that what often counts is less the individual components than the relationships between them over all different scales. There really is such a thing as society. The set of prices determined by a free market economy is therefore best viewed as an emergent property of the system as a whole, which cannot be determined by a reductionist analysis. The link between micro and macro is a nonlinear, fuzzy one.

"Markets are fair, and individuals have equal access to information." This assumption removes the requirement of modeling each individual in detail—we need only concern ourselves with what Jevons called the "average person." Everybody has the same pull in the market. But the reality is that the market is not square or balanced, so different people or firms have different amounts of power, and there is no meaningful average, just as there is no average length for a fractal coastline. As shown by the skewed distribution of global wealth in Figure 9.4, the dynamics of capitalism tend to accentuate differences, rather than repress them.

The main conclusion that follows from these axioms also appears unlikely from the perspective of the new sciences:

"Free markets drive the economy to a Pareto-optimal equilibrium that cannot be modified without making someone worse off." As a method of setting prices for many goods fostering innovation, and encouraging economic growth, markets are certainly a marvelous and indispensable tool. Economic theory about the benefits of markets is also responsible for much of the freedom of individual choice that we enjoy today. But the neoclassical idea that selfish behavior will automatically lead to a good society represents an astonishing inversion of both common sense and basic moral teachings. Neoclassical economists took Adam Smith's theory of the invisible hand to extremes and divorced it from its original context. Their philosophy suited the Victorian era of colonial expansion, but things have changed—and in a nonlinear world, continuing in a straight line often gets you into trouble.

A corollary to Pareto optimality is that any form of government regulation or nonmarket activity detracts from the optimal market solution. In a world of extreme inequalities, this theory seems like a utopian dream, or an excuse to maintain the status quo. The reality is that wealth gets siphoned up from the poor to the rich in a way that is neither just nor efficient. Most people in third world countries would argue with the idea that resources (including themselves) are optimally allocated; and the skewed distribution of world wealth is hardly consistent with the utilitarian notion of "the greatest happiness for the greatest number."

After Vilfredo Pareto obtained his PhD in 1870 for his work on *Equilibrium in Solid Bodies*, it was not a huge leap to switch to the new, equally mechanistic science of economics. The main axioms of neoclassical economics are exactly the ones required to model the economy as a kind of solid body obeying rational mechanics— but none of them stands up to rational analysis. Nor do the conclusions based on those axioms accurately resemble the real world.

Neoclassical economics doesn't have a leg—or an axiom—to stand on. If it were a bridge, it would fall down. So what good is it? And why is it still around?

COUNTERFEIT SCIENCE

The main arguments usually heard in favor of the neoclassical approach are the following:

- The model is based on rigorous mathematics.
- Many of the assumptions can be relaxed and the theory still works.
- It is useful to have a standard model that can be easily shared.
- The model can be used to make predictions about the economy.

These are the standard defenses of mathematical models in any science. But in the case of economics, they seem a little counterfeit—they are not the real thing.

"The model is based on rigorous mathematics." While it is true that neoclassical economics is based on mathematics, it is only rigorous if you accept the axioms. Gérard Debreu described "the acid test" for theories "of removing all their economic interpretations and letting their mathematical infrastructure stand on its own." But if you question the axioms, the whole structure collapses.[11]

"The assumptions can be relaxed and the theory still works." Many economic papers have explored the effect of relaxing or modifying one or more assumptions in a controlled way, while still retaining the overall framework. For example, economists can test the effect of asymmetric information or bounded rationality or endogenous preferences that allow some degree of flexibility. These lead to modifications to the model, and provide a defense against criticism ("we already took that into account"). But the problem does not lie in one or two areas that can be treated independently. Attempting to adjust the model in this way is similar to the efforts of ancient astronomers to fix their earth-centered, circle-based model of the cosmos with the addition of epicycles. A more radical change is required.

"It is useful to have a standard model that can be easily shared." The existence of a standard, basic model is certainly useful from a procedural point of view. It aids communication between economists from different countries or backgrounds, just as a musical score allows different musicians to play the same tune. But the model can then become a kind of dynamical attractor itself, and take precedence over the observed economy. Mathematical models are useful tools, but they should not play the same central role in a social science such as economics as they do in an area such as physics. As Benoit Mandelbrot wrote, "little good can come ... when a science yields to the social pressures that reward modelling and theorizing while scorning 'mere' description without 'theory'."[12]

"The model can be used to make predictions about the economy." Milton Friedman, who served as economic adviser for Nixon and Reagan, once argued that the assumptions of a theory don't matter, so long as it makes accurate predictions.[13] Mainstream economics tells us some useful things about the behavior of idealized markets, and captures part of the story. However, economics is not exactly the poster child of success for mathematical prediction. Economists routinely fail to forecast booms or recessions.[14] Indeed, a major coup of neoclassical economics was the efficient market hypothesis, which explained away the inability of economists to predict the future. Their insights into policy questions, such as the effect of raising taxes or cutting welfare, have also proved unreliable. After the fall of the Soviet

Union, neoclassical economists descended into the area armed with all sorts of firm prescriptions and predictions for a new capitalist society. Their ignorance of social and political factors that don't appear in the models, such as huge asymmetries of power, meant the result was not stability but chaos.[15] In Africa, institutions such as the World Bank and the International Monetary Fund have had far longer to experiment with neoclassical reforms, with little sign of success. The utopians of the modern era are not tree-hugging environmentalists, but rather starry-eyed economic advisers who believe that once authoritarian rule is removed—from the Soviet Union in the 1990s or Iraq in the 2000s—free markets will magically appear and solve all problems. They always seem surprised and a little let down when people don't conform to the ideals of rational economic man.

The real reasons for the longevity of the neoclassical model have less to do with science, and more to do with the social dynamics of the universities that propagate it, and its appeal to a particular mind-set. The economist Rebecca Blank describes the process by which students are recruited into the field: "In introductory undergraduate microeconomics courses I have the sense that the following scenario is frequent: out of a class of one hundred students, ninety-nine will listen to the lectures and think to themselves, 'Although interesting, this is sort of crazy; nobody really thinks this way.' Those students do what they must to pass the course and forget it soon afterwards. But the one remaining person in that class lights up. This is almost always a male. He realizes this model describes the way that he thinks and acts. To that person, the economic model *is* intuitively obvious. It is that one person who is most likely to become an economist. Small wonder then that fifteen years later, sitting around the lunch table with a group of other similar selectively chosen economists, everyone believes that the standard economic model indeed describes how most people think about the world. It's certainly the way most people who choose to study economics think about the world."[16] The process seems to resemble the recruitment procedure of a latter-day Pythagorean cult, intent on preserving its ancient teachings.

Clearly not all economists subscribe to the neoclassical view, or practice it, but it still forms the core of economic theory as taught in our most influential universities.[17] It is amusing to contrast the work experience of most academic economists—that is, cranking out rarely read papers and applying for government grants in order to attain tenure and its protection from ever being fired—with the unbridled capitalism depicted in the neoclassical model. Heraclitus wrote: "Pythagoras, the son of Mnesarchus, practiced inquiry most of all men and having made a selection from these writings made for himself a wisdom, a polymathy, an evil art."[18] It's starting to sound like a warning.

GOOD VERSUS EVIL

Given that neither the axioms nor the conclusions of neoclassical economics stand up to scrutiny, it follows that the equations are not an accurate model of a market economy. They give a distorted, oversimplified picture that represents only one side of a far more complex reality. But how about free markets themselves? Are they good, evil, or a fuzzy mix of the two?

Economists—be they in academia, government, or private institutions—are trained to shy away from such a direct phrasing of the question. The field has long modeled itself after objective sciences such as chemistry and physics, and aims to make purely neutral statements about the economy that are untainted by political or ethical considerations. It accomplishes this aim by radically dividing the world into objective and subjective components. Preferences are assumed to be known and fixed, so they can be modeled objectively, but the reasons for the preferences are assumed to be entirely subjective. It is thus impossible to say that any kind of behavior is better than any other. And because society is just the sum of individuals, there is no reason to distinguish between the utility of a single person, and the utility of society as a whole. The economy is therefore a machine for maximizing utility that does not need to be guided by political or ethical considerations. Value judgments are unnecessary, because the market is always right.

In real life, though, the needs of the individual, and the needs of society, often come into direct conflict. A classic example is how society deals with common areas—of land, ocean, or sky—that are owned by no individual. Aristotle wrote: "For that which is common to the greatest number has the least care bestowed upon it."[19] Garrett Hardin raised the same point in a 1968 paper called *The Tragedy of the Commons*, which described a kind of parable.[20] A number of individual animal herders all have access to an area of common pasture. For each herder, rational self-interest dictates that they should exploit as much of the land as possible. But if they all do this, then the result is overgrazing, so the land is of no use to anyone. The invisible hand does not maximize utility as advertised, but does the opposite.

A neoclassical solution may be to get rid of the commons and make all resources privately owned. In theory, the price demanded by the owners would then go up as the resource neared depletion, thus decreasing demand. However, this is based on the idea that the invisible hand can correctly measure both utility and scarcity, and set prices accordingly. In practice, neither resource owners nor customers can see into the future. Often, they are equally surprised when the resource runs out.

Perhaps the most graphic example so far has been the collapse of fisheries such as Grand Banks off Nova Scotia. Instead of prices smoothly increasing until supply and demand came into happy equilibrium, the fish population just suddenly died. As economists Ronald Colman and Hans Messinger observed, "Economic performance of Newfoundland and Nova Scotia benefited from record fish landings up to the very moment of the collapse of the Atlantic ground-fish stocks."[21] The reason was that biological systems are unaware of the economic laws of supply and demand. One thing that mathematical studies of chaotic biological systems have helped explain (see the bifurcation diagram in Figure 6.5, which was first discovered in studies of fish populations) is that if population levels go below a certain threshold, they are at risk of sudden collapse—a kind of fatal bifurcation. Biologists don't know exactly where that threshold is, and neither do fishermen, or eaters of fish and chips. For fishermen to hold back when price signals warn of collapse is like a smoker who waits for signs of cancer before giving up cigarettes: it's too little too late. Because neoclassical economics sees the economy as being at equilibrium, it has no sense of time or the future; and because it sees the economy as rational and enlightened, it does not allow for the indeterminacy of natural systems.

Even with nonliving resources such as gold or oil, it is not easy to measure exactly how much is left in the ground, or predict how quickly it will be used. A primary determinant of resource prices is the cost of extraction, which doesn't necessarily blow up as the source nears depletion—especially since technology will improve with any increase in price. The cost of a barrel of oil depends on many factors, such as Middle East politics or refinery outputs or hurricanes in the Gulf of Mexico, but there is no way you could use it to accurately estimate the remaining amount.

Even when a resource is relatively abundant, the dynamic of the invisible hand means that it will tend to be exploited at the fastest rate possible, rather than conserved for future generations. An example is the Athabasca oil sands in Northern Alberta, named for the Athabasca River, which flows through the area. Indigenous people used to scoop the bitumen from the riverbanks to waterproof their canoes. Today, companies such as Syncrude and Shell use giant trucks the size of houses to strip-mine the earth. The procedure is extremely intensive in labor, land, and energy. It is also hugely damaging to the environment. The emissions from the extraction procedure mean Canada has no chance to meet the levels it agreed to in the Kyoto climate treaty. Common sense would imply that a go-slow approach would allow the land more time to repair, and would also preserve some of the resource for future generations. The invisible hand—and the Alberta government's economic advisers—say otherwise.[22] The result is that woods, meadows, and wetlands are being transformed into something like the lunar surface.

A similar problem affects the Amazon rainforest, which is being cut down at record rates because the land is cheap and can be used to grow soy or cattle. As with the boreal forest being flattened for the Albertan oil sands, the trees are believed to play an essential role in moderating the earth's climate. The dynamic in either case is similar to that of the market's treatment of natural heritage (see "How to be complex" in Chapter 4). Resources that take a long time to develop (millennia in the case of oil fields) are exhausted or destroyed in the name of short-term efficiency. Countries such as Canada or Brazil appear to do well by exporting natural resources—the numbers look good—but they give up environmental capital in exchange, at rates that may look foolishly cheap in 100 years' time.

When Adam Smith first proposed the existence of an invisible hand, he was talking about a specific kind of market, where a number of producers compete openly to sell similar products to informed consumers. However, the theory doesn't apply at the boundary of the market with the natural world. Transactions involving resources, or pollution, do not take place in a human market. We don't produce the resources ourselves, or purchase them from the earth: they are just there in the ground. The earth cannot negotiate payment, any more than it can resist the pollution that a chemical company dumps in a stream. Nor can future generations make a claim for their share of resources—they haven't been born yet.

None of this has been a serious problem for orthodox theory because everything outside the current human economy is labeled an externality and ignored or discounted. As mentioned in Chapter 1, some economists maintain that physical resources aren't even necessary, because everything can be substituted for money. If we are sufficiently wealthy, then we don't need land or forests or oceans or clean air. We just need cash. (Of course, if this were true, then there should be no objection to closing off huge areas of land and oceans to be kept solely as natural reserves. The result would be to decrease our access to natural resources, but according to theory that would only spur our ingenuity and promote economic growth.)

Just as markets fail with the earth's natural resources, so they fail with the most basic human resource—our health. America's market-based health care system relies on each individual purchasing his or her own insurance, or having it supplied by his or her employer. Multiple companies compete to sell the insurance, and the market is highly fragmented. The result is a plethora of insurance forms and documentation for patients and doctors to fill out, which means a substantial portion of health care costs goes towards paperwork. Those with good insurance receive the best medical care in the world. However, the cost of insurance has skyrocketed in recent years, and so, increasingly, many people are going without. The only health care they receive is in the emergency room (which is often paid for by the taxpayer). By overall metrics, such as longevity, infant mortality, and so on, Americans have ended up with arguably the worst system of any industrialized country, despite the fact that they pay more than twice as much per capita. As Arnold S. Rahlman of the Harvard Medical School put it, those who deny the evidence of these problems "are either blinded by unshakeable faith in market ideology or are biased by their interests in businesses that profit from the privatization of health care."[23]

America's health care system probably boosts its GDP because people are afraid to lose their jobs and medical insurance. Have an accident when you are unemployed, and you may end up bankrupted from medical expenses. Because people with low incomes can't afford health care and therefore are at greater risk of developing serious health problems, the system acts as a feedback mechanism that accentuates the income gap. Meanwhile the demand for expert medical personnel draws highly trained doctors and professionals away from other countries that are in far more need. According to a report cited by the World Bank, for every twenty-two nurses that Grenada trains, they only keep one.[24] Globally, access to health care and life-saving drugs is as skewed as the income distribution.

Free markets are an excellent way to set prices for many goods, and their ability to unleash the creative spirits of entrepreneurs is well known. They provide a kind of laboratory in which strong businesses succeed and poor ones fail, and thus promote the growth of the economy, and in many respects the evolution of society. But they run into trouble when left alone to deal with the really important issues—health, the environment, the distribution of food, the world we will leave our children. And their main talent at generating economic growth of the type measured by GDP is itself becoming a problem. In 1953, President Eisenhower's Council of Economic Advisors declared, "The American economy's ultimate purpose is to produce more consumer goods." However, it is possible to have too much of a good thing. The drive for growth helped build the country up after World War II, but the solution to our current problems surely does not lie in a consumerist utopia of more and more stuff.

Perhaps the hardest thing for us to accept is that economic growth has a shadow side. We think of growth as healthy and positive, while stagnation or recession are equated with hardship, waning power, and decay. But quality of life cannot always be measured by economic indices, and as we press harder against the constraints of the planet, continued expansion brings problems such as pollution, environmental degradation, and overcrowding. The problem is not that "all economic growth is evil"—only that, while unrestrained economic growth may once have been a good thing, the fuzzy balance is tilting increasingly towards the negative.

Neoclassical economics was invented at a time when the world population was about a billion people, as compared to today's 6.5 billion. It is only in recent decades that we have begun to impact natural systems such as forests, oceans, and the atmosphere on a truly global scale—and realize that these systems have a value greater than the sum of their resource stocks. The economy has also changed in other ways. Resources are still important, but the economy is increasingly shifting from a linear, frontier-style economy to one based on a complex web of services and collaborations. The growth of the information economy has highlighted the importance of networks and communication. Women have taken on an increasingly large role in the "official" economy. Even money has lost much of its stability, moving from a stand-in for gold, to something as slippery and hard to pin down as a pool of mercury.

While mainstream economic theories have remained Pythagorean—straight, square, individualistic, fixed—the economy, as if in protest, has become increasingly nonlinear, skewed, networked, and fluid. From the point of view of neoclassical economics, the defining features of the modern economy resemble a dark and unfathomable problem. As with a Victorian explorer lost in a jungle, the old maps don't work anymore.

POST-PYTHAGOREAN ECONOMICS

So where can we find a better map for exploring the terrain of the modern economy? Here is a summary of a post-Pythagorean economics. None of these points is particularly surprising or original, but they have all been downplayed or ignored by orthodox economics. The only thing to have changed since the 1960s is that we can now demonstrate many of them using mathematics.

- The economy must be viewed as part of the larger ecosystem. We need to shift from a short-term "bloom" economy to one that can prosper over the long term.
- Measures of progress, such as GDP, should be replaced or at least complemented by fuzzy estimates that attempt to account for nonnumeric qualities, such as sustainability. The main factor that distinguishes our economy from the ecosystem is that we use money. But money is just a convention, and not everything in life can be reduced to exact numbers.
- Our wealth is measured not just by net worth, but also by

networks. This is especially true today as electronic networks such as the World Wide Web grow in size, complexity, and economic importance. When you're embedded in a network, the selfish pursuit of short-term profit may not be the most successful strategy, or the best ideology. Mechanisms for cooperation are as important as those for competition.

• The economy exhibits emergent features that must be understood holistically, rather than through right-handed, reductionist logic. There is no one-size-fits-all economic policy that can be dictated from above; and knowledge of local culture and history is often more useful than facility with abstract equations.

• Our economic system is based on a male paradigm that values "active" theorizing over "passive" observation, and results in the undervaluation of nonmarket activities such as child rearing. To balance the economy, we need first to balance our priorities, and abandon rigid and inflexible ideologies.

• A free market economy is a dynamic system that never reaches an optimal equilibrium (indeed, the whole notion of optimality makes little sense in a fluid, constantly adapting system). It can be incredibly creative in the way it generates solutions for problems; but it can also destroy natural resources, and produce huge social inequities. We need to cultivate the useful side of the money-based economy, while limiting its excesses.

• The economy is wild and unpredictable. We can't perfectly control it, but we can build fences to protect things we value—such as natural resources, social equality, and other species. We can also make the financial system more robust by demanding that institutions such as banks protect against extreme events, rather than the "normal" variation.

• Our economy is not always rational or efficient. It is creative, temperamental, ingenious, energetic, occasionally self-destructive, and subject to unexpected seizures. Its energy is out of balance.

- The free market does not automatically produce a just society—instead its natural tendency is to produce almost unimaginable inequalities of wealth. Neoclassical economists see most regulations that aim to reduce such inequalities as "unnatural" impositions that distort free markets. But it's the other way around. Money isn't natural; it's a societal invention that should not take precedence over other forms of social arrangement.

- The boundary between good and evil is not a straight line. It would be better described as a fractal, dynamic, fuzzy set, where good and evil interpenetrate one another like the water and sand of a beach in a shifting tide. To negotiate it requires a rich and complex system of ethics, not reductionist economic laws.

The shape of our current economic system has been strongly influenced by neoclassical dogma. The switch to a post-Pythagorean framework will therefore have huge implications. Just as free markets liberate the "animal instincts" of entrepreneurs to create innovative products, so the alternative ideas discussed in this book—from areas such as ecological, complexity, feminist, post-autistic, and green economics—will liberate social and environmental innovations that meet needs such as fairness and sustainability. Of course, the exact effect of such a fundamental change is hard to predict. We are at the stage where the supports of the old structure have been found corroded, but the new one has yet to be erected in its place. All we have are sketches of ideas, many untried or still in the experimental stage. If there is one thing they have in common, it is a tendency to employ a mix of techniques: when faced with a demanding task, it helps to use both the left and the right hands. There is also no single best solution. Tackling our complex and often contradictory problems will require complex and contradictory approaches.

One way of moving towards a sustainable economy is to invent prices for so-called ecosystem services, such as forests or rivers. In principle, we could calculate the value of the Amazon for preventing global warming, or the environmental cost of Alberta oil sands extraction, and then charge companies for the damage they cause. Companies would therefore be forced to absorb these externalities, rather than pass them on to current or future generations. However, while it may be possible to estimate whether we are on a sustainable path now—in other words, to determine whether things are getting in a fuzzy sense worse or better—it is far harder to make calculations that depend on an uncertain future. Cost estimates rely on the modeling of economic and climatological effects, which are beyond our computational ability.[25] And even if a forest is assigned a price, that doesn't protect it from destruction—it only acts as a delay until the price of wood goes up.

Another approach is to create a legal boundary around things we want to protect. An example is the auction system proposed by Herman Daly (Chapter 1), where natural resources such as forests are sold to the highest bidder at a controlled rate. This would tend to drive the price up to that of the nearest renewable substitute, which would be chosen by the market, not the government. It also separates out the problems of resource depletion, and resource allocation. The auction system is designed to take care of the former, and market forces are harnessed for the latter—this is an argument for more markets, not less. In desperate cases, such as collapsing fisheries, complete bans are necessary.

Of course, such measures are unacceptable from a neoclassical viewpoint, because they impose new constraints on the market, and are therefore inefficient. But neoclassical economics hasn't proved very useful at saving fish, and it doesn't seem any better suited to saving the planet. The only way to stop the excessive and dangerous exploitation of natural resources—be they animal, mineral, or vegetable—is to make it illegal, or at least suitably expensive, and enforce the penalties with something like the rigor we apply to our credit system. Governments can also strengthen recycling and pollution regulations, and use techniques such as emissions trading so that business costs more accurately reflect their impact on the environment. Advanced technology (such as nuclear power) and economic growth of a certain kind will help—rich societies often do a better job of caring for their local environments—but while they are part of the fuzzy solution, we can't rely on them completely.

The problem of social inequality eludes simple market solutions because it is an intrinsic feature of markets. Wealth begets more wealth, in a positive feedback loop. Money therefore tends to become concentrated in the hands of the few, and often with those who work with the stuff. Bankers in cities such as London and New York earn huge annual bonuses—as much as 50 million dollars for a top trader—while health care workers in the same cities struggle to afford rent in inflated housing markets.[26] This isn't because bankers are more "good" than nurses; it's just a consequence of market dynamics—a kind of market illogic. On a global scale, the imbalances are truly obscene, and threaten even rich countries with instability, for example, in the form of social unrest or terrorism.

One way to reduce these imbalances is by transferring money through mechanisms such as progressive taxation (Buffet recently noted that he pays tax at a much lower rate than his staff), salary caps within companies or industries, and debt cancellation for poor nations (see "Poor law" below).[27] Again, these would be considered suboptimal and inefficient by orthodox theory, and perhaps they would lead to a lower GDP. Certainly none of them will work as long as society gives its tacit approval of wealth disparities. The metaphor of the economy as a rational, deterministic machine is counterproductive because it absolves us of responsibility and acts to distance us emotionally from the misfortunes of others.

We also need new ways to address the basic issues that underlie poverty. Of course there is no easy solution to this multifaceted problem, but it surely requires an economic theory, and a practice, that acknowledges the power of local networks and social capital.[28] An example is micro-credit schemes such as those run by the Grameen Bank. Muhammad Yunus started the bank in the 1970s in Bangladesh, and it is now responsible for billions of dollars in loans. These are individually directed to entrepreneurs in poor areas (usually women—apparently they are a better credit risk). To encourage repayment, the bank sets up small "solidarity groups" whose members act as co-guarantors. Micro-credit is by no means a silver bullet to end poverty, and it won't in itself build the state institutions or large employers that help drive a strong economy, but it seems a pragmatic way to convert social capital into financial currency.

Another major reform to our economic system would be to change the legal definition of corporations to reflect the triple bottom line of people, planet, and profit. In the United States, as Joel Bakan noted, corporations are "set up by statute to serve the best interest of the shareholder, and that's creating wealth. Any manager or director who actually pursued the triple bottom line at the expense of shareholder interests would be acting illegally."[29] Given that corporate "personhoods" are our society's most powerful players, perhaps it's time to relax that restriction. Policies such as globalization and free trade, which encourage corporations to move wherever is cheapest or has the weakest social or environmental regulations, also appear driven more by the needs of multinationals than those of the real people whose lives are affected. The world may look very different if our leaders spent less time listening to the neoclassical economists who sit at their right hand, and paid more attention to the diversity of voices that are being raised in opposition.

Any lasting change presupposes a major shift in the way we think and feel about money, not just in the banks and universities and company boardrooms, but also at every level of society. Government laws and regulations can correct some of capitalism's excesses, but their problem is that they are exerted from the top down. Companies can always find a way to work around regulations, if there aren't broader constraints. Also, real change usually comes from the bottom up, because those at the top tend to protect the status quo. The first step is to rid ourselves of dead ideologies.

EARTHRISE

Neoclassical theory may obtain its power from its association with science and mathematics and number. But its real significance is not scientific, but rather ideological. Herman Daly once compared the World Bank to a church, full of fine, well-intentioned people who are "trying to do good in the world according to what its clergy learned in seminary. But the 'seminaries' are teaching bad theology. Bank economists, whether from Cameroon or California, all get their training in a handful of academic economics departments, and all learn basically the same economic theology."[30]

By claiming the status of an objective science, neoclassical economics attempts to remove ethical and political considerations from the economy, and reduce everything to number. Since money is a store of utility, it follows that wealth is good, and one's goodness is a number in a bank account. But money has no reality of its own. What matters in a civilization are what people do, how they feel, whether they have enough to eat, how they deal with their own waste, what kind of a culture they produce, and how they provide for future generations. Money, if taken too seriously, becomes a distraction. The obsession with numerical targets makes us lose track of what really counts.

Our economic problems are related to a mechanistic, Pythagorean mind-set that divides us from nature, and from each other. The scarcity of neoclassical economics becomes a self-fulfilling prophecy. Instead of allocating resources efficiently, taking into account the rights of future generations, it simply exhausts them. To overcome the Pythagorean divide, we therefore need to shift from a reductionist, mechanistic view of the economy, to one that sees the economy as a complex, creative, organic entity. This requires a change not just in economics, but also in consciousness.

The philosopher Owen Barfield has described such a transformation.[31] He divided the development of human consciousness into three phases: original (unconscious) participation, separation, and final (conscious) participation. The first phase, stretching from the Palaeolithic to roughly late Bronze Age or early Iron Age, was characterized by an instinctive affinity between man and nature, and the celebration of lunar and earth goddesses. Humans lived in a spirit world—when they looked at the moon, they saw it as an extension of their own existence. Man and nature were not separate, but were made of the same stuff.

The second phase represented an abrupt withdrawal and

separation from nature. We stood back from the world so as to be able to understand and gain power over it. We plotted the movements of the moon and planets and learned to predict them. The shift coincided with what Joseph Campbell called solarization—the replacement of female moon and earth deities with their masculine, solar equivalents.

The third stage, according to Barfield, represents a return to nature—not to our original unconscious relationship, but to one where we can consciously participate in nature through imagination. As in a balanced marriage, we are together but separate at the same time. We are two sides of the same coin.

A prime example of solarization was the Delphic oracle in ancient Greece. According to Greek mythology, the oracles were originally provided by Gaia, the earth goddess, and read out by a deity known as Sibyl, who was associated with the moon goddess Artemis.[32] The young god Apollo killed Gaia's protector, the serpent called Python, and took over the oracle. From then on, he was known as the Pythian Apollo. He later took over from Helios as the god of the sun.

In many ways, Pythagoras was the human personification of the solar, separation phase. He was named after the Pythian oracle, and was believed by his followers to have been fathered by Apollo himself. His reductionist, mathematical approach to nature, which attempted to reduce the world to number, has dominated our civilization for 2,500 years; and his list of opposites, which divided phenomena into two opposing classes, served as a kind of template for western scientific thought.

In a very real sense, we are all Pythagoreans. We are all the children of Apollo. We carry around with us a set of ideas that is 2,500 years old. The reason neoclassical economics can so often be presented as some kind of received truth is that its concepts and images are deeply rooted in our psyches. It is an example of what the literary critic Northrop Frye called "mythological conditioning."[33] And it has had an enormous effect on the way our societies treat money. The numbers on the bills have taken on the same magical qualities—beauty, stability, power, goodness—as the integers did for the Pythagoreans. The priests who mediate its powers are the neoclassical economists who still dominate the discussion at universities, governments, and institutions such as the World Bank and IMF.

While the Pythagorean approach has worked wonders in sciences such as physics and chemistry, its application to the social science of economics has been less successful—and has led to some truly perverse consequences. Economics has convinced us that in a world blessed with riches, the main threat is scarcity. It has taught us that selfishness is good. It explains that skill or luck at accumulating money is the same as virtue; and it rationalizes a system where a single person can have the wealth of an entire country. It teaches that we should plunder the earth, pollute the atmosphere, destroy species, and risk the uncontrolled warming of the planet just to make money.

These are the things they teach in schools and universities. It is what the experts from rich countries tell those in developing countries. Coins and banknotes have changed from a convenient device for facilitating trade to a substance that divides people from nature and one another. All this in the name of good.

As psychologist Jules Cashford wrote, the solar stage of consciousness, when taken to excess, can be described as "blinding, over-simplified, inflexible, intransigent, dogmatic, obdurate, literal, over-idealistic, prone to polarization and abstraction."[34] It sees the world in terms of harsh, fixed polarities—the bright light of good versus the dark shadow of evil. The moon, in contrast, has always been the symbol of change and transformation and subtle gradations. It is therefore fitting that the transition to Barfield's stage of conscious participation may have been when the astronauts went to the moon and took a photograph of the earthrise from the moon's point of view. For at that moment, when our image was captured in the silver of the photographic film, our consciousness was reflected back on itself.[35] We saw the world, not as an inanimate lump of matter, but rather as a complex living being. The wall between man and nature began to crumble.

Lao-tzu said, "He who knows others is clever; he who knows himself is enlightened." The Chinese character *ming*, for enlightened, is drawn as a union of the images of moon and sun, which embody the principles of yin and yang respectively.[36] When we went to the moon, we started to know ourselves.

The practitioners of neoclassical economics still stumble on, handing out their prescriptions and advice; the gatekeepers of academia still defend their fragile and brittle theory against the assaults of observation or common sense or alternative points of view. But they are out of touch with a world that is changing around them. And despite their efforts, a new, post-Pythagorean economics is being forged that sees the human economy as just one part of a larger ecosystem; and sees life on this planet as a gift rather than a dismal, money-grubbing struggle against scarcity.

The old myths about the moon and planets don't carry the weight that they used to. With the bright city lights, we barely even notice the celestial bodies. And we don't rely on stories to explain the moon because the *Apollo* astronauts already went there and checked it out. We have gained much in our knowledge of the universe, but at the same time another part of our consciousness has atrophied—we have lost a sense of our place. So perhaps the aim of science and economics should not be just to make predictions or perform calculations, but also to revitalize our imaginations, and serve as a source for stories. As physicists Nigel Goldenfeld and Leo P. Kadanoff wrote, "Up to now, physicists looked for fundamental laws true for all times and all places. But each complex system is different; apparently there are not general laws for complexity. Instead, one must reach for 'lessons' that might, with insight and understanding, be learned in one system and applied to another. Maybe physics studies will become more like human experience."[37] Post-Pythagorean economics does not offer a simple, one-size-fits-all solution for all the world's problems; but it may help us see the issues in a new way, and suggest perhaps surprising solutions.

The astronomer Fred Hoyle predicted in 1953: "Once a photograph of the earth, taken from the outside, is available—once the sheer isolation of the earth becomes plain—a new idea as powerful as any in history will let loose."[38] He was right. And one result of that idea is that half a century later, in the early years of the new millennium, the sun is finally setting on neoclassical economics—and the earth is rising.

POOR LAW

"Morals reformed—health preserved—industry invigorated—instruction diffused—public burthens lightened—Economy seated, as it were, upon a rock—the gordian knot of the Poor-Laws are not cut, but untied—all by a simple idea in Architecture!" Thus was the promise of Jeremy Bentham's Panopticon: a plan for "any sort of establishment, in which persons of any description are to be kept under inspection; and in particular to penitentiary-houses, prisons, houses of industry, workhouses, poor-houses, lazarettos [quarantine stations], manufactories, hospitals, mad-houses, and schools."[39] The founder of utilitarianism was also a designer of prisons.

The idea of the Panopticon was to divide a building into radial cells around a central tower that contained a single observer. Windows on the outside of the building meant that the inhabitants of the cell were backlit, and a series of screens prevented them from seeing the observer. All inhabitants of the complex would therefore constantly feel themselves to be under observation, and would regulate their own behavior out of fear—even if the observer took a break for a cup of tea. The construction of prisons for criminals and debtors was booming in the Victorian period, and the Panopticon was, its inventor believed, an efficient way to keep costs down.

Bentham spent much of his time and fortune developing the Panopticon, but one was never built. However, his vision was eventually realized in a somewhat different form. Today, many of us live in a kind of virtual Panopticon—especially if we go into debt. It is known as the credit rating system.

In the United States, for example, companies known as credit bureaus assess creditworthiness. Everyone gets a three-digit credit score, which determines whether (and at what interest rate) they can get a credit card or a mortgage or a bank loan. If you miss a payment, go bankrupt, or otherwise misbehave, then the credit bureau finds out and you soon find yourself with "bad credit." In a society that associates money with status and virtue, bad credit means you're bad. As it says in the Old Testament: "Evil men borrow and cannot pay it back" (Psalms 37:21).

For many years, Americans couldn't find out their own credit scores. The information was reserved for the observer— the money-lending institutions. The law was changed in 2001 so that consumers can now obtain their scores, but in practice very few do.

The system has its benefits, especially for moneylenders and those with good credit. It is a way of identifying what Adam Smith called the "slothful, effeminate, and voluptuous" characters who are bad for industry. However, the information is widely shared, and often contains errors. Critics also point out that it drives consumers with bad credit towards exploitative companies who offer them credit then charge them punitive interest rates, thus driving them further into debt.

Indeed, society's attitude towards debt is reminiscent of the moral rigidity of the Victorian era. Where this does create a serious problem is with the issue of third world debt. Our governments could have torn it all up decades ago, but instead we allow much of it to linger as if in a last attempt to satisfy some kind of penny-pinching, moralistic principle. It's time to let the debtors out of jail. (See the "Drop the Debt" campaign at http://www.jubileeusa.org/.)

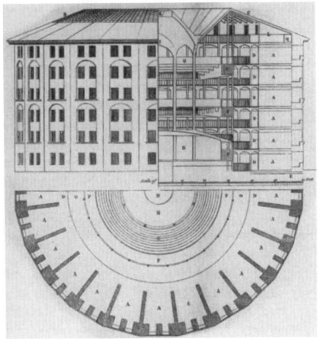

Figure 10.1. Bentham's Panopticon.

HOW TO BE POST-PYTHAGOREAN

It wasn't easy to be a Pythagorean, back in the sixth century B.C. Their sect resembled a quasi-religious cult that made rigorous demands of its members. To join the inner circle, known as the *mathematikoi*, you had to surrender all personal possessions, give up eating meat, adopt an ascetic lifestyle, and study for five years under a vow of silence. Only then were you deemed ready to gain access to Pythagoras' secret teachings.

Fortunately, it is much less demanding to be a post-Pythagorean. There aren't really any secret teachings, and there's no need to remain silent. It mostly comes down to common sense. (It doesn't even have a single name—I call it post-Pythagorean here, but other people have their own names.) The only demand it makes is that, because the economy is more than a clockwork machine, we must be more than unthinking cogs. It's not that it's more political, just that it makes the politics explicit rather than hiding it behind pseudoscience.

In neoclassical economics, the free market economy is seen as the optimal outcome of mechanistic forces. It therefore follows—rather ironically, given the creed's Pythagorean roots—that selfishness is good. Any attempt to reform the system by imposing ethical constraints or social responsibility on individuals and corporations just misses the point.[40] There isn't much need to think, vote, or act on difficult issues, because all will be taken care of by the market.

However, if the economy is a kind of organic entity we can consciously shape, then—as in the examples below—we often have to make decisions based on something other than money or selfish desire. Of course, it isn't the case that what was once good is now suddenly totally evil. But there is a shift underway from an extreme view to one that is more fuzzy and balanced.

Economic growth

Neoclassical: A rapidly expanding economy means that in money terms, we get richer sooner.

Post-Pythagorean: But we aren't necessarily happier or better off, after the hidden environmental and social costs are taken into account. Prosperity for the long term demands a balanced approach towards growth.

Energy

Energy fuels the economy. Human ingenuity will come up with new sources when we need them.

Oil supplies are declining. We need to develop alternatives, but should also cap energy use. Added benefit: less pollution.

Urban design

People want space, so if they are willing to tolerate long commutes to live in a big house, that is their free choice.

Sprawl is inefficient and happens because commuters don't pay the true cost of pollution or land use. The design of cities is key to building a sustainable economy. Added benefit of living closer together: strengthened social capital.

Tax

Resources generate economic growth, so we should encourage extraction through low taxes.

Given that resources are finite and must be shared with future generations, we should shift taxes from labor and income towards resource use and pollution.

Globalization and free trade

According to neoclassical theory, we're all the same under economic law, and national boundaries just get in the way.

According to the data, income differences have increased under globalization. A little local self-sufficiency makes the world economy both more robust, and more complex and interesting.

Birth control

Every new body is another consumer.

Time to give the planet a break. Part of the battle is to improve sexual equality around the world.

Defense spending

Defense is a major part of the world economy—and if a war breaks out, the extra military spending actually boosts GDP (as long as you don't lose).

Defense spending is an indicator of skewed economic logic. In an era of asymmetric conflict, buying elaborate hardware mainly helps corporations and their shareholders.

Land development

Green spaces that aren't doing anything should be developed.

Those green spaces are doing something—they develop and support life.

Consumption

If we keep shopping it helps the entire economy and boosts GDP.

Of course, stuff is highly important. But there is such a thing as overkill.

Advertising

Advertising is just a way for businesses to supply information to rational consumers, and the expense can often be written off against tax.

Neuroscience and common sense show that advertisements manipulate consumers by appealing to their emotions. They make people spend their savings (or their credit cards) on things they don't really want or need. They should be taxed and regulated accordingly.

Policy making

Decisions should be based as far as possible on objective economic criteria and hard numbers.

Concepts such as "efficiency" or "market forces" or "economic growth" are not value free or apolitical, and their uses aren't always appropriate.

Education and ideology

Neoclassical economics embodies the one true light of truth. Educators at elite institutions such as Harvard and MIT help spread the good word to the people who count.

To overcome problems such as pollution, overcrowding, resource exhaustion, and insane social inequalities, we have never been in greater need of a diverse range of new ideas. Most of the action is in smaller centers outside the mainstream. New textbooks that emphasize a plural approach to economics are also starting to appear.[41]

○ APPENDIX
NORMAL VERSUS POWER LAW

Many forms of economic data, such as stock market fluctuations or wealth rankings, have traditionally been modeled using a normal distribution (otherwise known as the bell curve), but are actually much better fitted by a power-law distribution. As Figure A.1 shows, the two are quite different. The data in the left panels are normally distributed, and simulate some typical height data for males in meters, with a mean of 1.75 and standard deviation 0.09. The data in the right panels have the same mean, but are distributed according to a power law. Each contains 5,000 points.

The top two panels show twenty random samples from each data set. The uniformly distributed data stays close to the mean, but the power-law data is far wider (note the different vertical scales). The histograms in the middle panels bin the data into different height ranges. For the normal data, the largest bin is the one containing the mean—most samples are near-average—while for the power law the largest bin is the first—most samples are short. The bottom panels show the samples arranged in descending order of height. The normal data is symmetric around the mean—as many samples are below average height as above it. However, the power-law data are highly skewed, so that the largest sample is around 100 (only the top fifty heights are shown). In a normal world, everyone has about the same height, while in the power-law world, most people are short but there are a few 100-meter-tall monsters. Economically, we're in the latter situation.

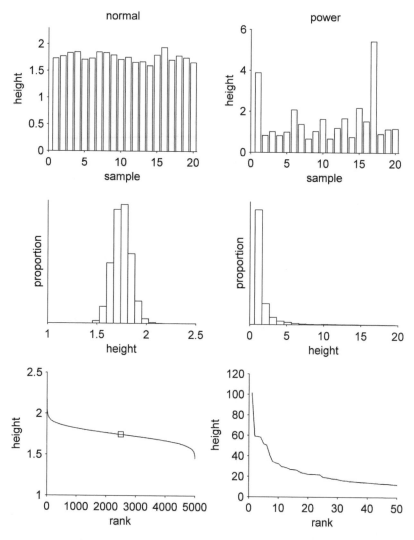

Figure A.1. Comparison of normally distributed height data (left panels) with power-law data (right panels).

NOTES

INTRODUCTION

1 Young Generation. (1967, Jan. 7). *TIME*.

2 See: Davis, M. (2006). *Planet of Slums*. New York: Verso.

3 One study showed that "only the top 10 percent of the income distribution enjoyed a growth rate of real wage and salary income equal to or above the average rate of economy-wide productivity growth." Dew-Becker, I., & Gordon, R. J. (2005). *Where Did the Productivity Growth Go? Inflation Dynamics and the Distribution of Income* (NBER Working Paper 11842).

4 Stern Review on the Economics of Climate Change. (2006). Retrieved Apr. 24, 2007, from http://www.sternreview.org.uk.

5 Retrieved Mar. 2, 2007, from http://www.paecon.net.

6 Dangers of an unfettered market: George Soros interview. *Wall Street Week with FORTUNE* [Television broadcast]. Retrieved Nov. 24, 2007, from http://www.pbs.org/wsw/tvprogram/sorosinterview.html.

7 Guthrie, W. K. C. (1962–1981). *A History of Greek Philosophy* (6 vols.). Cambridge, U.K.: Cambridge University Press, p. 177.

8 Lederman, L. & Teresi, D. (1993). *The God Particle: If the Universe Is the Answer, What Is the Question?* New York: Houghton Mifflin, p. 346.

9 Koestler, A. (1968). *The Sleepwalkers*. London: Hutchinson, p. 25.

10 Rosen, R. (2000). *Essays on Life Itself*. New York: Columbia University Press, p. 63.

11 Some of these ideas were first presented in: Orrell, D. (2006, Sep.-Oct.). Post-Pythagorean Economics. *Adbusters*, 67.

Chapter 1

1 Zimmerman, R. (1998). *Genesis: The Story of Apollo 8.* New York: Four Walls Eight Windows, p. 206.

2 Apollo Astronauts. (1969, Jan. 3). *TIME.*

3 Quoted in Zimmerman, 1998, p. 238.

4 Woods, D. & O'Brien, F. (2006). *Apollo 8* Flight Journal. Retrieved Nov. 3, 2006, from http://history.nasa.gov/apo8fj/index.htm.

5 Rowell, G. (1995, Sept.). The power of one—how individuals have succeeded in preserving wilderness. *Sierra.*

6 Tucker, I. B., III (1995). *Survey of Economics.* New York: West Publishing Co.

7 Quoted in Guthrie, 1979, p. 207.

8 Guthrie, 1962, p. 221.

9 Malthus, T. R. (1836). *Principles of Political Economy.* London: Kelley, p. 227.

10 Genesis 1:28 King James version.

11 Defoe, D. (1709, July 2). *A Review of the State of the British Nation.*

12 Solow, R. (Professor). (1974) Richard T. Ely Lecture, The Economics of Resources or the Resources of Economics. *American Economic Review, 64,* 1–14. In macroeconomics texts, aggregate production is usually written as a function of capital and labor stocks, with no consideration for resources. See: Daly, H. E. (1996). *Beyond Growth: The Economics of Sustainable Development.* Boston: Beacon Press, p. 47. See also: Sterman, J. D. (2002). All Models are Wrong: Reflections on Becoming a Systems Scientist. *System Dynamics Review 18*(4), 501–31.

13 Boulding, K. E. (1966). The Economics of the Coming Spaceship Earth. In H. Jarrett (Ed.), *Environmental Quality*

in a Growing Economy (pp. 3–14). Baltimore: Resources for the Future/Johns Hopkins University Press.

14 Zimmerman, 1998, p. 60.

15 Gannon, S. (2007, March 10). "Ashamed of all that clutter? We'll help you hide it." *The Globe and Mail.*

16 The ecological footprint of the average North American may be equivalent to that of twenty or more people living in a poor country. Wackernagel, M., & Silverstein, J. (2000). Big things first: focusing on the scale imperative with the ecological footprint. *Ecological Economics, 32,* 391–94.

17 Diogenes Laertius (1853). *Lives of the Philosophers.* Translated by C. D. Yonge. London: Henry G. Bohn, p. 376.

18 Beckerman, W. (1974). *In Defence of Economic Growth.* London: Jonathan Cape.

19 Genesis: 1:28–30.

20 For a good discussion of this topic, see Czech, B. (2000). *Shoveling Fuel For a Runaway Train: Errant Economists, Shameful Spenders, and a Plan to Stop Them All.* Berkeley: University of California Press, Berkeley, p. 105.

21 See Lovelock, J. (2006). *The Revenge of Gaia: Why the Earth Is Fighting Back—and How We Can Still Save Humanity.* London: Penguin, p. 22.

22 Homer-Dixon, T. (2006). *The Upside of Down: Catastrophe, Creativity, and the Renewal of Civilization.* Toronto: Knopf, p. 90.

23 Robbins, L. (1994). An Essay on the Nature and Significance of Economic Science. In D. M. Hausman (Ed.). *The Philosophy of Economics* (2nd ed.). Cambridge, U.K.: Cambridge University Press, pp. 83–110. (Original work published 1935).

24 Brandt, B. (1995). *Whole Life Economics: Revaluing Daily Life.* Gabriola Island, B.C.: New Society, p. 207.

25 Mill, J. S. (1909). In W. J. Ashley (Ed.), *Principles of Political Economy*. London: Longmans, Green and Co. (Original work published 1848).

26 See Daly, H. E. (Ed.). (1980). *Economics, Ecology, Ethics: Essays Toward a Steady-State Economy*. San Francisco: W. H. Freeman. One of Daly's mentors was Nicholas Georgescu-Roegen, who long argued that economic theory didn't just violate ecological principles, it violated basic laws of physics, such as conservation of mass. See: Georgescu-Roegen, N. (1971). *The Entropy Law and the Economic Process*. Cambridge, MA: Harvard University Press. See also: Daly, H. E. (2007). *Ecological Economics and Sustainable Development, Selected Essays of Herman Daly*. Northampton, MA: Edward Elgar, pp. 125–37.

27 A good example is the Alberta oil sands, where companies can write off 100 percent of the cost of capital upgrades. Leatherdale, L. (2007, June 3). How Much is Enough? *Toronto Sun*. Steve Laut, who is president of Canadian Natural Resources Ltd., the country's second-highest producer, said, "any significant change—or any change—to the royalty system could [produce] a drastic—I mean drastic—reduction in activity in Alberta." But other countries, such as Venezuela, Russia, or Nigeria, charge far greater royalties. Ebner, D. (2007, August 18). As Big Oil pumps Alberta for profit, the province's royalty take is shrinking. *The Globe and Mail*. See also http://www.oilsandswatch.org/.

28 Czech, 2000, p. 105. To get an idea of the difficulties involved, see also: http://steadystate.org/Foundation-of-a-New-Conservation-Movement.pdf.

29 Wackernagel, M. & Rees, W. (1996). *Our Ecological Footprint: Reducing Human Impact on the Earth*. Philadelphia, PA: New Society Publishers.

30 See http://www.ecofoot.net.

31 O'Neill, M. (2007, June 26). Meet the Bookkeeper: An Interview with Mathis Wackernagel of Global Footprint Network. Retrieved Nov. 24, 2007, from http://www.tree hugger.com/files/2007/06/meet_the_bookke_1.php.

32 There are many examples; one is the B001 eco-district in Malmo, Sweden. See http://www.map21ltd.com/scan-green/b001.htm. See also http://www.oneplanetliving.org/.

33 Cashford, J. (2002). *The Moon: Myth and Image*. New York: Four Walls Eight Windows, p. 8.

34 Lietaer, B. (2001). *The Future of Money: Creating New Wealth, Work and a Wiser World*. London: Century, p. 47. This book gives a good introduction to complementary currencies.

35 See: Daly, 2007, p. 114.

Chapter 2

1 Nietzsche, F. (1995). *The Birth of Tragedy*. New York: Dover, p. 17. (Original work published 1872).

2 Images from NASA retrieved Nov. 3, 2006, from http://lunar.arc.nasa.gov/science/phases.htm.

3 Retrieved Sep. 22, 2006, from http://www.thesmokinggun.com/archive/0803051jimi10.html.

4 Whiteley, S. (1992). *The Space Between the Notes: Rock and the Counter-Culture*. New York: Routledge, p. 27.

5 Iamblichus (1918). *Life of Pythagoras*. (T. Taylor, Trans.). Hollywood, CA: Krotona, p. 60. (Original work translated 1818).

6 Iamblichus, 1918, p. 60.

7 Davis, D. (2003, Oct. 14). The day José changed the anthem forever. *Detroit Free Press*.

8 National anthem best sung in English, Bush declares.

(2006, April 29). *The Globe and Mail.*

9 Tempelman-Kluit, A. (2006, May 25). When a sturdy steed is what you need ... *The Globe and Mail.*

10 Blair, B. (1994). Interview with Lotfi Zadeh, Creator of Fuzzy Logic. *Azerbaijan International 2*(4).

11 Quoted in Kosko, B. (1993). *Fuzzy Thinking: The New Science of Fuzzy Logic.* New York: Hyperion, p. 3.

12 Nietzsche, F. (2003). *Beyond Good and Evil.* London: Penguin, p. 55. (Original work published 1886).

13 The expression goes back to 1849, when Thomas Carlyle described the new science of economics as "a dreary, desolate, and indeed quite abject and distressing one; what we might call, by way of eminence, the dismal science." Carlyle, T. (1849). Occasional Discourse on the Negro Question. *Fraser's Magazine for Town and Country 40,* 670–79.

14 Bentham, J. (1907). *Introduction to the Principles of Morals and Legislation.* Oxford: Clarendon Press, p. 1.

15 Jevons, W. S. (1957). *Theory of Political Economy* (5th ed.). New York: Kelley and Millman, pp. xvii–xviii. (Original work published 1871).

16 Jevons, 1957, p. 11.

17 Honoré, C. (2004). *In Praise of Slowness: How a Worldwide Movement Is Challenging the Cult of Speed.* New York: HarperCollins.

18 Boss, S. (2006). *Green with Envy: A Whole New Way to Look at Financial (Un)Happiness.* New York: Warner, p. 170. Newman, K. (1989). *Falling from Grace: The Experience of Downward Mobility in the American Middle Class.* New York: Vintage. Of course poor people can also suffer from social isolation.

19 Schumacher, E. F. (1968). Buddhist Economics. *Resurgence 1*(11).

20 Mickleburgh, R. (2006, Sept. 9). Dalai Lama brings teens a message of compassion. *The Globe and Mail.*

21 Crawford, T. (2006, Sept. 10). Dalai Lama speaks with scientists about stress. *Victoria Times Colonist.*

22 Pew Research Center. Are We Happy Yet? Retrieved Nov. 24, 2007, from http://pewresearch.org/pubs/301/are-we-happy-yet.

23 See for example: Fombonne, E. (1995). Depressive disorders: time trends and possible explanatory mechanisms. In M. Rutter & D. J. Smith, (Eds.), *Psychosocial Disorders in Young People: Time Trends and Their Causes* (pp. 544–615). Chichester: John Wiley & Sons.

24 General Social Surveys, 1972–2004. Retrieved Jul. 3, 2006, from http://sda.berkeley.edu.

25 One day I was exiting the station and saw a man lying flat on his back unconscious. Everyone was streaming around him as if he were an obstacle. He had a briefcase next to him, and he didn't look like a drunk. I stopped a woman to ask if she had a mobile phone. She looked inconvenienced, and then agreed to call an ambulance. The psychology professor Robert Levine had a similar experience in New York—as he put it, "Not one of the passing herd seemed to notice that the obstacle was a man"—which motivated him to make a study of how helpful people were in different cities. The main correlation he found was that helpfulness was "inversely related to a country's economic productivity." Levine, R. (2001). "Cross-Cultural Differences in Helping Strangers." *Journal of Cross-Cultural Psychology* 32, 543–60.

26 Inglehart, R. (2004). Subjective well-being rankings of 82 societies. Retrieved Jul. 3, 2006, from http://www.worldvaluessurvey.org/library/latestpub.asp.

27 Mill, J. S. (1907). Posthumous Essay on Social Freedom.

Oxford and Cambridge Review.

28 Hyman, H. H. (1942). The psychology of status. *Archives of Psychology, 269,* 5–91.

29 Data is until 1986, when Gallup stopped asking the question. Rainwater, L. (1990). *Poverty and equivalence as social constructions.* (Luxembourg Income Study Working Paper 91). Center for Policy Research/The Maxwell School, Syracuse, NY.

30 Daly, H. E. (1968). On Economics as a Life Science. *Journal of Political Economy 76,* 392–406.

31 They were trying to avoid European Union penalties that are imposed when the budget deficit rises above 3 percent of GDP. Oldest profession helps enlarge Greek GDP by 25%. (2006, Sept. 30). *The Globe and Mail.*

32 Kennedy, R. F. (1968, Mar. 18). Address. University of Kansas. Lawrence, Kansas.

33 Daly, H. E., & Cobb, J. B., Jr. (1989). *For the Common Good: Redirecting the Economy toward Community, the Environment, and a Sustainable Future.* Boston: Beacon Press.

34 Anielski, M. (2007). *The Economics of Happiness: Building Genuine Wealth.* Gabriola Island, B.C.: New Society.

35 Jevons, W. S. (1890). In R. Adamson & H. A. Jevons (Eds.), *Pure Logic and Other Minor Works.* New York: Macmillan & Co.

36 Daly, 1996, p. 2.

37 Nietzsche, 2003, p. 157.

38 Andriantiatsaholiniaina, L. A., Kouikoglou, V. S., & Phillis, Y. A. (2004). Evaluating strategies for sustainable development: fuzzy logic reasoning and sensitivity analysis. *Ecological Economics 48,* 149–72.

39 Collins, J., & Porras, J. I. (1994). *Built to Last: Successful Habits of Visionary Companies.* New York: Harper-Business.

40 See http://www.blendedvalue.org.

41 See http://www.earthinc.org.

Chapter 3

1   Aristotle (1908). *Nicomachean Ethics, Book V.* (W. D. Ross, Trans.). Retrieved Nov. 24, 2007, from http://classics.mit.edu/Aristotle/nicomachaen.5.v.html.

2   Guthrie, 1962, pp. 221–22.

3   Johnson, L. W., & Wolbarsht, M. L. (1979). Mercury Poisoning: A Probable Cause of Isaac Newton's Physical and Mental Ills. *Notes and Records of the Royal Society of London, 34,* 1–9.

4   *Treasury Papers, ccviii,* 43. See: http://www.pierre-marteau.com/editions/1701-25-mint-reports/report-1717-09-25.html.

5   Jevons, 1957, p. 48.

6   Ibid., p. 64.

7   Ibid., p. 86.

8   Ibid., p. 94.

9   Ibid., p. 147.

10 Fama, E. F. (1965). Random walks in stock-market prices. *Selected Papers of the Graduate School of Business, 16.* Chicago: University of Chicago Press.

11 Arrow, K. J. (1984). *The Economics of Information.* Cambridge, MA: Belknap Press of Harvard University, p. 80.

12 Erdös, P., & Rényi, A. (1959). On random graphs. *Publicationes Mathematicae, 6,* 290–97.

13 Milgram, S. (1967). The small-world problem. *Psychology Today, 1,* 61–67.

14 Guare, J. (1990). *Six Degrees of Separation: A Play.* New York: Vintage.

15 Kleinfeld, J. (2002). The small world problem. *Society, 39,*

61–66.

16 Another reason is related to an earlier and even more famous experiment of Milgram's, which showed how people
were easily influenced by the power of scientific authority
to the point where they were willing to administer electric
shocks to innocent people if ordered to do so by a scientist.
Milgram showed how subjects could be made to inflict
what they thought were enormous, life-threatening electric
shocks to another person (actually an actor) if ordered to
do so by someone they thought was an experimental scientist. The "six degrees" result was the finding of a renowned
scientist from a top university—Milgram himself—and
like the folders sent to participants, the research came em-
bossed with the gold letters of Harvard. It had credibility.
Milgram, S. (1974). *Obedience to Authority: An Experimental View*. New York: HarperCollins.

17 The Internet Movie Database was first launched as a news-
group database in 1990, and went on the World Wide Web
in 1993. See http://www.imdb.com.

18 The Oracle of Bacon site was created by Brett Tjaden in
1996. See http://oracleofbacon.org/.

19 Batagelj, V., & Mrvar, A. (2000). Some analyses of Erdos
collaboration graph. *Social Networks*, *22*, 173–86.

20 See the Erdos Number Project at
http://www.oakland.edu/enp/trivia.html.

21 Albert, R., Jeong, H., & Barabási, A.-L. (1999). Diameter of
the World Wide Web, *Nature*, *401*, 130–31.

22 Watts, D. J., & Strogatz, S. H. (1998). Collective dynamics of
"small world" networks. *Nature*, *393*, 440–42.

23 Liljeros, F., Edling, C., Amaral, L., Stanley, E., and Åberg, Y.
(2001). The web of human sexual contacts. *Nature*, *411*,
907–08. Results were for a sample size of 2,810 people.

24 Smith, A. (1776). *An Inquiry into the Nature and Causes of the Wealth of Nations.* McMaster archive online. Retrieved Nov. 24, 2007, from http://socserv.mcmaster.ca/econ/ugcm /3ll3/smith/wealth/wealbko1.

25 Dr. Kathleen Carley quoted in: Kolata, G. (2005, May 22). "Enron Offers an Unlikely Boost to E-Mail Surveillance." *New York Times.*

26 Newman, M. E. J., Strogatz, S. H., & Watts, D. J. (2001). Random graphs with arbitrary degree distributions and their applications. *Physical Review E, 64,* 1–17.

27 Bowley, G. (2006, Oct. 27). The high priestess of internet friendship. *Financial Times.*

28 Barabási, A.-L. (2003). *Linked: How Everything Is Connected to Everything Else and What It Means for Business, Science, and Everyday Life.* Cambridge, MA: Plume, p. 211.

29 See the journal *Review of Network Economics* at: http://www.rnejournal.com/index.html.

30 Ferber, M. A., and Nelson, J. A. (Eds.). (1993). *Beyond Economic Man: Feminist Theory and Economics.* Chicago: University of Chicago Press, p. 82.

31 Lederman, L. (1993). *The God Particle: If the Universe Is the Answer, What Is the Question?* New York: Houghton Mifflin, p. 348.

32 Hobson, J. A. (1914). *Work and Wealth: A Human Valuation.* London: Macmillan.

33 Barabási, 2003, p. 212.

34 Frank, R. H., Gilovich, T., & Regan, D. T. (1993, Spring). Does Studying Economics Inhibit Cooperation. *Journal of Economic Perspectives, 7*(2), 159–71.

35 Monaghan, P. (2003). Taking On "Rational Man." *Chronicle of Higher Education, 49*(20), A12.

36 Vohs, K. D., Mead, N., & Goode, M. (2006). The Psycho-

logical Consequences of Money. *Science, 314,* 1154–56.

37 It is interesting to note that children appear to do best not when they are educated to be selfish, but rather when they participate from an early age in household chores that benefit the whole family. Studies have shown that activities such as picking up toys, taking out the garbage, making the bed, or setting the table not only give the parents a break, but also instill values such as responsibility and empathy. Furthermore, it seems that the tasks should not be linked to an allowance, because this confuses the idea of making a contribution with managing money. Neoclassical economics, if applied to children, would be a recipe for producing spoiled brats. Eddie, D. (2006, Sept. 30). It's like you think I'm your slave or something. *The Globe and Mail.* Involving children in household tasks: Is it worth the effort? (2002). *ResearchWorks,* University of Minnesota College of Education and Human Development. Retrieved October 5, 2006, from http://www.education.umn.edu/Pubs/Research-Works/Rossmann.html.

38 McPherson, M., Smith-Lovin, L., & Brashears, M. (2006). Social Isolation in America: Changes in Core Discussion Networks Over Two Decades. *American Sociological Review, 71,* 353–75. Of course, it is hard to define what "important" means. See Bearman, P. S. & Parigi, P. Cloning Headless Frogs and Other Important Matters. *Social Forces, 83*(2).

39 Putnam, R. D. (2000). *Bowling Alone: The Collapse and Revival of American Community.* New York: Simon & Schuster.

40 The phrase was probably coined in: Jacobs, J. (1961). *The Death and Life of Great American Cities.* New York: Random House.

41 Harrison, L. E., & Huntington, S. P. (2001). *Culture Matters:*

How Values Shape Human Progress. New York: Basic Books.
42 Hobson, 1914.

Chapter 4

1 Quoted in Zimmerman, 1998, p. 44.
2 Anonymous. (1957, October 4). *BBC News 4* [Television broadcast]. London: British Broadcasting Corporation. Retrieved Nov. 24, 2007, from http://news.bbc.co.uk/onthis-day/hi/dates/stories/october/4/newsid_2685000/2685115.stm.
3 Whitehouse, D. (2002, October 28). First dog in space died within hours. London: British Broadcasting Corporation. Retrieved Nov. 24, 2007, from http://news.bbc.co.uk/1/hi/sci/tech/2367681.stm.
4 See: http://www.teachingamericanhistory.org/library /index.asp?document=176
5 Quoted in Zimmerman, 1998, p. 275.
6 On the invisible hand, Smith also wrote: "The rich ... are led by an invisible hand to make nearly the same distribution of the necessaries of life, which would have been made, had the earth been divided into equal portions among all its inhabitants, and thus without intending it, without knowing it, advance the interest of the society, and afford means to the multiplication of the species." (*Wealth of Nations*, Part IV, Chapter 1). The question of wealth distribution is discussed in Chapter 9.
7 "Accumulate, accumulate! That is Moses and the prophets!" Marx, K. (1867). *Capital*. Retrieved Apr. 2, 2007, from http://www.marxists.org/archive/marx/works/1867-c1/ch24.htm.
8 Tomorrow Is Three Suits. (1964, Feb. 21). *TIME*.
9 The Austrian economist Friedrich Hayek had already pointed out in 1948 that the economy is far too complex to

compute. Hayek, F. A. (1948). *Individualism and Economic Order.* Chicago: University of Chicago Press.

10 Guy, R. K. (1985). John Horton Conway. In Albers and G. L. Alexanderson (Eds.), *Mathematical People: Profiles and Interviews* (pp. 43–50). Boston: Birkhauser.

11 See for example http://www.bitstorm.org/gameoflife/.

12 Mill, J. S. (1843). *System of Logic.* London: Longmans, Green, Reader, and Dyer.

13 Arthur, W. B. (1994). Bounded Rationality and Inductive Behavior (the El Farol Problem), *American Economic Review, 84,* 406–11.

14 See for example Lux, T. & Marchesi, M. (1999). Scaling and criticality in a stochastic multi-agent model of financial market, *Nature, 397,* 498–500.

15 Horgan, J. (1995, June). From Complexity to Perplexity. *Scientific American 272,* 104–109.

16 See Cashford, 2002, p. 290.

17 Yeats, W. B. (1900). The Philosophy of Shelley's Poetry. Edward Larrissey (Ed.) *W.B. Yeats: A Critical Edition of the Major Works.* Oxford: Oxford University Press, 1997, p. 351.

18 Sperry, R. W. (1981, December 8). Some Effects of Disconnecting the Cerebral Hemispheres. Nobel Lecture. Nobel Foundation. Stockholm, Sweden.

19 See the World Health Organization factsheet on epilepsy at: http://www.who.int/mediacentre/factsheets/fs168/en/.

20 Sperry, R. W., & Gazzaniga, M. S. (1967). Language following surgical disconnection of the hemispheres. In: F. L. Darley (Ed.), *Brain Mechanisms Underlying Speech and Language* (pp. 108–21). New York: Grune and Stratton.

21 Sperry, R. W. (1975, Aug. 9). Left-brain, right-brain. *Saturday Review,* 30–33.

22 Gazzaniga, M. S., & LeDoux, J. E. (1978). *The Integrated*

Mind. Plenum Press, New York, pp. 152–53.

23 Andrews, E. L. (2005, Aug. 25). 'Maestro' leaves stellar record and murky legacy. *International Herald Tribune.*

24 Knight, F. H. (1921). *Risk, Uncertainty, and Profit.* Boston: Houghton Mifflin.

25 Midgley, M. (2000). *Gaia: The next big idea.* London: Demos, p. 14.

26 Koestler, A. (1969). In A. Koestler & J. R. Smythies (Eds.), *Beyond Reductionism: New Perspectives in the Life Sciences.* London: Hutchinson. See also Koestler, A. (1967). *The Ghost in the Machine.* London: Hutchinson.

27 See Waldrop, M. M. (1992). *Complexity: The Emerging Science at the Edge of Order and Chaos.* New York: Simon & Schuster; and Kaufman, S. (1995). *At Home in the Universe: The Search for the Laws of Self-Organization and Complexity.* Oxford: Oxford University Press.

28 Computer versions of complex adaptive systems also exist. One of the better known is a kind of computer game called Sugarscape, which involves agents swarming like ants over an imaginary landscape looking for sugar. Each agent has slightly different characteristics, so some can move faster or need more food. They can also reproduce through a process in which a couple's attributes are randomly mixed up to produce a new agent. If the parameters are set up correctly, then the emergent behavior is quite lifelike—the agents self-organize into groups, trade back and forth, and come into conflict when sugar runs low. The program has been used to study everything from economics to warfare. See http://www.brook.edu/es/dynamics/sugarscape/default.htm.

29 Arthur, W. B. (1999). Complexity and the Economy. *Science, 284,* 107–109.

30 Beinhocker, E. D. (2006). *Origin of Wealth: Evolution, Complexity, and the Radical Remaking of Economics*. Boston: Harvard Business School Press, p. 97.

31 Hayek, F. A. (1967). The Theory of Complex Phenomena. In F. A. Hayek (Ed.), *Studies in Philosophy, Politics, and Economics* (pp. 22–42). London: Routledge & Kegan Paul. Schumpeter, J. A. (1942). *Capitalism, Socialism and Democracy*. New York: Harper & Row.

32 See http://www.cmit.csiro.au/research/special/green/nemp.cfm.

33 Venezuela's president, Hugo Chavez, is a believer in old-school socialism. He told a London audience in 2006: "We may not live to see our dream of socialism come true. But the younger people will see this wonderful, luminous world, believe me." Sengupta, K. (2006, May 15). Britain's left-wing 'aristocracy' greet their hero Chavez. *Independent*. If his dream does come true, it will be on the back of oil profits.

34 Geospatial Agent-Based Reasoning. Retrieved July 1, 2006, from http://www.nutechsolutions.com.

35 See: http://www.strathcona.org/History/Foundation.html.

36 Mason, R. et al. (1999, Spring). The Economics of Heritage Conservation: A Discussion. *The Getty Conservation Institute Newsletter 14*(1).

37 Jacobs, Jane (1961). *The Death and Life of Great American Cities*. New York: Vintage, p. 432.

Chapter 5

1 Cashford, 2002, p. 282. The moon is not always female. In Britain, for example, the moon was considered male until the sixteenth century. However, as Cashford notes, it always seems to represent archetypal feminine functions

such as fertility and regeneration.

2   Physicist Leon Lederman, on discovering evidence of parity violation: "My breathing was becoming difficult, my
palms were wet, my heartbeat accelerated, I felt light-
headed—many (not all!) of the symptoms of sexual
arousal. This was big stuff." Lederman, 1993, p. 272.

3   Keller, E. F. (1985). *Reflections on Gender and Science*. New
Haven: Yale University Press, p. 69. See also: Wertheim, M.
(1995). *Pythagoras' Trousers: God, Physics, and the Gender
Wars*. New York: Norton.

4   As its full title suggests, this prize was created in 1969 by
the Bank of Sweden, not Nobel. Some of his surviving
family say he wouldn't have approved of the use of his
name. I will call it the Bank of Sweden Prize, because that's
what it is.

5   Ferber and Nelson, 1993, pp. 75–76.

6   Nelson, J. A. (1996). The Masculine Mindset of Economic
Analysis. *The Chronicle of Higher Education*, 42, B3.

7   Nelson, 1996.

8   De Botton, A. (2004). *Status Anxiety*. Toronto: Penguin, p. 203.

9   See http://sda.berkeley.edu/cgi-bin/hsda3.

10 Roddick, A. (2003, June 19). Editor for the Day. *Independent*.

11 Pigou, A. C. (1932). *The Economics of Welfare* (4th ed.). London: Macmillan and Co. (Original work published 1920).

12 Reynolds, L. G. (1988). *Economics: A General Introduction*.
Homewood, IL: Irwin. Quoted in Ferber & Nelson, 1993, p. 5.

13 Colman, R., & Messinger, H. *Economic Performance and the
Wellbeing of Canadians*. Retrieved Jul. 1, 2006, from
http://economics.ca/2004/papers/0295.pdf.

14 More Canadian women bringing home the back bacon:
StatsCan. (2006, August 23). *CBC News*. Retrieved Sep. 9,
2006, from http://www.cbc.ca/news/story/2006/08/23/

women-breadwinner.html.

15 Putnam, 2000.

16 Ferber, M. A., & Birnbaum, B. G. (1980). Housework: Priceless or valueless? *Review of Income and Wealth, 26,* 387–400.

17 See, for example, Ben-Ner, A., & Putterman, L. (2000). Some implications of evolutionary psychology for the study of preferences and institutions. *Journal of Economic Behavior and Organization, 43*(1), 91–99.

18 Ghiselin, M. T. (1974). *The Economy of Nature and the Evolution of Sex.* Berkeley, CA: University of California Press, p. 247.

19 Dawkins, R. (1976). *The Selfish Gene.* Oxford: Oxford University Press.

20 Lewontin, R. C. (1991). *Biology as Ideology: The Doctrine of DNA.* Concord, ON: Anansi. Midgley, M. (1985). *Evolution as a Religion: Strange hopes and stranger fears.* London: Methuen.

21 In an interview published in *Woman's Own,* Thatcher said, "There's no such thing as society. There are individual men and women and there are families." Keay, D. (1987, Oct. 31). Aids, education and the year 2000! *Woman's Own,* 8–10.

22 Anthropologists use the phrase "altruistic punishers" to describe the observation that humans tend to cooperate with each other, but will punish non-cooperators. See Fehr, E., & Gächter, S. (2002). Altruistic punishment in humans. *Nature, 415,* 137–40.

23 Smith, A. (1790). *The Theory of Moral Sentiments.* London: A. Millar. Online version at http://www.econlib.org.

24 Friedman, M. (1962). *Capitalism and Freedom.* Chicago: University of Chicago Press.

25 Klein, N. (2000). *No Logo: Taking Aim at the Brand Bullies.*

New York: Picador. Klein describes herself as a feminist in: Viner, K. (2000, September 23). Hand-to-brand-combat (part two). *The Guardian.* "I am a feminist and this is a feminist book."

26 While neoclassical economics focuses on objectivity and pretends to be above politics, it is actually profoundly political, because it rationalizes the decisions of a privileged class—those in power. Again, this has gender implications. If employers choose to pay women less than men for doing the same tasks, the theory implies this isn't a form of discrimination, it's just rational behavior. As economist Diana Strassman puts it, "the notion of people as independent agents and unique selves, responsible for only their own needs, reflects a disproportionately male, adult and privileged world view." Strassman, D. (1999). Feminist Economics. In J. Peterson & M. Lewis (Eds.), *The Elgar Companion to Feminist Economics*, pp. 360–373. Northampton, ME: Edward Elgar.

27 Julie A. Nelson, J. A. (2003). *Clocks, Creation, and Clarity: Insights on Ethics and Economics from a Feminist Perspective.* (GDAE Working Papers 03-11). Tufts University, Medford, MA.

28 Daly, 1996, p. 153.

29 Meagher, G., & Nelson, J. (2004). Survey Article: Feminism in the Dismal Science. *Journal of Political Philosophy*, 12(1), 102–26. Working copy at http://ase.tufts.edu/gdae/about_us/cv/nelson_papers/survey_feminism_dismal.doc.

30 For a discussion of endogenous preferences, see: Bowles, S. (1998). Endogenous Preferences: The cultural consequences of markets and other economic institutions. *Journal of Economic Literature, 36*, 75–111.

31 Ferber & Nelson, 1993, p. 65.

32 See Fullbrook, E. (2003). *The Crisis in Economics: The Post-Autistic Economics Movement: The first 600 days.* New York: Routledge. Also: Fullbrook, E. (Ed.). (2007). *Real World Economics: A Post-autistic Economics Reader.* London: Anthem.

33 See the *Student Petition of Autisme-Economie* (June 2000) at http://www.paecon.net/PAEtexts/a-e-petition.htm.

34 Gutenkunst, R. N., Waterfall, J. J., Casey, F. P., Brown, K. S., Myers, C. R., & Sethna, J. P. (2007). Universally Sloppy Parameter Sensitivities in Systems Biology. *PLoS Computational Biology*, 3, e189. See also my book *Apollo's Arrow* for a discussion of biological models: Orrell, D. (2007). *Apollo's Arrow.* Toronto: HarperCollins.

35 See: http://www.life.com/Life/cover_search/view?coverkeyword=astronaut&startMonth=9&startYear=1959&endMonth=10&endYear=1959&pageNumber=1&indexNumber=2.

36 Nolen, S. (2003). *Promised the Moon: The Untold Story of the First Women in the Space Race.* New York: Four Walls Eight Windows. See also Cobb, J. (1997). *Jerrie Cobb, Solo Pilot.* Tulsa, Okla.: Jerrie Cobb Foundation. Available from the J. Cobb Foundation.

37 Retrieved Nov. 10, 2006, from http://spaceblog.xprize.org/page/2/.

38 Brizendine, L. (2006). *The Female Brain.* New York: Random House.

39 Barres, B. (2006). Does gender matter? *Nature, 442,* 133.

40 According to Lee Smolin, there is also "blatant prejudice" against women in physics. Smolin, L. (2006). *The Trouble With Physics: The Rise of String Theory, the Fall of a Science, and What Comes Next.* New York: Houghton Mifflin, p. 336.

Chapter 6

1   Chaucer, G. and Mann, J. (2005). *The Canterbury Tales: (original-spelling edition)*. New York: Penguin, p. 653.

2   Lietaer, 2001, p. 36. For data on price ratio, see: Lalor, J. J. (Ed.). (1899). *Cyclopaedia of Political Science*. New York: Maynard, Merrill, and Co. Online version at http://www. econlib.org/LIBRARY/YPDBooks/Lalor/llCy960.html.

3   Aristotle, *De Mundo* 392a.

4   Jevons, 1957, p. 94.

5   Arrow, K. J., & Debreu, G. (1954). Existence of a Competitive Equilibrium for a Competitive Economy. *Econometrica, 22*(3), 265–90.

6   Radner, R. (1968). Competitive equilibrium under uncertainty, *Econometrica, 36*, 31–58. Quoted in Ormerod, 1994, p. 90.

7   As economist Richard H. Day noted in 1985, fluctuations in the economy were assumed to be caused by "the superimposition of random shocks on what is (usually) assumed to be a stable deterministic linear process." Day, R. H. (1985). Dynamical Systems Theory and Complicated Economic Behavior. *Environment and Planning B: Planning and Design, 12*, 55–64.

8   The models may have a dynamic or stochastic component to capture fluctuations around that equilibrium.

9   The model contains many parameters, which control things such as how interest rates affect consumption, how wages affect desire to work, how easily companies can substitute labor and capital, and so on. These are determined by running the model against historical conditions, and adjusting the parameters (within what are considered reasonable bounds) until the model behavior agrees with reality. For details, see: Bayoumi, T. A. (2004). *GEM: a new*

international macroeconomic model. Washington, D.C.: International Monetary Fund.

10 Big questions and big numbers. (2006, July 13). *The Economist.*

11 Ackerman, F. (2001). Autistic Economics vs. the Environment. *Post-Autistic Economics Newsletter, 5.*

12 Kehoe, T. J. (2005). An Evaluation of the Performance of Applied General Equilibrium Models of the Impact of NAFTA. In T. J. Kehoe, T. N. Srinivasan, & J. Whalley (Eds.), *Frontiers in Applied General Equilibrium Modeling: Essays in Honor of Herbert Scarf* (pp. 341–77). Cambridge, U.K.: Cambridge University Press.

13 See *Apollo's Arrow* for a discussion of economic forecasting.

14 Veblen, T. (1898). Why Is Economics Not an Evolutionary Science. *The Quarterly Journal of Economics, 12.*

15 As Veblen wrote, "marginal utility theory is of a wholly statical character. It offers no theory of a movement of any kind, being occupied with the adjustment of values to a given situation ... [No economists] in this line of research have yet contributed anything at all appreciable to a theory of genesis, growth, sequence, change, process, or the like, in economic life." Veblen, T. (1909). The Limitations of Marginal Utility. *Journal of Political Economy, 17,* 620–36.

16 Campbell, L., & Garnett, W. (1884). *The Life of James Clerk Maxwell, with selections from his correspondence and occasional writings.* London: MacMillan & Co., p. 362–66.

17 Quoted in Beinhocker, 2006, p. 49.

18 Verhulst, P.-F. (1845). Recherches mathématiques sur la loi d'accroissement de la population. *Nouv. mém. de l'Académie Royale des Sci. et Belles-Lettres de Bruxelles, 18,* 1–41. Verhulst, P.-F. (1847). Deuxième mémoire sur la loi d'accroissement de

la population. *Mém. de l'Académie Royale des Sci., des Lettres et des Beaux-Arts de Belgique, 20,* 1–32.

19 The system is known as the Lorenz '96 system, after its inventor Ed Lorenz. For details on the spectral bifurcation diagram, see: Orrell, D., & Smith, L. (2003). The spectral bifurcation diagram: Visualizing bifurcations in high-dimensional systems. *Int. J. Bifurcat. Chaos, 13,* 3015–27.

20 Lipsey, R. G., Steiner, P. O., & Purvis, D. D. (1984). *Economics.* New York: Harper & Row. Sections reproduced in: Scoffield, H. (2006, June 3). The Man Who Wrote the Book. *Globe and Mail.*

21 Mirowski, P. (2004). *The Effortless Economy of Science?* Durham, NC: Duke University Press.

22 Lillo, F. & Doyne Farmer, J. (2005). The key role of liquidity fluctuations in determining large price fluctuations. *Fluctuation and Noise Letters, 5*(2), 209–16.

23 Part of the problem for business managers is that such systems are very hard for the human brain to understand because with complex feedback loops the whole notion of cause and effect breaks down. Sterman's team has developed a number of "management flight simulators" that allow business students to improve their intuition. Sterman, J. (2000). *Business Dynamics: Systems Thinking for a Complex World.* New York: McGraw-Hill. See also Sterman's homepage at http://web.mit.edu/jsterman/www/.

24 Sensier, M., & van Dijk, D. (2004). Testing for volatility changes in U.S. macroeconomic time series. *Review of economics and statistics, 86*(3), 833–39.

25 As chaos theorist Doyne Farmer said of financial forecasting, "the dimensionality of the market is sufficiently high that [chaos theory techniques] are not useful." Quoted in Halpern, P. (2000). *The Pursuit of Destiny: A History of Pre-*

diction. Cambridge, MA: Perseus, p. 185.

26 Meadows, D. H., Meadows, D. L., Randers, J. and Behrens III, W. (1972). *The Limits to Growth.* New York: Universe Books.

27 Greenspan, A. (2003, Aug. 29). Monetary Policy under Uncertainty. Federal Reserve Bank of Kansas City. Jackson Hole, Wyoming. See: http://www.federalreserve.gov/boarddocs/speeches/2003/20030829/default.htm.

28 As Sterman wrote: "Developing the capacity to see the world through multiple lenses and to respect differences cannot become an excuse for indecision, for a retreat to impotent scholasticism. We have to act. We must make the best decisions we can despite the inevitable limitations of our knowledge and models, then take personal responsibility for them. Mastering this tension is an exceptionally difficult discipline, but one essential for effective systems thinking and learning." Sterman, 2002.

29 Thomasson, L. (2007, Aug. 15). U.S. Stocks Drop, Erasing S&P 500's Gain for 2007; Banks Fall. Retrieved Aug. 15, 2007, from http://www.bloomberg.com.

30 Tett, G., & Gangahar, A. (2007, Aug. 14). Limitations of computer models. *Financial Times.*

31 An example of this is the DICE model of the economic effects of climate change, available online at http://www.econ.yale.edu/~nordhaus/homepage/dicemodels.htm. The welfare of anyone around in 2025 is weighted at less than 2 percent of the 1995 value. See Sterman, 2002.

32 See the Terra Trade Reference Currency website at http://www.terratrc.org.

33 This interpretation is opposite to that of the so-called butterfly effect, which states that it does have to be this way, because a butterfly flapped its wings somewhere on the

other side of the world. As I argue in *Apollo's Arrow*, the real world doesn't follow such simple deterministic laws.

Chapter 7

1 Woods & O'Brien, 2006.

2 Image from Bunbury, E. H. (1883). *A History of Ancient Geography among the Greeks and Romans from the Earliest Ages till the Fall of the Roman Empire*. London: John Murray.

3 http://turnbull.mcs.st-and.ac.uk/~history/Biographies/Euclid.html.

4 Quoted in: Machamer, P. (Ed.). (1998). *The Cambridge Companion to Galileo*. Cambridge, U.K.: Cambridge University Press, pp. 64–65.

5 Woods & O'Brien, 2006.

6 From the preface to Newton's *Principia* (1687); see: http://en.wikisource.org/wiki/Philosophiae_Naturalis_Principia_Mathematica/Preface.

7 For the Koch curve, a measurement with step length ε gives a length $L=F\varepsilon^{1-D}$, where F is some constant. A reduction in step length to $\varepsilon/3$ gives a result longer by a factor $4/3$, so $4/3L= F(\varepsilon/3)^{1-D}$. Dividing the two equations gives $4/3= (1/3)^{1-D}$ and solving for D gives the result. For the Sierpinski gasket, an increase of resolution by a factor two will reveal three new copies, so a similar analysis gives $D=\log(3)/\log(2)$.

8 The word "pathological" is often used by scientists to describe natural phenomena that don't fit in with their theories. For example, climate features not captured by model equations are called pathological, even though it would make more sense to describe the climate system as natural, and the model as pathological. See *Apollo's Arrow*, p. 294.

9 Ordnance Survey Boundary Line data at 1:10000 scale, Oc-

tober 2001. See http://www.ordnancesurvey.co.uk/osweb-site/freefun/didyouknow/. CIA data from http://www.cia.gov.

10 Data from Peitgen, H. O., Jurgens, H., & Saupe, D. (1992). *Chaos and fractals: new frontiers of science*. New York: Springer-Verlag.

11 Adapted from an image at http://en.wikipedia.org/wiki/Mandelbrot_set.

12 Mandelbrot, B. & Hudson, R. L. (2004). *The (mis)Behavior of Markets: A Fractal View of Risk, Ruin and Reward*. New York: Basic, p. 167.

13 Lo, A. W. & MacKinlay, A. C. (1999). *A Non-Random Walk Down Wall Street*. Princeton: Princeton University Press, p. 4.

14 Woods & O'Brien, 2006.

15 The diameter of the largest crater, Korolev, is 437 kilometers. See the Lunar and Planetary Institute website at http://www.lpi.usra.edu.

16 See information from Natural Resources Canada at http://geoscape.nrcan.gc.ca/vancouver/earth_e.php.

17 Taleb, N. N. (2007, Oct. 23). The pseudo-science hurting markets. *Financial Times*. See also: Taleb, N. N. (2006). *The Black Swan: The Impact of the Highly Improbable*. London: Penguin.

18 See Mandelbrot & Hudson, 2004, for a discussion. Also: Peters, E. (1994). *Fractal Market Analysis: Applying Chaos Theory to Investment & Economics*. New York: John Wiley & Sons.

19 Greenspan, 2003.

20 As economist Allen Sinai also pointed out, Greenspan "didn't go to one of the top schools ... I think that was an advantage. He didn't get brainwashed into one of the doctrines." Andrews, E. L. (2005, Aug. 26). 'Maestro' leaves stel-

lar record and murky legacy. *International Herald Tribune.*
21 Homer-Dixon, 2006, p. 90.
22 Ricardo, D. (1821). *On the Principles of Political Economy and Taxation.* London: John Murray.
23 Ralston Saul, J. (2005). *The Collapse of Globalism: And the Reinvention of the World.* Toronto: Penguin.
24 Buono, M. J., & Kolkhorst, F. W. (2001). Estimating ATP resynthesis during a marathon run: A method to introduce metabolism. *Advances in Physiology Education,* 25(2), 70–71.
25 For U.S. data, see Axtell, R. L. (2001). Zipf Distribution of U.S. Firm Sizes. *Science,* 293, 1818–20.

Chapter 8
1 Woods & O'Brien, 2006.
2 De Botton, 2004, p. 204.
3 Conrad, J. (1926). *Last Essays.* London: J. M. Dent, 19–20.
4 Gillham, N. W. (2001). *A Life of Sir Francis Galton: From African Exploration to the Birth of Eugenics.* New York: Oxford University Press, p. 76.
5 Cornford, F. M. (1922). Mysticism and Science in the Pythagorean Tradition. *The Classical Quarterly,* 16, 137–50.
6 Quoted in: Miller, P. L. (2008). Greek Philosophical Dualism. In Myers, E., Lange, A., & Styers, R. (Eds.), *Light against Darkness: Dualism in Ancient Mediterranean Religion and the Contemporary World* (pp. 111–56). Leiden.
7 Plato (1957). *The Republic.* Translated by Benjamin Jowett. New York: Heritage Press. Available online at: http://classics.mit.edu/Plato/republic.8.vii.html.
8 Quoted in Koestler, 1968.
9 Bentham quoted in Jevons, 1957, p. 24.
10 Pareto, V. (1897). The New Theories of Economics. *J. Pol*

Econ, 5, 485–502.

11 Veblen, T. (1909). The Limitations of Marginal Utility. *Journal of Political Economy*, 17.

12 The New York–based Astrology Fund, for example, is run according to a "mathematical psychology based on astronomy." Goff, S. (2007, May 26). It's an all-star performance. *Financial Times*.

13 Dismal science, dismal sentence. (2006, Sept. 9). *The Economist*.

14 Buffet, W. (1989, Feb. 28). Chairman's Letter to the Shareholders of Berkshire Hathaway Inc. See also Lo & MacKinlay, 1999, p. 14.

15 The 1776 committee in charge of designing the Great Seal of the United States described this as "The Eye of Providence."

16 Kahneman, D., & Tversky, A. (1979). Prospect Theory: An Analysis of Decision Under Risk. *Econometrica*, 47, 263–91.

17 From Kahneman's autobiography, retrieved Sept. 24, 2007, from http://nobelprize.org/nobel_prizes/economics/laureates/2002/kahneman-autobio.html.

18 Bechara, A. (2004). The role of emotion in decision-making: Evidence from neurological patients with orbitofrontal damage. *Brain and Cognition*, 55, 30–40.

19 McClure, S. M., Laibson, D. I., Loewenstein, G., & Cohen, J. D. (2004, Oct. 1). Separate Neural Systems Value Immediate and Delayed Monetary Rewards. *Science*, 306, 503–507.

20 Kosfeld, M., Heinrichs, M., Zak, P. J., Fischbacher, U., & Fehr, E. (2005, June 2). Oxytocin increases Trust in Humans. *Nature*, 435, 673–76.

21 Quoted in: Moye, C. (2007, Sept. 16). All in the mind. *Financial Times*.

22 Simon, H. A. (1957). A Behavioral Model of Rational

Choice. *Models of Man, Social and Rational: Mathematical Essays on Rational Human Behavior in a Social Setting.* New York: Wiley. See also: Simon, H. A. (1992). *Economics, Bounded Rationality and the Cognitive Revolution.* Brookfield, VT: Edward Elgar.

23 Taub, S. (2007, April 20). The Top 25 Moneymakers: The New Tycoons. *Alpha Magazine.* Trading algorithms based on patterns in past data can work well for a while, but tend to break down when others detect the same pattern. As Rob Buckland of Citigroup put it, "If everybody back-tests the same data, they will probably end up with the same strategy." My computer guessed wrong. (2007, Sept. 2). *Economist.* Another illustration of the risks involved was the 2006 collapse of the Amaranth hedge fund, after a bet on natural gas prices resulted in a $6.6 billion loss in just two weeks.

24 Economist Rhonda M. Williams notes the "recurrent tendency in neoclassical economics to construct African-Americans as fundamentally pathological and thus unable to compete effectively in existing capitalist economies." In Ferber & Nelson, 1993, p. 146.

25 Image from NASA: http://visibleearth.nasa.gov/view_rec.php?vev1id=5826.

26 De Botton, 2004, p. 53.

27 McLaughlin, D. (1998). Silent Spring Revisited. Retrieved Jun. 12, 2007, from http://www.pbs.org/wgbh/pages/frontline/shows/nature/disrupt/sspring.html.

28 See Czech, 2000. See also the True Cost Economics campaign at http://www.adbusters.org.

29 Tyedmers, P. (2003). Fisheries and Energy Use. In C. Cleveland (Ed.), *Encyclopedia of Energy* (pp. 683–93), (Vol. 2). San Diego, CA: Academic Press/Elsevier.

30 Malcolm X (1965, March). In G. Breitman (Ed.). (1990).
    Malcolm X Speaks. New York: Grove, p. 199.
31 O'Neill, 2007.
32 Atom Powered World Absurd, Scientists Told. (1933, Sept.
    12). *The New York Herald Tribune.*
33 Strauss, L. L. (1954, Sept. 16). Speech to the National Asso-
    ciation of Science Writers. New York, New York.
34 See: Taverne, D. (2005). *The March Of Unreason.* Oxford:
    Oxford University Press.

Chapter 9

1   Available online at: http://classics.mit.edu/Aristotle/cate-
    gories.3.3.html. See also Miller, 2008.
2   Quoted in Lederman, 1993, p. 273.
3   Available online at: http://classics.mit.edu/Aristotle/
    rhetoric.3.iii.html.
4   Quoted in Zimmerman, 1998, p. 238.
5   Jevons, 1957, p. xxiii.
6   Bentham, 1907, p. 31.
7   Ibid., p. 64.
8   Akerlof, G. A. (1970). The Market for 'Lemons': Quality
    Uncertainty and the Market Mechanism. *Quarterly Journal
    of Economics, 84*(3), 488–500.
9   Pareto, 1897.
10 Mandelbrot, B. (1982). *The Fractal Geometry of Nature.*
    New York: W. H. Freeman, p. 404.
11 See: http://www.forbes.com/lists/2005/54/Rank_1.html.
12 The source for this data was a figure in: Sorensen, A. T.
    (2004). *Bestseller Lists and Product Variety: The Case of
    Book Sales.* Research paper. Stanford University, Palo Alto,
    California.
13 On Amazon, the relationship between book sales and rank

is approximately given by a power law with exponent of −0.87. While the sales are dominated by the top-ranked books, Amazon still makes a substantial profit from the few million books that only sell two copies or less a month. See Brynjolfsson, E., Hu, Y., & Smith, M. D. (2003). Consumer Surplus in the Digital Economy: Estimating the Value of Increased Product Variety at Online Booksellers. *Management Science, 49*(11), 1580–96.

14 A rather more detailed model, but with similar dynamics, is given in: Bouchard, J. P., & Mezard, M. (2000). Wealth condensation in a simple model of economy. *Physica A, 282,* 536. Power-law distributions appear in agent-based simulations of a range of different systems. Of course, the fact that a simulation can be tuned to produce a realistic-looking distribution does not mean it accurately captures the dynamics of the underlying system.

15 Answer: Gene Cernan, on the 1972 *Apollo 17* mission, was the twelfth and last person to set foot on the moon.

16 Davies, J. B., Sandstrom, S., Shorrocks, A., & Wolff, E. N. (2006). *The World Distribution of Household Wealth.* World Institute for Development Economics Research of the United Nations University (UNU-WIDER).

17 Wealth varies with rank to the power -0.67, while the number of people with a particular wealth varies with wealth to the power -2.5. In general, if a plot of wealth versus rank follows a power law with exponent -k, then the number of people with a particular wealth follows a power law with exponent −$(1+1/k)$.

18 Dragulescu, A., & Yakovenko, V. M. (2001). Exponential and power-law probability distributions of wealth and income in the United Kingdom and the United States. *Physica A, 299,* 213–21.

19 Dew-Becker, I., & Gordon, R. J. (2005, Dec.). *Where Did the Productivity Growth Go? Inflation Dynamics and the Distribution of Income.* (NBER Working Paper 11842).

20 Piketty, T., & Saez, E. (2006, Jan.). *The Evolution of Top Incomes: A Historical and International Perspective.* (NBER Working Paper 11955).

21 The rich, the poor and the growing gap between them. (2006, Jun 15). *Economist.*

22 Ibid.

23 Romero, S. (2000, Feb. 15). Rich Brazilians Rise Above Rush-Hour Jams. *New York Times.*

24 McGregor, R. (2006, Nov. 21). China's poorest worse off after boom. *Financial Times.*

25 As a mathematical convenience, many modern texts actually assume a "continuum of firms," which means not just infinite, but uncountable.

26 As mentioned in "How to be fractal," in Chapter 7, company size also follows a power-law distribution.

27 The rich, the poor and the growing gap between them. (2006, Jun. 15). *Economist.*

28 Duncan, D. E. (2003). Reversing Bad Truths. *Discover, 24,* 20.

29 Birchall, J., & Yeager, H. (2006, Aug. 16). Wal-Mart takes the fight to its critics. *Financial Times.*

30 Sanfey, A. G., Rilling, J. K., Aronson, J. A., Nystrom, L. E., & Cohen, J. D. (2003). The neural basis of economic decision making in the ultimatum game. *Science, 300,* 1755–57. See also: Cassidy, J. (2006, Sept. 18). Mind Games. *New Yorker.*

31 Wolfensohn, J. D. (2000, August 19). Globalization and the Human Condition. Celebrating the 50th Anniversary of the Aspen Institute. (Symposium). Aspen, Colorado. See also Daly, 2007, p. 195.

32 Homer-Dixon, 2006, pp. 191–92.

33 Ibison, D. (2006, Sept. 16). Swedes ponder life outside the comfort zone. *Financial Times.*

34 According to Forbes.com in September 2006, Adelson "made almost $1 million an hour since the 2004 Forbes 400 list was published." See also Roberts, S. (2006, Sept. 29). Rise of the £1,000 hotel room. *Financial Times.*

35 Daly, 1996, p. 212.

36 Quoted in Daly, 1980, p. 333.

37 A study by McKinsey & Company showed that "from 1991 to 2000, market and industry factors drove about 70 percent of the returns of individual companies, company-specific factors only about 30 percent." De Swaan, J. C., & Harper, N. W. C. (2003). *The McKinsey Quarterly, 1.*

38 As just one example, in 2006 Robert Nardelli was paid $210 million when he resigned from Home Depot after six years of disappointing performance. See Golden handshakes. (2007, Jan. 4). *Economist.* The article notes, "In 2006, the Securities and Exchange Commission introduced new rules that will force firms to disclose more about how various top bosses are compensated."

39 Buffet, W. (2006, Feb. 28). Chairman's Letter to the Shareholders of Berkshire Hathaway Inc.

40 Giles, C. (2007, July 22). Backlash in rich nations against globalisation. *Financial Times.*

Chapter 10

1 Men of the Year. (1969, Jan. 3). *TIME*, p. 17.

2 Jevons, W. S. (1886). *Letters and Journal of W. Stanley Jevons.* London: Macmillan & Co.

3 Bentham, 1907, p. 31.

4 The good company. (2005, Jan. 20). *The Economist.*

5 Keen, S. (2001, July). Economists Have No Ears, *Post-Autistic Economics Newsletter*, 7, 4.

6 Keynes, J. M. (1936). *The General Theory of Employment, Interest, and Money*. New York: Harcourt Brace Jovanovich, p. 383.

7 See Mirowski, P. (1989). *More Heat than Light: Economics as Social Physics, Physics as Nature's Economics*. Cambridge: Cambridge University Press.

8 "A survey commissioned by the American Psychological Association (APA) found that seventy-three percent of Americans single out money, with thirty-three percent saying it is a very significant factor contributing to stress. Work, physical health and children follow next." As Tax Deadline Approaches Americans Say Money Is Number One Cause of Stress. (2004, March 31). *American Psychological Association*.

9 Edgeworth, F. Y. (1881). *Mathematical Psychics: An Essay on the Application of Mathematics to the Moral Sciences*. London: Paul.

10 Hobson, 1914.

11 The love affair between economics and pure mathematics is rather one-sided and unrequited—Norbert Wiener, for example, wrote that "economists have developed the habit of dressing up their rather imprecise ideas in the language of the infinitesimal calculus ... To assign what purports to be precise values to such essentially vague quantities is neither useful nor honest, and any pretense of applying formulae to these loosely defined quantities is a sham and a waste of time." Wiener, N. (1964). *God and Golem, Inc.* Cambridge, MA: M.I.T. Press, p. 89.

12 Mandelbrot, 1982, p. 461.

13 Friedman, M. (1953). *Essays in Positive Economics*. Chicago:

University of Chicago Press.

14 As the economist Alan Kirman, director of studies at L'Écoles
   des Hautes Études en Sciences Sociales in France, noted:
   "Almost no one contests the poor predictive performance of
   economic theory. The justifications given are many, but the
   conclusion is not even the subject of debate." Quoted in
   Beinhocker, 2006, p. 59. See also *Apollo's Arrow* for a discussion of economic prediction.

15 Cohen, S. (2000). *Failed Crusade: America and the Tragedy
   of Post-Communist Russia*. New York: Norton.

16 Ferber & Nelson, 1993, pp. 142–43.

17 An example is Martin Feldstein, who long taught the introductory economics class at Harvard University, and according to the *New York Times* was the "scholarly mentor
   to Bush's team." Leonhardt, D. (2002, Dec. 1). Scholarly
   Mentor To Bush's Team. *New York Times*.

18 Heraclitus, fragment 129.

19 Aristotle (1905). *Politics*. Translated by Benjamin Jowett.
   Oxford: Oxford University Press. Retrieved Oct 20, 2006,
   from http://classics.mit.edu/Aristotle/politics.2.two.html.

20 The title referred to an earlier 1833 parable by William
   Forster Lloyd.

21 Colman & Messinger, (2004, June). *Economic Performance
   and the Wellbeing of Canadians*. Paper presented at the
   Canadian Economic Association Annual Meeting, Toronto,
   Ontario.

22 In August 2007, the Alberta premier Ed Stelmach was holding up the adoption of a cap-and-trade system to limit
   greenhouse gas emissions in Canada. "We've had over
   500,000 new Albertans move to the province within the
   last six years. They all demand energy, they drive and they
   all live in homes that have to be heated." Why are they

there? Because of the unrestrained exploitation of the oil sands. Anonymous (2007, Aug. 10). No cap-and-trade system but premiers move forward. Retrieved Aug. 12, 2007, from http://www.CTV.ca. See also: Marsden, W. (2007). *Stupid to the Last Drop: How Alberta Is Bringing Environmental Armageddon to Canada (And Doesn't Seem to Care).* Toronto: Knopf.

23 Rahlman, A. S. (2007, Aug. 15). What Canadians should learn from the U.S. health care disaster. *Globe and Mail.* For statistics, see National Center for Health Statistics (2004). *Health, United States, 2004, With Chartbook on Trends in the Health of Americans.* Hyattsville, Maryland.

24 Faini, R. (2006). *Remittances and the Brain Drain.* (IZA Discussion Paper 2155). Lapper, R. (2007, Aug 27). The tale of globalisation's exiles. *Financial Times.*

25 As discussed in Chapter 6, macroeconomic models are highly unreliable. They can't predict the next recession, let alone the effect on the economy of climate change. And climate models are no better: a single model can give vastly different answers just by making small modifications to its structure. The problem is that both the economy and the climate system are dominated by an interacting network of positive and negative feedback loops, which elude prediction. See *Apollo's Arrow.*

26 In the U.K. in 2007, one report said, "the average house price in 99 per cent of towns was too rich for the typical nurse." Chisholm, J. (2007, April 13). House price rises show signs of slowing. *Financial Times.*

27 Clark, A. (2007, Oct. 31). I should pay more tax, says US billionaire Warren Buffett. *The Guardian.*

28 As economist Deepa Narayan wrote, "Social capital ... forms the underpinnings of poverty and prosperity."

Narayan, D. (1997). Voices of the Poor: Poverty and Social Capital in Tanzania. *Environmentally Sustainable Development Monograph 20.* World Bank, Washington, D.C.

29 Hart, J. (2006, May-June). The New Capitalists. *Utne Reader.* See also: Bakan, J. (2004). *The Corporation: The Pathological Pursuit of Profit and Power.* New York: Free Press.

30 Daly, 1996, p. 10.

31 Barfield, O. (1988). Saving the Appearances: A Study in Idolatry. 2nd ed. Middletown: Wesleyan University Press. (First published 1957).

32 Jules Cashford wrote, "according to Pausanias, 'Sibyl' was another name for Artemis, which may be why Plutarch says the face of the Sibyl can be seen in the Moon. 'The ancients,' comments the Roman Lydus, 'regarded the Moon as the leader in all divination.'" Cashford, 2002, p. 286.

33 Frye, N. (1982). *The Great Code: The Bible and Literature.* New York: Harcourt Brace Jovanovich.

34 Cashford, 2002, p. 173.

35 "The event, and primarily its image," writes Cashford, "was greeted throughout the world with the same wonder that abounds in early mythopoetic thought, as though the human imagination had once again been awakened." Cashford, 2002, p. 364.

36 Cashford, 2002, p. 293.

37 Goldenfeld, N., & Kadanoff, L. P. (1999). Simple Lessons from Complexity. *Science, 284,* 87–89.

38 Quoted in Cashford, 2002, p. 364.

39 Bentham, J. (1995). In M. Bozovic (Ed.), *The Panopticon Writings.* London: Verso.

40 According to that neo-Victorian organ *The Economist,* such reforms are "based on a faulty—and dangerously faulty—

analysis of the capitalist system they are intended to re-deem." The good company. (2005, Jan. 20). *The Economist.*

41 The Revolution Will Begin with a Textbook [Part Two]. (2007, Jan.-Feb.). *Adbusters, 69.*